IMAGINATIVE LITERATURE I

from Homer to Shakespeare

Imaginative Literature I

from Homer to Shakespeare

By

Mortimer J. Adler

and

Seymour Cain

Preface by

Saul Bellow

Author, *The Adventures of Augie March*

ENCYCLOPÆDIA BRITANNICA, INC.

Chicago • London • Toronto • Geneva

PRINTED IN THE U.S.A.

PREFACE

Imaginative Literature I examines several masterpieces of ancient literature and of the literature of the Middle Ages and the Renaissance which aim at a total view of human life. Dante's avowed purpose was to summarize existence in every aspect. He has left us, says our text, "a magnificent work of the imagination based on the Christian vision of reality." It is perhaps too much to say that Chaucer and Rabelais intended to depict a civilization, but that is what they have done, in effect, and a modern writer cannot help being impressed by the completeness of their work, its density, its vividness in particulars, its unfailing relevance, and the great range of it.

In modern times such unity is lacking. Sigmund Freud speaks somewhere of three revolutions which have overturned and dispersed the old visions. The Copernican revolution, he says, came first, removing man from the center of creation, and then came the Darwinian and lastly the Freudian discoveries which completed the dispersal. He might have added more reasons, but he has said enough for our purposes. We can no longer expect to relate man, nature, and God as the old world did.

Nevertheless, writers have continued, with varying degrees of success, the attempt to make an all-embracing synthesis. In the eighteenth century, the man of letters still considered himself a natural center or clearinghouse for every form of knowledge. Voltaire thought it his proper function to interpret Newtonian physics to the educated French reader. The writer had not yet given way to the specialist and would not grant that a good intelligence might be unable to keep pace with all the new developments. But knowledge was growing more diverse and civilization more complex, and it seemed too much to expect the poet to dominate it as Dante had done. Goethe, in *Faust,* took the difficulty itself as one of his themes. In the nineteenth century, Balzac, in his series of novels, the *Comédie humaine,* tried to create a realistic encyclopaedia, to include all of science, politics, art, belief, and manners in a single imaginative scheme, but his interests were more narrowly social and biological than those of the old masters and he did not succeed, fascinating though he often is, in speaking for an entire civilization.

In the twentieth century, novelists such as Thomas Mann and James Joyce are very like their contemporaries, the universal historians, the Spenglers and the Toynbees. They combine cultural history with art, and offer to interpret the human condition in its entirety. Joyce's *Ulysses* and Mann's *The Magic Mountain* and *Dr. Faustus* have some of the scope of epic poetry. But there is something inside-out about these books. The reader soon finds that Joyce is very well acquainted with Homer, Dante, Rabelais, and Shakespeare. *Ulysses,* like *The Divine Comedy,* is an allegorical work; it is also a compendium, a sort of summary of everything that man in the Western world has become. But it is a parody of earlier masterpieces, deliberately a parody, a sometimes funny, sometimes frightening contrast of ancient and modern. And if the *Aeneid* is the epic of a great historical beginning, Mann's *Dr. Faustus* may be read as the poem of the undoing of a people and a civilization, the collapse of Germany into barbarism.

A modern writer finds in the literature of antiquity and the Renaissance the most generous and noble images of human existence. There men are godlike or even partly divine. In the modern age, poets and novelists have studied man in his commoner, more familiar condition. They have written realistically of everyday life, of the *merely* human. Still, whatever they create, they cannot help but look back to Homer, Chaucer, and Shakespeare from whom they have inherited their conceptions of literary form, of character and action.

In applying what he has inherited to modern experience,

the modern writer will inevitably find himself trying to establish whether the living man can be measured by the same measure as the Homeric, the Euripidean, the Chaucerian, the Shakespearean man. If he finds it absolutely impossible to use the same measure, he may be driven to conclude that the gulf between past and present is too wide to bridge and that there are perhaps two different types or orders of humanity—one heroic, discernible in the past; the other contemporary and negligible.

American writers have always been peculiarly sensitive to this difficulty. Nathaniel Hawthorne in the introductory chapter of *The Scarlet Letter,* called "The Custom-House," speaks of "the materiality of this daily life pressing so intrusively" upon him and blames himself for turning away from it and flinging himself "back into another age." "The wiser effort," he says, "would have been to diffuse thought and imagination through the opaque substance of today, and thus to make it a bright transparency." It is from Shakespeare and the ancient classics that the nineteenth-century American derives the ideal of "a bright transparency." It can have no other source.

Later in the same century, Walt Whitman called for a new art, appropriate to a democracy. As the great civilizations of the past, based on the institutions of slavery and feudalism, created typical works of genius, so America, too, must originate not only a great art but a new sort of nobility of character deriving from this art. "A great original literature is surely to become the justification and reliance (in some respects the sole reliance) of American democracy," he wrote in *Democratic Vistas*. "Few are aware," he said, "how the great literature penetrates all, gives hue to all, shapes aggregates and individuals, and, after subtle ways, with irresistible power, constructs, sustains, demolishes at will." In Whitman's view, the development of American democracy would never be complete without a literature equal in scope and power to the literature of the old world. He summoned poets to write such a literature.

Few writers anywhere have denied the tradition outright. William Blake who warned against it—"We do not want either

Greek or Roman models if we are but just and true to our own imaginations"—was, however, in love with Chaucer, Shakespeare, and Milton. I assume that he was concerned about the connection between art and an ongoing life. This connection, never neglected by the great poets of the past, may have seemed to Blake endangered by the idolatry of the antiquarians, those who wished to freeze the classics, and to keep them forever, golden but frozen, in the past.

That his fears were not illusory was shown in our own times by writers such as Ezra Pound, Wyndham Lewis, and others, men of genius some of them, who turned past and present into opposites and used the energy and beauty of Greece, Rome, and the Renaissance for destructive ends, political as well as aesthetic, denouncing modern life in the name of a departed glory, contrasting that glory with the chaos and dissolution of a civilization whose end they wished to hasten.

These classics, however, belong to anyone who has the ability to take them, to everyone who understands and is moved by them. They are not transmitted in an inert state from generation to generation. Those who read them are changed by them. They are sources not only of wisdom and pleasure but of energy and power. We must learn to live with their greatness.

Saul Bellow

FOREWORD

I

This Reading Plan is an aid to the appreciation and understanding of great works of imaginative literature from Homer to Shakespeare. It is followed by another Reading Plan, *Imaginative Literature II,* covering works from Cervantes to Dostoevsky. You need not have done the readings in previous Reading Plans to follow the discussions in this one. Sometimes we refer to a previous Reading Plan for some special insight it may add. For instance, in the guide to the Fifth Reading, *The Divine Comedy,* we refer to the discussion of the "Paradise" canticle of this work in the Reading Plan *Religion and Theology.*

How to Use the Reading Plan. The Reading Plan contains three parts: (1) a list of readings, (2) guides to each of the readings, and (3) suggestions for additional readings.

1. *The Reading List.* This Reading Plan comprises eight readings, consisting of whole works that vary considerably in length. Proper enjoyment and understanding of these works require that each reader pursue a reading at his own pace. Hence, there are no specific time limits set for these readings. Some of the selections, the drama readings, for instance, may take only two weeks. Others, such as the long epics, may take a month or two.

2. *The Guides.* These are intended to help the reader who is on his own, without a teacher or other study aids. They provide relevant background material and stimulate appreciation and understanding of the readings. Background material

may include information about the particular historical setting in which the work was written—tradition, culture, contemporary conditions, and literary movements. It may also tell us something about the author—his life, character, other writings, and his place in literature—and about the composition of the particular book. Each guide also includes a comprehensive summary of the work, together with salient citations from the text. This summary refreshes your memory of the work, sets forth the substance in a methodical manner, and provides the basis for our discussion in the final section of the guide.

The discussion raises thoughtful questions about the form, content, and style of the work—for instance, whether it is an epic and what an epic is, or whether the work is a unified whole, or why the author handled a situation in one way rather than another. These questions are intended to arouse your awareness and appreciation of literary values and meanings. They do not have any simple "yes" or "no" answers, but call for a sensitive and thoughtful response to the reading. A brief discussion follows each question, in order to indicate its significance and suggest some possible answers. The discussions do not provide any final or "right" answers—indeed, they sometimes provide contradictory answers. They are simply suggestions intended to stimulate your own awareness and understanding, and to get you started on answering the questions yourself.

The guide concludes with a set of "Self-Testing Questions," which are quite distinct from the discussion questions. These questions, dealing with particular details of the text, call for a definite answer. They are intended to help you test the thoroughness and retentiveness of your reading. You can keep score on yourself by checking the list of answers on pages 232-233.

3. *Additional Readings.* We have added a list of books that will help you in the reading and appreciation of imaginative literature. These range from philosophical works on literary criticism to practical aids to reading poetry and prose. We have also included works on the other aspects of imaginative literature—moral, religious, and social.

II

The term "literature" refers generally to any written matter. The works of Locke, Berkeley, and Hume are just as much a part of English literature as those by Shakespeare, Milton, and Keats. But the term is also applied in a special sense to lyric poetry, drama, epic, the novel, the short story, and other forms of imaginative writing. This is the type of literature with which we are concerned in this Reading Plan—"imaginative literature."

It is sometimes difficult, by merely formal criteria, to draw the line between imaginative literature and other literature. Plato uses dramatic dialogue and myths to express philosophical principles and problems. The works of Plutarch, Tacitus, and other historians are models of literary structure and style. Portraits of actual men and events often have the same literary qualities as portraits of fictional characters and events.

Despite the borderline cases and the common literary excellence of the two types of literature, however, it is obvious that they are different types with different functions. Imaginative literature presents a fictional world, not the factual world of historians and biographers. It appeals to our imagination, our emotions, our sense of delight, our intimate personal experience, not to the powers of disinterested thought required by the scientists and philosophers. De Quincey's distinction between "the literature of power"—the emotionally moving—and "the literature of knowledge"—the intellectually instructive—is to the point in most cases.

It may be illuminating to note that imaginative literature is often more akin to the oral sagas, legends, folk tales, and romances of an earlier period of culture than to "the literature of knowledge." Homer's epics are closely related to the oral chants sung by ancient bards at banquets or around the campfire. Chaucer and Cervantes openly mimic the form of oral storytelling in their works, and reflect the avid audience listening to the telling of a good yarn. The oral bard was a man talking or singing to men, using his face, body, gestures, and especially the sound of his voice. Something of these elemental qualities is expressed in written works in other ways. Rhetorical power, the "gift of gab," the love of word sounds and combinations, the powerful or tender organ tones of the human voice—these are to be found in great imaginative writers all through the ages—in Aristophanes, Rabelais, Shakespeare, Milton, Fielding, Melville, Joyce, and Dylan Thomas, our twentieth-century embodiment of the ancient bard.

Reading imaginative literature, therefore, is not just a visual process of discerning symbolic signs on a piece of paper; it is also a process of hearing sounds, either in the mind's ear or through oral recitation. It is a response to the human voice, to the human breath and pulse, to the throbbing life, which no electronic reading machine can detect or interpret. Through the "physical" sound and rhythm of words, as well as through their logical sense, imaginative writers engage our imagination and feeling and afford us enjoyment.

While sharing these characteristics with oral works—and the elements of narrative interest, verbal power, and sheer delight are always there—imaginative literature in the West has achieved complex and refined forms, technical sophistication, and a range of subject matter appropriate to an advanced stage of culture. Some of the greatest minds in the Western world have devoted themselves to the creation of imaginative literature, and they have usually been conscious inheritors of the culture of the past and active participants in the culture of their own day. Their works raise questions of form and substance, of manner and matter, of the intent and result of literary expression.

III

Unfortunately, or perhaps fortunately, there is only one formal work of literary criticism in the *Great Books of the Western World,* Aristotle's *Poetics.* In the guides, we have often cited Aristotle's distinctions in order to illuminate our reading and to suggest other distinctions, where Aristotle's seemed inadequate or irrelevant. We have also cited biographical, historical, and critical works where they shed light on the author and his work. But, on the whole, we have proceeded from the actual texts to the general questions they call forth on the function, forms, and nature of imaginative literature.

Among the questions that have recurred persistently are these:

1. *Questions about formal kinds or "genres."* Philosophers and literary critics have distinguished various kinds of imaginative writing, that is, definite forms or species, as in animal life. For example, Aristotle in the *Poetics* distinguishes tragedy, epic, and comedy. As we read the specific works in the Reading Plan, we may find it interesting and illuminating to discern the particular forms of literature that they represent. We may find that certain works make previous definitions of a form questionable, possibly calling for a redefinition or even for the naming and definition of a new form. Does Aristotle's analysis of the structure of tragedy, for instance, apply to the serious dramas of Euripides and Shakespeare? Are Ulysses and Aeneas proper heroes for an epic poem? These are the sorts of formal questions that are raised in our discussion of the readings.

2. *Questions about the effectiveness of literary devices.* Writers in all ages have used various devices to obtain their effects. The further away we get from an era and its literary conventions, the more we tend to question the effectiveness of these devices. We can, however, try to discern what the author was trying to do and to see whether or not the particular devices he used detract from the work's plausibility and our enjoyment of it. Questions such as these are raised by the lengthy digressions in the *Odyssey* and by the intervention of the gods in the works of Euripides and Virgil.

3. *Questions about the literary style and rhythm.* One of the essential marks of literary excellence is the use of language. This is obvious in great works of prose as well as in verse. Because most of the readings in this Reading Plan are translations, we have given little space to discussions of verse rhythms or the fine points of prose style. However, in the cases of Chaucer and Shakespeare, we have dwelt at length on their language and their verse forms, and raised the question of the relation of form and content. In the case of some of the translations, notably Rogers' translation of Aristophanes and Urquhart and Motteux's translation of Rabelais, the origi-

nal has carried over with enough force to be observed and commented upon.

4. *Questions of the moral effects of literature.* Many of the works discussed have raised questions of morality and obscenity since they were first published. Homer scandalized Plato, Rabelais shocked St. Francis de Sales, and Shakespeare is still being expurgated in high school texts. Hence, we have discussed questions of propriety, good taste, and the moral effects of literature as they arise with the reading of a work. Certainly the ribaldry of Aristophanes, Chaucer, and Rabelais requires some discussion even in so presumably "free" and "open" an age as this. These are the types of work that raise the question of morality and censorship discussed by Plato, Milton, Tolstoy, and other great writers in our tradition. The possibility of religious or political offense involved in many of our readings, both comic and serious, raises a somewhat similar type of question.

CONTENTS

A NOTE ON REFERENCE STYLE

In referring to *Great Books of the Western World,* the same style is used as in the *Syntopicon.* Pages are cited by number and section. In books that are printed in single column, "a" and "b" refer to the upper and lower halves of the page. In books that are printed in double column, "a" and "b" refer to the upper and lower halves of the left column, "c" and "d" to the upper and lower halves of the right column. For example, "Vol. 53, p. 210b" refers to the lower half of page 210, since Vol. 53, James's *Principles of Psychology,* is printed in single column. But "Vol. 7, p. 202b" refers to the lower left quarter of page 202, since Vol. 7, Plato's *Dialogues,* is printed in double column.

THE READING LIST

1 Homer, *The Odyssey*. Vol. 4, pp. 183-322.

2 Euripides, *Medea, Electra,* and *Orestes*. Vol. 5, pp. 212-224, 327-339, 394-410.

3 Aristophanes, *The Clouds, The Birds,* and *The Lysistrata.* Vol. 5, pp. 488-506, 542-563, 583-599.

4 Virgil, *The Aeneid.* Vol. 13, pp. 103-379.

5 Dante, *The Divine Comedy*. Vol. 21.

6 Chaucer, *The Canterbury Tales*. Vol. 22, pp. 159-550.

7 Rabelais, *Gargantua and Pantagruel.* Vol. 24.

8 Shakespeare, *Othello, King Lear,* and *Macbeth.* Vol. 27, pp. 205-310.

HOMER

The *Odyssey*

Vol. 4, pp. 183–322

This is the story of the adventures of Ulysses, who fought ten years at Troy and wandered for another ten years before getting home again. Men have been listening to the tale of his journeys for almost three thousand years. Lawrence of Arabia, one of the great translators of the *Odyssey*, said: "The Odyssey by its ease and interest remains the oldest book worth reading for its story and the first novel of Europe."

The book holds our interest, like many a great novel, by following its hero through a series of dangers, struggles, escapes, obstacles, and successes to a triumphant conclusion. Monsters, gods, beautiful women, villainous men, kings, slaves, shipwrecks, battles, domestic life, and farming—all these are included in the pages of this book. And the leading characters are unforgettable—Ulysses, the cunning, crafty, self-reliant hero; his wife Penelope, who slyly delays the day of reckoning with her suitors; their son Telemachus, who is too weak to hold his own as a man, a youth in search of his father; Laertes, the father of Ulysses, wasting away in sorrow for his long-lost son; and the devoted slaves and servants, Eumaeus and Euryclea, loyal to the end. And all of these events and persons are expressed in good, clear, simple, solid language, that makes us see and hear, that gives us the illusion of actual experience.

This story of the wanderings of Ulysses has become through the centuries the literary model and example for human exile and wandering in general. Indeed, this has become so accepted that we use the term "odyssey," with a small "o," to indicate any long series of journeys. In our own century, the Irish novelist James Joyce found in this ancient Greek poem the basic theme for his story of a modern Everyman, and he called it *Ulysses*.

GUIDE TO

First Reading

I

We have no certain knowledge about the authorship of the *Odyssey* or how it was composed. Some scholars have held that it had no single author, but was a gradual accretion of materials from many sources—individuals, tradition, and folklore. They held this to be true of the *Iliad,* too. According to one scholarly view, prominent in the nineteenth century, the two works were written by different authors in different times. Our translator, Samuel Butler, shared this view and added the guess that the author of the *Odyssey* was a woman. Most present-day scholars, however, hold that, although the materials probably came from many sources, a single author gave them their literary unity and form, and wrote both the *Iliad* and the *Odyssey*. The author, it is calculated, probably lived in the ninth century B.C.

Although we have no certain historical knowledge, we do have many legends about the author; for instance, that he was a Greek from Asia Minor, probably born in Smyrna or Chios, and that in his old age he was a blind, mendicant minstrel. A famous ancient verse alludes to the poet's poverty and homelessness:

> Seven cities warred for Homer being dead,
> Who living had no roof to shroud his head.

The "seven cities" were Smyrna, Rhodes, Colophon, Salamis, Chios, Argos, and Athens—all claiming to be the birthplace of Homer.

The reason that the seven cities were eager to claim Homer as a native son was that he had become the educator of Greece, the bearer of culture and wisdom, the object of universal veneration—indeed, his works were practically the Bible of ancient Greece. Later Greek poets used Homer's themes, many of the greatest Greek dramas were suggested by Homer's stories, and popular Greek religion was affected by his portraits of the gods. Homer was generally regarded as a fountainhead of wisdom and learning. (Later philosophers, such as Plato, questioned Homer's authority and influence.)

The events narrated by Homer are set in about the twelfth century B.C.—the so-called Homeric Age. A patriarchal, agrarian economy prevailed, with close kinship ties, and family-centered production, the master often working along with the women and the slaves. Government was by a council of nobles usually under the leadership of a king, who may or may not have been hereditary. The king himself was one of the nobles, like Ulysses and Menelaus, and the kingdoms were small city-states, such as Ithaca and Sparta. In addition to the nobles, slaves, and servants, there were craftsmen, merchants, sailors, minstrels, physicians, and heralds. Feasting, athletic contests, dancing, and the songs and stories of minstrels like Homer provided the recreation. The gods were worshiped through sacrifices, libations, and prayers; and hospitality to strangers was a religious duty.

The Trojan War which is the background of the *Iliad* and the *Odyssey* was probably a historical event. The traditional date of the fall of Troy, or Ilium, is 1184 B.C. The explorations of the famous archaeologist Schliemann in the nineteenth century indicated that there had really been a siege and fall of Troy. Homer used much legendary material, including the legend that the war started because the Trojan prince Paris stole Helen, the beautiful wife of Menelaus, King of Sparta. The *Iliad* deals with the tenth year of the war, just before the fall of Troy. The latter event, brought about by the trick of the wooden horse, with the Greeks hidden in it—the "Trojan Horse"—is told in the *Odyssey* (pp. 201d-202a, 227a-b, 248b), not in the *Iliad*.

II

The *Odyssey* begins in the tenth year after the fall of Troy. Ulysses alone, of the surviving Greek heroes, has failed to return home. He has had to suffer ten years of wandering because he has offended the sea-god, Neptune, and his men have perished because they offended the sun-god, Hyperion. The invocation to the muse at the very beginning sets the theme of the *Odyssey* and tells us Ulysses' situation.

TELL ME, O MUSE, of that ingenious hero who travelled far and wide after he had sacked the famous town of Troy. Many cities did he visit, and many were the nations with whose manners and customs he was acquainted; moreover he suffered much by sea while trying to save his own life and bring his men safely home; but do what he might he could not save his men, for they perished through their own sheer folly in eating the cattle of the Sun-god Hyperion; so the god prevented them from ever reaching home. Tell me, too, about all these things, O daughter of Jove, from whatsoever source you may know them.

So now all who escaped death in battle or by shipwreck had got safely home except Ulysses, and he, though he was longing to return to his wife and country, was detained by the goddess Calypso, who had got him into a large cave and wanted to marry him. But as years went by, there came a time when the gods settled that he should go back to Ithaca; even then, however, when he was among his own people, his troubles were not yet over; nevertheless all the gods had now begun to pity him except Neptune, who still persecuted him without ceasing and would not let him get home. (p. 183a-b)

The *Odyssey* consists of twenty-four books. We may divide them neatly into two halves—Books I-XII, dealing with events prior to Ulysses' return to Ithaca, and Books XIII-XXIV, dealing with events after his return. The first twelve books may again be divided neatly, into three parts: Books I-IV set the scene before Ulysses enters the story, Books V-VIII tell of Ulysses' journey from Calypso's island to the land of the Phaeacians, Books IX-XII present Ulysses' story of his adventures from the time he left Troy to the time he was stranded on Calypso's island.

The first four books open with a council of the gods on Olympus, discussing Ulysses' plight. Jove, the ruler of the gods, and Minerva, the goddess of arts and crafts, favor Ulysses. Minerva goes to Ithaca to bring courage and hope to Ulysses' son, Telemachus, and to send him in search of his father. In Ithaca, a host of suitors for the hand of Penelope, the presumed widow of Ulysses, are eating her and Telemachus out of house and home. The suitors insist on banqueting free of charge in the house of Ulysses until Penelope makes up her mind whom she will wed. Once Penelope tricked the suitors by asking them to wait until she finished weaving a shroud for her father-in-law, Laertes. She kept them waiting three years, until she was discovered weaving the web in daylight and unstitching it at night. The suitors are still furious at her deceit and are determined to plague her until she makes a choice.

Minerva, disguised as an old friend of Ulysses, tells the despairing Telemachus to rely on his father's ingenuity and the aid of heaven to bring him safely home. She holds up Orestes, who killed the murderer of his father, Agamemnon, as a model for him to follow in the pursuit of fame. With this end in view —renown—she sends him to the courts of Pylos and Sparta, in quest of news of his father. Menelaus, the famous King of Sparta, gives him the good news that his father is still alive. Proteus, "the old man of the sea," has told Menelaus that Ulysses is "alive but hindered from returning" by the nymph Calypso, who holds him captive on her island.

Meanwhile, in Ithaca, the suitors, angered and fearful because Telemachus has slipped away, plot to kill him on his return. A group of the suitors sail out to wait in ambush for Telemachus' ship. This is the situation in Ithaca as Book IV ends, and we do not return to it until Book XV.

The second four books of the *Odyssey* (Books V-VIII) also begin with a council of the gods, where Minerva again pleads Ulysses' cause. Jove decrees that Ulysses shall return home by way of Scheria, the land of the Phaeacians, and he sends Mercury, the messenger of the gods, to advise the nymph Calypso of his will. Calypso is angry and grieved at the divine decree that bids her send away the man she loves.

"... I found the poor creature sitting all alone astride of a keel, for Jove had struck his ship with lightning and sunk it in mid ocean, so that all his crew were drowned, while he himself was driven by wind and waves on to my island. I got fond of him and cherished him, and had set my heart on making him immortal, so that he should never grow old all his days ..." (p. 209b)

But Ulysses, crying his heart out with homesickness, does not return her feeling; he has tired of her and only goes to bed with her because that is her desire. In spite of Calypso's divine beauty and immortality, he wants to get back to his home and his merely human wife, and he is willing to endure whatever suffering is in store in order to attain that goal.

Ulysses, aided by Calypso, prepares a raft and provisions and sets out to sea. After many days he sights the Phaeacian coast, but his old enemy Neptune, the sea-god, gives "the man of troubles" a rough time before he reaches land. He survives a terrible storm, the destruction of his raft, and two nights and days in the water before he makes shore. The next day he is awakened by the shouts of the Phaeacian princess Nausicaa and her maids, who are playing ball near the river. Ulysses flatters the Princess into giving him food and clothing, and he gets the King, Alcinous, to promise him aid in getting home to Ithaca. A new ship, with a picked crew, is prepared for Ulysses.

But before Ulysses leaves, there is a feast with minstrelsy and athletic games in his honor. Ulysses is touched to tears as he listens to the blind minstrel sing of the quarrel between Ulysses and Achilles, and of the Trojan horse. His weeping attracts the attention of the King, who insists that Ulysses tell the assembled company all about himself.

Ulysses' story of his journey from Troy to Calypso's island (which takes up Books IX-XII) is a story of hardship and suffering, of human cunning and courage, as well as of foolishness and weakness, in the face of all kinds of troubles and perils. Ulysses tells how he overcame sweet enchantresses, horrible monsters, human weaknesses, a journey to Hades, and shipwreck. The figures and events in this tale have long played a part in shaping human imagination. We have heard or read of them in our childhood. Here they are presented in their uncensored fullness, with all the attractive and repellent details.

Ulysses and his men encountered their first great temptation in the land of the Lotus-eaters, who offered them food

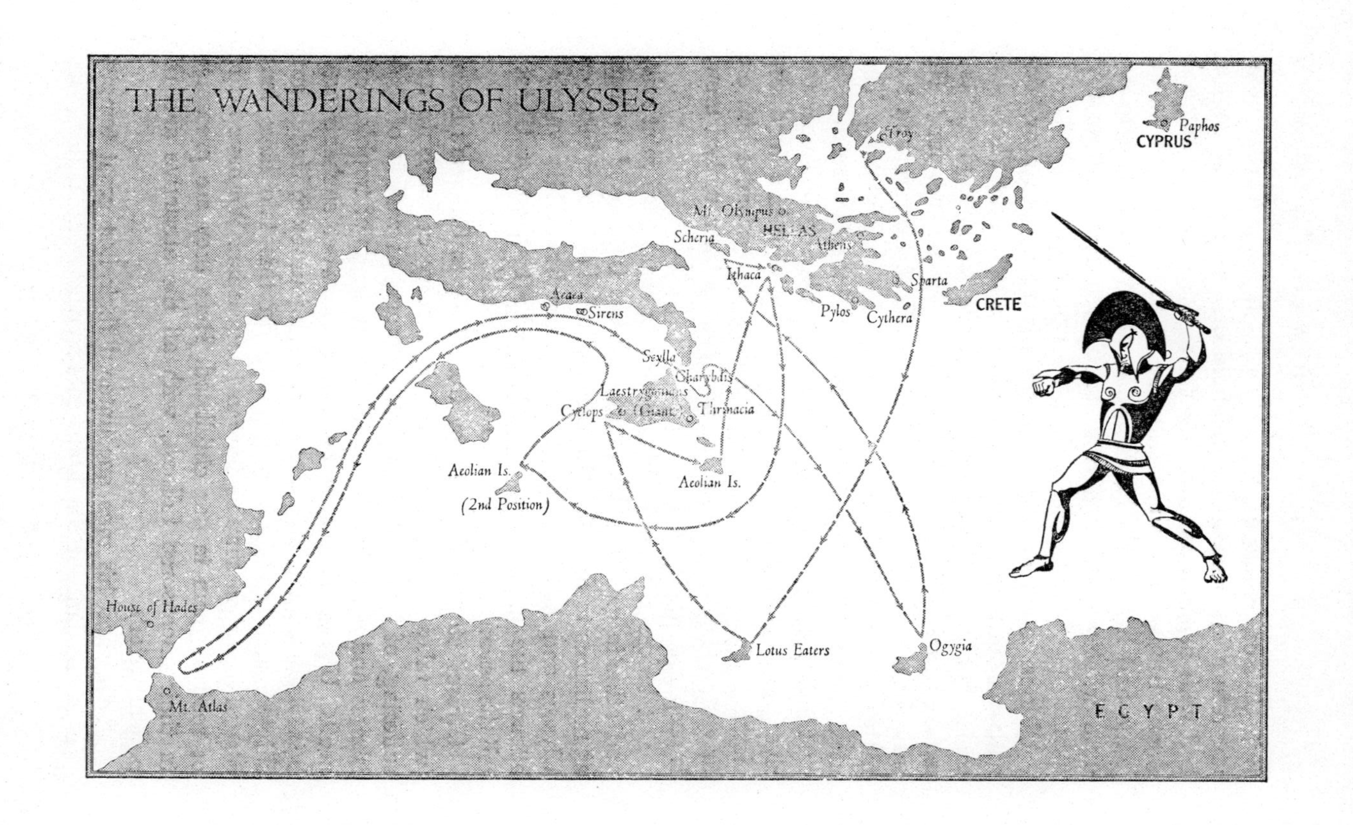
THE WANDERINGS OF ULYSSES
Troy
Paphos
CYPRUS
Mt. Olympus
HELLAS
Scheria
Athens
Ithaca
Sparta
CRETE
Pylos
Cythera
Aeaea
Sirens
Scylla
Charybdis
Laestrygonians
Cyclops
(Giant)
Thrinacia
Aeolian Is.
(2nd Position)
Aeolian Is.
House of Hades
Mt. Atlas
Lotus Eaters
Ogygia
EGYPT

to make them forget all about home and duty; the men who ate of the lotus had to be forced aboard ship and bound fast. Next they contended with the Cyclops, the one-eyed giant who shut them up in his cave and ate them, two to a meal. Ulysses, through his cunning, succeeded in boring out the giant's one eye and managing the escape of himself and the surviving men. The Cyclops, amazed and furious that "a little insignificant weakling" had blinded him, prayed to his father, Neptune, to

> "'. . . grant that Ulysses may never reach his home alive; or if he must get back to his friends at last, let him do so late and in sore plight after losing all his men [let him reach his home in another man's ship and find trouble in his house].'" (p. 234d)

Neptune heard his blinded son's prayer and bore Ulysses a perpetual grudge thereafter.

Ulysses and his men next reached the island of Aeolus, who has charge of the winds. Aeolus shut up all the winds in a sack on Ulysses' ship, save for the West wind which blew them home. But in sight of Ithaca, almost in earshot of home, the men, jealous lest Ulysses might have personal booty in the sack, opened it and let loose the winds that blew them back to where they had started. "We were lost through our own folly," Ulysses rightly says; indeed, he was so vexed that he felt like jumping into the sea and ending it all, but he decided to carry on.

Next they ran into the Laestrygonians, the man-eating ogres who made a meal of all the Greeks save Ulysses and his immediate crew. The survivors then met a new peril in the enchantress Circe, who invited some of them in to drink and dine, got them to forget about their homes, and then turned them into swine. But Ulysses, aided by Mercury, circumvented Circe's wiles and ensured that, though he went to bed with her, she should not unman him; and he also made her turn his men back into human form. A pleasant year of wining and dining followed, during which Ulysses enjoyed the charms of Circe, but he still insisted on going home at the end of the year.

First, however, he had to go to Hades, the land of the

dead, to obtain a prophecy about his future from the Theban seer Teiresias. The descent to Hades is one of the most impressive scenes in the *Odyssey,* as the pale, bloodless shades throng to the blood that has come from Ulysses' sacrifice. Teiresias drinks the blood (capacity to reason and speak is linked with the blood) and prophesies that Ulysses and his men will get home if they do not molest the cattle of the sun, which they will soon encounter. Ulysses also meets his mother, who has died of grief at his long absence, but he is unable to embrace her, for the dead are bodiless phantoms. There follow several processions of famous figures: women of myth and legend, Ulysses' dead comrades, and the great mythical heroes, including Hercules. Ulysses wants to see even more, but he prudently beats a retreat back to his ship, lest Proserpine send up the horrible Gorgon head to turn him into stone.

After this interlude at Hades' gate, Ulysses started homeward once more and met new temptations and perils. First, there were the Sirens, female creatures, who draw men to forgetfulness and death through the sweet enchantment of their songs. Next, there was the passage between the monster Scylla and the whirlpool of Charybdis (this is where the familiar phrase "between Scylla and Charybdis" comes from). The six-headed monster snapped up six of Ulysses' men, one to a mouth, before Ulysses' ship got through. Says Ulysses, "This was the most sickening sight that I saw throughout all my voyages." Lastly, there were the cattle of the sun, a final temptation which proved the undoing of Ulysses' men. In spite of all warnings, when they got hungry they ate the cattle, and Jove in punishment wrecked their ship. All the men drowned save Ulysses, who was washed ashore on Calypso's island.

This is the end of Ulysses' story.

III

The last half of the *Odyssey,* Books XIII-XXIV, forms a single unit and presents a simple story, compared with the many episodes of Books I-XII. We might entitle this story "The

Return of Ulysses" or "Ulysses' Revenge." This single theme is the essence of the final twelve books of the *Odyssey*, and though it is presented in a more leisurely way than a Western movie or television horse opera, the climax is the same, with the hero and his few trusted allies slaughtering a horde of enemies. There is also a final scene of reconciliation and peace when the suitors' feuding kinfolk and Ulysses bury the hatchet. But this is a leisurely story, as we have said, with many digressions, especially the tall tales told by Ulysses to conceal his identity, many recognition scenes in which his identity is made known, and many acts of intervention by the gods.

This story begins with the return of Ulysses to Ithaca in the Phaeacian boat. Mercury transforms Ulysses into a wrinkled old man, so that he may conceal his identity, explore the lay of the land, and carefully plot his revenge. He takes refuge in the hut of his swineherd Eumaeus, who does not recognize the old beggar and offers him hospitality out of religious impulse (Jove is the friend of beggars and rewards charity to them). Meanwhile, Telemachus comes home from Sparta and Pylos, under Minerva's protection, and evades the ambush set by the suitors. He sees omens of Ulysses' revenge—an eagle with a white goose in its talons, a hawk bearing away a dove.

The first recognition scene occurs when Telemachus goes to Eumaeus' hut immediately on his return. Ulysses does not reveal his identity at first but probes his son and questions his inaction in the face of the suitors' monstrous behavior. Finally, with the aid of a retransformation effected by Mercury, Ulysses appears in his own form to his son, but Telemachus (who is too young, anyway, to have known a father gone twenty years) is awestruck at the sudden change and thinks Ulysses is a god. Says Ulysses,

> "I am no god, why should you take me for one? I am your father, on whose account you grieve and suffer so much at the hands of lawless men." (p. 274a)

> ". . . There is no other Ulysses who will come hereafter. Such as I am, it is I, who after long wandering and much hardship have got home in the twentieth year to my own country. . . ." (p. 274b)

He tells his son that they will conquer the hundred-odd suitors with the aid of Jove and Minerva.

Ulysses then returns to his incognito form so that he may better spy out those of his own household to determine who is with him and who is against him. When Ulysses returns to his house after twenty years' absence, disguised as an old beggar, he is humiliated and insulted—by his own goatherd and by two of the suitors, who throw stools at him. The second recognition scene comes when Euryclea, his old nurse, sees an old scar he got as a boy.

> As soon as Euryclea had got the scarred limb in her hands and had well hold of it, she recognized it and dropped the foot at once. The leg fell into the bath, which rang out and was overturned, so that all the water was spilt on the ground; Euryclea's eyes between her joy and her grief filled with tears, and she could not speak, but she caught Ulysses by the beard and said, "My dear child, I am sure you must be Ulysses himself, only I did not know you till I had actually touched and handled you." (p. 294a)

Ulysses makes Euryclea keep silent so that he may retain his incognito and safely consummate his revenge.

The revenge, prefigured by dreams and omens, takes place on the occasion of a shooting contest staged by Penelope to decide who will win her hand. Whichever of the suitors can string the bronze bow of Ulysses and send an arrow through the handle holes of twelve axes, set up in a row, will win. But none of the suitors is able to accomplish this, and the old beggar (Ulysses) alone succeeds. Now Ulysses reveals his identity to the suitors and announces their doom.

> "Dogs, did you think that I should not come back from Troy? You have wasted my substance, have forced my women servants to lie with you, and have wooed my wife while I was still living. You have feared neither God nor man, and now you shall die." (p. 306b)

> "Though you should give me all that you have in the world both now and all that you ever shall have, I will not stay my hand till I have paid all of you in full. You must fight, or fly for your lives; and fly, not a man of you shall." (p. 306d)

Ulysses then wreaks his revenge, aided by Telemachus, Eumaeus, and another loyal servant, as well as by Minerva.

who makes the suitors' spears miss and terrifies them by her "deadly aegis." (See *Iliad,* p. 37c.) Ulysses slaughters the suitors unmercifully, sparing only the minstrel and the herald. He also has Telemachus hang twelve servant girls who have been insolent to Penelope and Telemachus, and who have slept with the suitors. The goatherd who insulted Ulysses and aided the suitors in the struggle is horribly mutilated and eviscerated, and his parts are thrown to the dogs. After these gory goings-on, the hall is purified with fire and sulfur, and a grim pretense of music and dancing is put on, so that the suitors' kin will not know what has happened. Says Ulysses,

> ". . . When one man has killed another, even though he was not one who would leave many friends to take up his quarrel, the man who has killed him must still say good bye to his friends and fly the country; whereas we have been killing the stay of a whole town, and all the picked youth of Ithaca. . . ." (p. 313b-c)

But before Ulysses deals with the kinfolk he has to reveal his identity and return to his wife and father. The recognition scene with Penelope takes an odd turn. Uncertain whether to embrace him or probe him, she decides to put his identity to the test. Ulysses is quite nettled at this.

> "My dear," said he, "heaven has endowed you with a heart more unyielding than woman ever yet had. No other woman could bear to keep away from her husband when he had come back to her after twenty years of absence, and after having gone through so much. But come, nurse, get a bed ready for me; I will sleep alone, for this woman has a heart as hard as iron." (pp. 313d-314a)

But he convinces her by the knowledge he has of the special bed he made from an olive-tree stump. The long-separated couple embrace and go "joyfully to the rites of their old bed."

In the final recognition scene, with his old father Laertes, Ulysses remains crafty to the end, no matter how piteous the sorrow of the old man. He conceals his identity behind a cock-and-bull story that includes good news about Ulysses.

> A dark cloud of sorrow fell upon Lærtes as he listened. He filled both hands with the dust from off the ground and poured it over his grey head, groaning heavily as he did so. The heart of Ulysses was touched,

and his nostrils quivered as he looked upon his father; then he sprang towards him, flung his arms about him and kissed him, saying, "I am he, father, about whom you are asking—I have returned after having been away for twenty years . . ." (p. 320b)

The old man is convinced by certain proofs that it is indeed his son, and offers up thanks to Jove for doing justice.

The story ends on a note of reconciliation and peace, as Minerva intervenes to stop the battle between the suitors' kin and Ulysses and his men. She orders that the dispute be settled without bloodshed. She makes "a covenant of peace between the two contending parties." These are the last words of the *Odyssey*.

IV

Let us now glance briefly at the main characters of the *Odyssey*. Ulysses, the hero of this work, is not the usual noble character of high tragedy or storybook romance. His main traits are craftiness and tenacity. Time and time again we are told that he is cunning, devious, cautious, suspicious. He does not trust even the gods or people who have gone out of their way to befriend him. When the sea-goddess Ino gives him a veil to save him from drowning, he is mistrustful and decides not to take a chance on the veil until his raft is broken into pieces. He had refused to go to sea in the first place until the nymph Calypso had first sworn that she intended him no harm. When he gets back to Ithaca and does not recognize the place, he suspects that the Phaeacians—who have incurred divine punishment in bringing him home—have deceived him. He does not even trust Minerva when she tells him he is in Ithaca, for which she upbraids him good-humoredly.

"You are always taking something of that sort into your head," replied Minerva, "and that is why I cannot desert you in your afflictions; you are so plausible, shrewd, and shifty . . ." (p. 258c)

As she says, anyone else returning after a long absence would go straight home to his family, but he has to be crafty and test his wife first. He is "a shifty, lying fellow," who instinctively prefers falsehood, deceit, and tricks. But it is this that has helped him to survive. Minerva says she never really worried about how he would come out in the end. It was his craftiness that defeated the Cyclops and flattered Nausicaa into aiding him.

But Homer does not make his hero conform to a single mold. Ulysses is not always prudent and cautious. It was his cupidity for a present that led to his capture by the Cyclops, and here he went against the sound counsel of his men. And he is valorous, eager to take anyone on, man or god, when the occasion requires it. Says Circe,

> " 'You dare-devil . . . you are always wanting to fight somebody or something; you will not let yourself be beaten even by the immortals . . .' " (p. 251b)

Also he has a rigorous sense of duty. When the time came to encounter Circe's enchantments and rescue his men, he pushed back timid counsels, and said, "but I must go, for I am most urgently bound to do so" (p. 239a). Again, however, Homer does not make him fit a logically consistent but unrealistic mold. Ulysses can be frightened by natural forces and by human odds that are too overwhelming. In his final battle against the suitors, he has to receive divine encouragement and intervention to bolster his shaken heart.

Ulysses is a braggart, always eager to sing his own praises as the craftiest and toughest of mortals. But a good deal of what he says is true, and apparently self-praise was not regarded as a defect in the Homeric era.

As for his relations with women, Ulysses is monogamous, but not fanatically so. He wants to get home to his own bed and wife, but Calypso does not have to twist his arm to get him to go to bed with her, nor does Circe, with whom he spends a pleasant year. Ulysses is a man en route, and he takes the sweet with the bitter on the long way home. The "double standard" for men and women seems to rule here, for although it is important that his wife be utterly faithful, Ulysses sees no need to justify his love life when he gets home.

Penelope, the main lady in this piece, is a bit harder to figure out. She appears different according to who is viewing her, so that it is not always clear what her real motivations are. She, too, seems to be a sly one who does not want to take any chances, and is waiting to see how things will turn out. She could refuse to marry again, but she does not. She does not think Ulysses will return, but she is not certain that he is dead.

The suitors resent the airs she puts on and suspect she enjoys being the center of attention. She is a lady who doesn't say "yes" and doesn't say "no," and uses considerable ingenuity in saying neither. She is also a sweet and charming woman, but not above wounding her importunate suitors with nasty, catty remarks on occasion. On the whole, Homer portrays her as the model of a faithful, devoted wife and mother, though Telemachus at times expresses irritation and suspicion about her actions, and Ulysses takes his own sweet time about confiding in her. But ultimately Homer makes it clear that she hates her suitors and wants her husband back.

Telemachus is cast in the ordinary, rather than in the heroic, mold. He has no great qualities of mind or character. He is pictured as weak, uncertain, untried, unsure of himself, a boy who needs his father. He is, perhaps, the most modern character in the story and could easily fit into a present-day play or novel. When we first meet him, he is a despairing youth, convinced that his father is dead, and impotent to stop the suitors from eating up his estate. Emboldened by Minerva's sponsorship, he tells his mother and the suitors that he is going to be master in his own house, but he soon has to be encouraged by Minerva again when the suitors refuse to act decently. She bids him be like his father, "not . . . either fool or coward," and sends him on a journey in quest of his father, so that he may gain renown, like Orestes. But Telemachus is no Orestes, for his words and actions are not self-initiated; indeed, he hardly acts at all, save as a supernumerary. Telemachus never becomes a hero.

His attitude is that "no matter how valiant a man may be he can do nothing against numbers, for they will be too strong for him" (p. 273a). He has no zeal to go down fighting singlehanded rather than endure indignity. He tells Ulysses that the odds against them are hopelessly great, and he has to be reassured that Minerva and Jove are their allies. He does not escape the suitors' ambush through his own craftiness and courage, but solely through divine intervention. When Ulysses is with him he talks up boldly to the suitors, and insists that now he has become a man. Homer indicates that this claim may be true, for he intimates that Telemachus could have strung Ulysses' bow (on the fourth try) and only makes a show of being too weak to defend himself. Indeed, he orders his mother back to her knitting and takes charge of the contest himself. He fights valiantly beside his father and intervenes magnanimously to save the lives of the minstrel and the herald. However, cruelty succeeds weakness and impotence. It is Telemachus who decides that the maidservants shall die the base death of hanging, and he participates in the horrible butchery of the goatherd.

V

Now let us glance briefly at the manner in which the *Odyssey* is told. The *Odyssey* is in form an epic poem. Epics are long narrative poems, written in sonorous, declamatory style, telling the story of legendary or historical heroes. Epics are the oldest form of Greek literature that has come down to us, and were originally recited by minstrels at public gatherings. Epic poetry is distinguished from lyric poetry, which consists of songs (in ancient times sung to a lyre) expressing personal feelings; and from dramatic poetry, which is recited by actors on the stage. Among the other epic poems in our set, besides Homer's *Iliad* and *Odyssey*, are Virgil's *Aeneid* and Milton's *Paradise Lost*.

One of the first things you will notice about the *Odyssey* is that it is repetitious. Situations, events, phrases (such as "rosy-fingered Dawn"), and dialogue are repeated again and again. If you miss some of the details about Ulysses' wanderings or the situation in Ithaca the first time you read about them, do not worry, they will be told again several times. You may find the repetitions annoying and want to skip them and get on with the story. But they were helpful to an audience that had to listen to this poem being recited, sometimes over a long period of time. In this "continued story" the minstrel tells his listeners what has gone before by repeating it at convenient spots in the narrative. We may also add that ancient audiences, unlike modern ones, found repetition enjoyable rather than tedious; just as people used to enjoy watching the same vaudeville acts year after year. Symphonic music and religious liturgy also depend a great deal on repetition.

Another thing you will notice about the *Odyssey* is the frequent digressions. Sometimes, as in Ulysses' story in Books IX-XII, these are structurally part of the main narrative, like sequences in the movies that "flash back" to show us what has taken place in the past. But sometimes the digressions contribute nothing directly to the course of the narrative, as Ulysses' cock-and-bull stories about himself when he is trying to preserve his incognito; the stories about their pasts by various minor characters, such as Eumaeus; and the wonderful little story in Book XIX about how Ulysses got his scar.

These digressions have been called "the retarding element" in Homer's poems, and received much attention from the famous German writers Goethe and Schiller, who considered "retardation" an essential element in epic poetry—relaxing the tension and keeping a leisurely pace—as contrasted with the constant ongoing tension to the point of climax in dramatic tragedy. Erich Auerbach said that this element in Homer derived from his essential tendency to make everything clear and explicit, to bring all the details to light. The poet finds this necessary even in a minor offshoot or bypath from the main story, just as an artist or craftsman does with details of a painting, building, or other object. Homer must fill in all the details, answering clearly and definitely questions of where, when, why, how, who. He is not content with a mere bare reference—he must spell it out, render it fully.

This capacity for clear, full detail is shown in all of Homer's descriptions, whether he tells about washing clothes, building a raft, or fighting a battle. This art of representing the concrete details of life makes the story and all the digressions so vivid that we have the illusion of being present at the events portrayed. Even his metaphors, his figures of speech, are taken from the ordinary life of home and field.

Another of the main elements in the *Odyssey* is the "recognition" scene. This is a special form of what Aristotle, in the *Poetics,* calls "discovery," the transition from ignorance to knowledge. (See Vol. 9, pp. 687b, 689d-690b.) Some of the most highly dramatic and poignant moments in the second half of the *Odyssey* come in the scenes when Ulysses' identity becomes known. The meaning of Ulysses' return is dramatized in these scenes through the speeches of Ulysses revealing his identity, and the responses of the persons to whom he makes his identity known. The speech and especially the response vary as Ulysses addresses his son, his nurse, his swineherd, the suitors, his wife, his father. The emotional depth of the characters and the situation is conveyed to the reader and shared with him through this device.

Despite its digressions and other "retarding" elements, the *Odyssey* is well plotted, and moves forward from beginning to end as an interesting, connected story. There is some question, though, as to whether or not the lesser characters in the *Odyssey* come out as individuals, fully presented as persons. The plot is the main thing here, and Homer's minor characters are usually thinly outlined, functioning as stock types or playing functional roles in the story. It is the story and the dialogue—which often consists of long speeches—that carry us along. We do not notice that we know almost nothing about Calypso, Circe, the many kings, and other supernumeraries in the story.

VI

What is the role of the gods in the Odyssey?

The gods intervene in the action. Neptune makes Ulysses' life miserable, but Minerva aids him. She usually assumes human form, that of actual living persons. Ulysses also is aided by various demi-gods, nymphs, enchantresses, and the like. The supernatural intervention and human action harmonize with one another. Ulysses is not saved by his own sagacity and courage alone. When the human or natural forces opposing him are too great, and all seems lost, the gods step in to help him.

Ulysses is the hero of extraordinary adventures and has an extraordinary triumph in the face of the greatest obstacles and dangers. The connection of the extraordinary with the supernatural is an ancient, primitive tendency, and good fortune, Lady Luck, is always a force to be reckoned with in human affairs. It was natural that Ulysses' survival and conquest should be associated with the supernatural powers believed to control human events in some measure.

Would the story be just as good, or even better, without these interventions by the gods? What would it gain in literary power? What would it lose? How would a modern author convey the elements of fate or fortune or other suprahuman powers that affect human life?

Are the suitors the villains of this story?

The suitors are clearly hateful to Ulysses and his household. Their behavior in loitering and roistering in another man's house is clearly wrong, and, further, offensive to the gods. But Homer, keeping himself out of the story as the impartial narrator, provides them with speeches in their own behalf. They claim that they are behaving the way they are only in order to force the dilatory and teasing Penelope to make up her mind. They say they do not want to eat up Telemachus' estate—and it is his, not hers, if Ulysses is dead—but only to bring the long courtship to a close.

It is not made clear, though, why they do not drop this matronly coquette and marry other women, as they say they could. Apparently it is not Penelope's charm and beauty that attracts them, but her being the presumed widow of the King of Ithaca. It seems that whoever marries her will be one up in the competition for the kingship—which is not hereditary and will not necessarily go to Telemachus if Ulysses is dead. It is charged that the chief suitor, Antinous—who is the real "heavy" in this piece—did not even want to marry Penelope, but only to be top man in Ithaca, at any cost—even if that means the murder of Telemachus. The motivations of the other suitors are not made clear. But Ulysses is not interested in distinguishing between them; a suitor is a suitor to him, and he kills them all—save for the minstrel and herald, who will sing his glory.

Would the story be more consistent and clear to you if Homer did not give the suitors some justification and reasonable motivation, and made them all black, and made Penelope all white, without a flaw or questionable trait? Or does it add something to the richness and reality of the story to make things more mixed and shaded?

Is Ulysses a proper hero for an epic poem?

The main subject of an epic is the action that takes place. If the events are extraordinary and the main character is heroic, as in the *Odyssey*, the requirements of epic are satisfied. The hero need not be a stainless, noble, and great person. It may be a problem, though, whether everyday life, which takes up a large part of this work, is compatible with the high tone required of epic poetry. *Tom Jones,* which is the subject of the Third Reading in *Imaginative Literature II,* also tells the story of a hero who passes through a series of adventures and misadventures. Is *Tom Jones* an epic? Does an epic have to be in poetry of highly dignified style? If so, does our translation by Samuel Butler, with its level, common English prose style, detract from the epic quality of the *Odyssey?* Does it make the poem more like a novel? Or is it substance alone, the content of the story, rather than the style and tone that decides whether a work is an epic?

Is Telemachus comparable to Shakespeare's Hamlet?

Hamlet is a prince whose uncle has killed his father and married his mother. He is directed by his father's ghost to revenge the horrible double crime of murder and incest. Hamlet goes through many twists of character and action before he accomplishes his revenge. Much has been made of the phase of indecision and introspection he passes through on the road to action.

Telemachus is the son of a king, too. But he does not know

whether his father is dead or alive, and nobody has married his mother yet. He despises the suitors as men inferior to his father and hates them for being insolent and eating up his estate, but there is no near relation involved, no incestuous staining of his father's marriage bed. He is not, like Hamlet, angry at his mother for the latter deed; but he is irritated with his mother about the whole situation.

What of Telemachus' indecisiveness? Is it like Hamlet's? Telemachus is not even sure that Ulysses is his father—"it is a wise child that knows its own father" (p. 185b). He is pessimistic and melancholy: "I inherit nothing but dismay" (p. 185c). He is "brooding and full of thought" (p. 187c). He talks up to the suitors, then weakens as they resist. He cannot act without Minerva's prodding and sponsorship. He seeks an explanation for his sad estate in his being from "a race of only sons," the only son of an only son. (See p. 273b.) As Hamlet puts on a show of madness, Telemachus puts on a show of weakness (and we are not quite sure whether either of them is just putting on a show). "Alas!" he cries, "I shall either be always feeble and of no prowess, or I am too young, and have not yet reached my full strength so as to be able to hold my own if any one attacks me" (p. 302c).

Both Hamlet and Telemachus end up by slaying their enemies. But is Telemachus ever central to the action in the *Odyssey*, as Hamlet is in Shakespeare's play? Does Telemachus ever make a decision on his own? Does Hamlet? Does the fact that Telemachus' father is alive and central to the plot and that Hamlet's father is only a ghost make any difference? Or is the will of Hamlet's father, though bodiless and absent, as effective as the will of Telemachus' father, who is present and active in the flesh? Does Hamlet act on his own, or does his father's will act through him, as the will of Ulysses acts through Telemachus?

Do the "retarding" elements help or hinder your enjoyment of the story?

Would the story run more smoothly or would it lack something if the digressions and "flashbacks" were omitted or reduced to brief notice? In the detailed story in Book XIX of how Ulysses got his scar, does the full, explicit account and rendering of the incident add richness and depth to the main narrative? Or does it detract instead, by centering our full attention on an incident not vital to carrying on the main story? Have you noted any other incidents and "flashbacks" in the *Odyssey* that receive this full treatment?

In other arts or in the various aspects of your life, do you find more enjoyment in getting directly to the point, as quickly as possible, and brushing aside all incidental details, whether they are enriching or not? Or do you prefer to take your time, pursue your enjoyment or appreciation at a leisurely pace, sipping slowly and not rushing toward the goal, not forcing the end, but retarding it instead?

Erich Auerbach has contrasted biblical with Homeric narration. He points to the story of the sacrifice of Isaac in Chapter 22 of Genesis as typical of the Bible in its bareness of narration, its neglect of specific details of place, time, manner, person, motivation. Yet we find such spare biblical tales loaded with meaning. Is the Homeric or the biblical way better suited to the telling of stories? Or are the biblical and Homeric stories told with a different intent, with a different vision of the world?

Is the Homeric way of spelling out the details, being so full and explicit, better suited to the representation of everyday reality and action? Can you think of modern storytelling that is bare and sparse, cutting out the details? How do Ernest Hemingway and Georges Simenon tell their stories—sparsely or fully? How about Joseph Conrad and Thomas Wolfe?

SELF-TESTING QUESTIONS

The following questions are designed to help you test the thoroughness of your reading. Each question is to be answered by giving a page or pages of the reading assignment. Answers will be found on page 232 of this Reading Plan.

1 Who is the daughter of Atlas?

2 What is the story of Agamemnon's murder and Orestes' revenge?

3 Who tried to inveigle the Greeks out of the Trojan horse?

4 Who is Jove's son-in-law?

5 Who is Arete?

6 What is the social state of the Cyclopes?

7 Who is Noman?

8 What is Moly?

9 What happened to Elpenor?

10 What is Achilles' attitude toward death?

Second Reading

EURIPIDES

Medea, Electra, Orestes

Vol. 5, pp. 212–224, 327–339, 394–410

Aeschylus, Sophocles, and Euripides were the greatest of the Greek tragic dramatists. Of the three, Euripides speaks the most directly to the modern reader. Aeschylus and Sophocles may possess greater depths or a nobler tragic vision, but their manner and matter is strange to us. As soon as we read Euripides, however, we recognize a familiar way of staging, characterization, and dialogue. How many generations of dramatists have learned from this ancient Greek? And where else have we seen those passionate, twisted individuals who follow their turbulent courses through his plays? As we read Euripides, we remember characters and incidents in Shakespeare, Ibsen, O'Neill, and other dramatists even closer to our time.

Euripides wrote some grim and terrible stories, with many stormy, amoral, and psychopathic characters; and some critics have therefore condemned his plays as shocking and perverted. But the weight of both critical and popular opinion through the ages has been that Euripides' best plays are great, well-made pieces of dramatic art that reveal the evil and suffering in human existence and man's tragic action in the face of these ills.

First, in the *Medea,* we have the story of a woman of tremendous passion and will, who wreaks a terrible revenge when her husband deserts her for another woman in order to better his position in the world. Through Euripides' art, this woman's agony and fury become understandable and believable, and Medea takes her place with the immortal characters of literature.

Second, in the *Electra,* we have the story of a horrible situation where a young man and a young woman feel bound to murder their mother in revenge for her murder of their father. The psychological understanding that Euripides displays of the motivations and consequences of such an act of vengeance is sure and subtle, and makes him congenial to the modern temper.

Finally, in the *Orestes,* we continue this terrible story in one of the most exciting and fast-paced of ancient dramas, as the brother and sister are brought to account for their deeds but struggle against the reckoning. This is a well-constructed and impressive thriller, replete with psychological sickness, violence, sudden turns of plot, and even humor.

GUIDE TO

Second Reading

I

Euripides, like his great predecessors, Aeschylus and Sophocles, wrote his dramas for production at the festivals in honor of Dionysius, the god of wine and fertility. The drama in ancient Athens was an element in public worship and was enacted in an outdoor theater, centered around the altar of the god. The word "tragedy" derives from a term meaning "goat song," which was probably a dithyramb, or choral song, for Dionysius. Possibly, as Aristotle suggests, dramatic tragedy developed from the Dionysian dithyramb. The themes of tragedy were derived from Greek mythology—the stories of gods and heroes—and were known to the audience beforehand. The distinction of the individual dramatist lay not in the originality of his story, but in the way he presented it. The dramatists competed with one another for first prize at the festivals each year.

One of the first things you will note about Greek tragedy is that it combines music and drama, like grand opera. Originally, the choral singing predominated, and only gradually did the dramatic action become central in tragedy. In Greek tragedy, the chorus acts as commentator, sets the mood, and prepares us for the action that is to come. Sometimes it enters into dramatic dialogue with the actors or even enters into the action (pounding on the door in the *Medea*). Greek tragedy is always enacted through some combination of choral songs and dramatic episodes.

The chorus and the actors were all men, even when the singers or characters were supposed to be women. The actors—three in number by Euripides' time—played several parts.

They wore masks which expressed their roles, wigs or headdresses, long robes, and buskins (shoes) with very thick soles to give them stature. Stage machinery was simple but effective. Light in these outdoor theaters was provided by the sun, and it was possible to roll up a chariot when the play called for it. Sound effects were not unknown to the ancients, and they had machines to simulate thunder and lightning. Two stage devices used quite frequently by Euripides were a platform wheeled out to present an interior scene, and a crane used to simulate flight—as when a god enters the action (the *deus ex machina*). At the very front of the theaters, where our stage is, was a building called the *skene* (whence our word "scene"). The inside of the *skene* was used as the actors' dressing room, and the façade (called *paraskenia* or *proscenium*) as the stage setting for the temple, palace, or

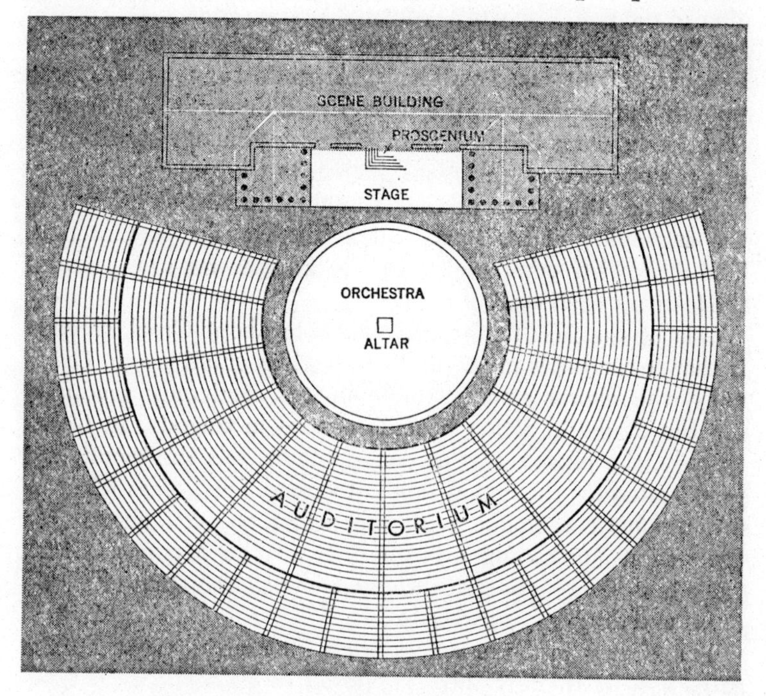

PLAN OF GREEK THEATER

house that was often the background in tragedy. Scene paintings were used to suggest other scenes. Dramatic action and choral singing took place in the large *orchestra* (dancing place) between the *skene* and the audience.

II

We have noted the social and religious setting of Greek tragedy as well as the material means with which it was presented. Now let us consider the essential nature and end of Greek tragedy that makes it understandable by modern readers far removed from its original setting and stage mechanics. We are fortunate in having in the *Great Books of the Western World* the classic attempt made by Aristotle to define tragedy and analyze its nature and purpose. Aristotle deals with tragedy in his *Poetics*. (See Vol. 9, pp. 684a-695a.)

Aristotle says that tragedy is an imitation of a serious action; presented through words, music, and other theatrical accessories; enacted rather than narrated (as is epic poetry, like the *Odyssey*); and arousing and releasing emotions of pity and fear in the spectators. By "imitation" Aristotle does not mean a mere copy of events, such as we get in photographs or newsreels, but a creative representation of essential and universal aspects of human existence. By "serious" action Aristotle means action involving persons of a higher type than the average, as opposed to the lower or ridiculous type of persons and actions presented in comedy. Since tragedy is an imitation *of action,* Aristotle considers plot the most important element, far more important than the music and stage properties, and even more important than the characters.

The ideal tragic plot for Aristotle is a unified whole in which all the parts contribute to the total dramatic effect. Hence a tragedy must deal with a single theme and be just the right size to be taken in at a single performance or reading, as opposed to long, rambling, episodic, disconnected presentation. This is the "unity of action," upon which Aristotle insists. Of the other "classic unities"—time and place—all he says is that tragedy usually tries to confine itself to a single day, but he says nothing at all about confining tragic action to a single place.

Since the end of tragedy is to arouse pity and fear, the ideal plot for Aristotle is one in which a person falls from high social position and good fortune to ignominy—from happiness to misery. Some complications are necessary to present such a reversal of fortune and to evoke the proper emotional response. Among such complications are happenings just the opposite of what the characters expected, and discoveries or recognitions (examples of which we have already considered in the First Reading). Suffering—murder, torture, wounds—is another essential element in the tragic plot.

The ideal tragic hero for Aristotle is a man somewhat above the average in virtue and character, but not perfect, for his fall from happiness to misery must occur because of some weakness in character or error in judgment on his part—a "tragic flaw." The hero's high place and fall may be intensified by making him a member of a great family, as is Orestes in *Electra* and *Orestes*. But he must fall and the play must have an unhappy ending. Here Aristotle points to Euripides as a model tragic poet.

> The critics, therefore, are wrong who blame Euripides for taking this line in his tragedies, and giving many of them an unhappy ending. It is, as we have said, the right line to take. The best proof is this: on the stage, and in the public performances, such plays, properly worked out, are seen to be the most truly tragic; and Euripides, even if his execution be faulty in every other point, is seen to be nevertheless the most tragic certainly of the dramatists. (Vol. 9, p. 688a)

The ideal tragic deed is one that occurs within the close bonds of friendship or kinship, such as the murder of parents by children, or of children by parents, for such an act arouses the greatest horror and pity. Aristotle opposes making use of stage effects (thunder, lightning, exciting music) to arouse such emotions, and he opposes using stage devices, such as the *deus ex machina,* to resolve matters that should be taken care of by the plot. He advocates treating the chorus as one of the actors, integrally related to the action, and not as a group that plays a merely ornamental or transitional role between dramatic episodes.

Aristotle knew that plays are meant to be played, that dramas must be acted; but he was convinced that a "mere reading of a play" will reveal the tragic theme and produce the tragic effect. (See Vol. 9, p. 698d.) Let us now try to be understanding and imaginative spectators of the dramas of Euripides through our reading alone—aided by this guide.

III

The *Medea* is probably the best known of Euripides' plays to modern readers. When it was first presented in Athens in 431 B.C., it was considered a very inferior production by the judges. But it soon rose to first rank as a model of Greek dramatic genius and was imitated or translated by later dramatists, all the way from the ancient Roman Seneca to the modern American Robinson Jeffers.

This strange and terrible play, with its perennial dramatic power, was based on the ancient Greek myth of Jason and the Golden Fleece. The Greek audiences which saw this play knew the traditional legend before they came to the theater. They came to see what new image the dramatist would create out of the fixed details of the old story.

In the myth, Jason was required by his wicked uncle, who was usurping his throne, to perform an impossible feat before he could become king—to obtain the Golden Fleece, which hung on an oak in the faraway kingdom of Colchis, guarded by a dragon that never slept. Jason sailed on the ship "Argo" with a crew of fifty great heroes—including Orpheus, Hercules, and Theseus—called the Argonauts. The King of Colchis agreed to give Jason the Golden Fleece if he would first yoke two fire-breathing oxen and sow the dragon's teeth. He was able to accomplish these feats only through the aid of Medea, the King's daughter, who had fallen in love with him and who possessed magic powers. She fled with Jason and the Argonauts when they escaped from Colchis with the Golden Fleece. Taking her brother along, she killed him, cut him into pieces, and scattered the pieces along the road to delay her father's pursuit.

When Jason returned to his homeland, his wicked uncle still denied him the throne. Medea tricked the usurper's daughters into cutting their father into pieces and boiling him, on the pretext that he would thereby be restored to youth. After the uncle died, his son banished Jason and Medea from the kingdom. They went into exile at Corinth, where they lived happily until Jason decided to divorce Medea in order to marry the daughter of the King of Corinth. Medea retaliated by making the Princess and the King suffer a painful death and by killing the two sons she had borne Jason. She then flew away to Athens in a chariot drawn by winged dragons. According to one account, the grief-stricken Jason committed suicide; according to another, accepted by Euripides, he was killed by a falling fragment of his old ship, the "Argo." In Greek religion, Medea was venerated as a goddess at Corinth, and especially adored in Jason's home province of Thessaly for her magic arts.

Euripides selects a single theme from this mass of legendary material—Medea's revenge against Jason for casting her down in order to rise in the world—and produces a powerful dramatization of the hellish fury of a woman scorned. The whole is staged in such a way that we may believe in and be moved by the appalling vengeance of a mother who would kill her own children in order to spite their father. Medea is a person with magic powers, but Euripides deals with her essentially as a woman, a woman of deep and dark emotions, a woman in a man-made and man-ruled world, and a foreigner (a "barbarian") in a Greek city-state. He fills out her character fully so that, though horrified, we may grasp imaginatively how she could come to do such deeds, how such things are humanly possible. Due note is taken of the gods and of fate, but the center of attention here is the human heart and human motivation—the action of a "proud restless soul, in the anguish of despair" (p. 213a).

When we first hear her voice, she expresses the wish to die at once, to gain release from the terrible agony that arises from being cast aside by her man. But we know from what her nurse says that her affronted love will seek compensation in harming others, even her own children.

. . . for dreadful is her wrath; verily the man that doth incur her hate will have no easy task to raise o'er her a song of triumph. (p. 212b-c)

And Medea herself soon makes it plain that she—a destitute and solitary foreigner, without a city or family to give her refuge—will seek vengeance on her husband, and on the King of Corinth and his daughter for the unhappiness that has befallen her.

But despite her passionate and proud nature, Medea's vulnerable position—unaided and lone in an alien land—forces her to alternate between fiery outspokenness and crafty deceit. When Creon, the King of Corinth, tells her she must leave Corinth immediately with her children—fearing the harm that may come from her wounded heart and her witchcraft—she wheedles a day's respite out of him to set her affairs in order. Actually she wants the additional time only in order to destroy him and his daughter and Jason, and she has only contempt for the man whose kindliness soon proves to be a foolish and fatal error.

In the first scene with Jason, apparently their first meeting since his new marriage, Medea tells him all she has done for him, how she saved his life and secured the Golden Fleece for him, betrayed her own family and country, only to be rewarded by his desertion. But Jason refuses to have a guilty conscience and defends what he has done. He says that it was "the Love-god" (Eros) (the term "Cypris" here is an epithet for Aphrodite, the mother of Eros) that saved him by making her love him, so she does not deserve the credit. Besides, he has more than repaid her by bringing her to Greek civilization; no one would ever have heard about her if she had remained in Colchis. Finally, he has married the Corinthian Princess merely as a matter of prudence, seeking future security for himself and his sons, and thus for her too. Medea retorts that he is a clever, lying villain who decided to insure his old age by getting rid of his inconvenient foreign wife and marrying the King's daughter. She hotly refuses to accept any aid from him to support her and the children in exile.

In this dramatic confrontation Medea has to alternate her passionate outspokenness with craft and guile in order to accomplish her purpose. First, she arranges with the King of Athens to give her sworn sanctuary in his kingdom. Next, she calls Jason back to tell him she is sorry about the way she talked to him; she was but a weak, childish woman, but now she has thought better of it and wants him to take care of the children. She asks Jason to take them to the Princess with fine gifts, especially prepared for her by Medea, so that she will be more ready to accept the boys into her home. Jason, fatuously and smugly, accepts the new turn as the victory of good sense over womanly weakness and vanity, and trots off toward his new bride, along with the boys and the gifts.

Medea's gifts are "a robe of finest tissue and a chaplet [crown] of chased gold" (p. 220a-b). The Princess, mollified by the fine gifts, puts them on and admires herself in the mirror, but she soon shrieks in agony, for the chaplet burns her to death and the robe—permeated with destructive drugs—consumes her flesh and bones. Her grief-stricken father, King Creon, clasps her in his arms and dies from contact with the robe, as the destructive drugs eat away his body too. All this happens offstage and we learn about it from a messenger as he tells it to Medea. She is exultant at the news.

But one more terrible deed remains to be done in order to strike down Jason—killing his children and hers (they have returned to the house before the deaths occurred). This deed —the most horrible of them all—is bound to strike Jason in his very vitals by rendering him childless. It is probably true, as he says, that he did not love the Corinthian princess, and King Creon means nothing to him personally, but the sons of his loins mean everything—his future, his descendants, his immortality. This blow will strike home, and Medea will have complete revenge.

Yet Medea in Euripides' play is a woman, and not a monster. She has to go through a struggle between the natural loving-kindness of a mother for her children and the furious vengeance of a woman scorned. In what is probably the most touching passage in the play (pp. 220d-221b), she goes through emotions of sorrow, horror, reluctance, abandonment of her awful purpose, acceptance of the necessity of her children's death. She goes forward and backward, from "I cannot . . . No, no, I will not do it," to "Out upon my craven heart!"—repenting of her soft words—back again to "Ah! ah! do not, my heart, O do not do this deed!" and then again to resolution, with a new note, "Die they must in any case," at the hands of Creon's avenging kin. Finally, after kissing and weeping over the boys, she sends them into the house, and realizes

At last I understand the awful deed I am to do; but passion, that cause of direst woes to mortal man, hath triumphed o'er my sober thoughts. (p. 221b)

And when she goes in to do the deed, convinced that she is saving the children from execution at harsher hands, she says,

. . . advance to the post whence starts thy life of sorrow! Away with cowardice! Give not one thought to thy babes, how dear they are or how thou art their mother. This one brief day forget thy children dear, and after that lament; for though thou wilt slay them yet they were thy darlings still, and I am a lady of sorrows. (p. 222c)

It is a terrible moment as we hear the piteous pleading of the boys for help against the murderous blows of their mother, and the chorus tries vainly to stop the murder (pounding on the barred doors of the house in the stage presentation). Jason arrives in the hope of saving the boys from the vengeance of Creon's kin, and finds that they have already been destroyed through the vengeance of the woman he deserted. The former hero, who in his glorious youth brought back the Golden Fleece from Colchis, and who has sought in middle age to obtain comfort and security through an opportunistic marriage, is now a pathetic figure. He has lost everything; and he is impotent to strike back against Medea, whose magic powers once brought him glory but now enable her to talk to him from "*mid air, on a chariot drawn by dragons*" (p. 223b). She even refuses to give him the boys' corpses "to bury and lament" and keeps them at her side. She curses him and prophesies his ignominious death. Jason complains to heaven about her deeds and wails a dirge for his sons, and the chorus chants the moral.

Many a fate doth Zeus dispense, high on his Olympian throne; oft do the gods bring things to pass beyond man's expectation; that, which we thought would be, is not fulfilled, while for the unlooked-for god finds out a way; and such hath been the issue of this matter. (p. 224c)

So ends the play.

This terrible tale, told in less than fifteen hundred lines of verse in the original, and staged in an hour or two, points out and reiterates many subthemes in addition to presenting fully the main theme. One of these subthemes is the destructive power of unshackled emotions, and hence the saving virtue of moderation. Another is the place of woman in a man's world (see Medea's acid comment, p. 214a-b), and the chorus' prophecy that a new day is dawning for woman (p. 215d). Another subtheme is the contrast of "barbarian," or foreigner, and Greek. And constantly reiterated is the idea that fate or the gods have ordained these terrible things, that what has happened was bound to happen.

The physical actions that are the occasion for the drama all occur off stage, and we learn about them from attendants, messengers, and the like. The chorus of Corinthian women comments on the action, advises the characters, and even enters the action at one point. Note also the role of Medea's nurse in the play. It is this minor character who briefs us on the situation at the start and drops hints at what further is to take place. She gives us this kind of information in the prologue—the monologue that starts off the play. This use of the prologue, which has a precedent in Aeschylus' *Agamemnon,* is Euripides' only important technical contribution to Greek tragedy. The earlier tragedies started with the entry and song of the chorus. Later tragedians started with a dramatic episode involving two or more actors. Euripides made the prologue a monologue that sets the scene and informs us about the situation.

IV

The *Electra* is another play about a woman's vengeance, but here the center is love and hate between parents and children, and here it is the children who slay the mother. And Electra, who has no magic powers at her disposal, works through menfolk and purely natural means. She is the motive power, but it is her brother, Orestes, who does the terrible deeds.

Again Euripides works with ancient mythical material. This myth had already been dramatized by Aeschylus and Sophocles. (See *Agamemnon, Choephoroe, Eumenides,* and *Electra,* pp. 52, 70, 81, 156.) Homer refers to it often in the *Odyssey,* as furnishing a contrast with the characters and events of his story. The ancient myth about "the house of Atreus," as it came down to Euripides, ran something like this:

Atreus, the King of Mycenae, inherited a curse from his father Pelops—the son of Tantalus and grandson of Zeus—and passed it on to his descendants. He intensified the ancestral curse through his own horrible act of killing his brother Thyestes' children and serving him a meal made from their flesh. This was in retaliation for Thyestes' seduction of the wife of Atreus. Later Thyestes and his son Aegisthus killed Atreus and took over his kingdom. The sons of Atreus—Agamemnon and Menelaus—fled to Sparta, where Agamemnon married Clytaemnestra and Menelaus married her sister Helen, whose beauty was to cause the Trojan War. Agamemnon regained the kingdom of Mycenae and ruled all Argos, or the Peloponnesus (according to some versions he killed or expelled his uncle Thyestes).

Agamemnon was chosen to lead the Greek forces against Troy in the war to return the abducted Helen to Menelaus. Agamemnon sacrificed his daughter Iphigenia to appease the anger of the goddess Artemis and to release the Greek forces which she had becalmed and decimated by plague at Aulis. Clytaemnestra never forgave Agamemnon for this, and while he was gone she took Aegisthus as her lover. When Agamemnon returned from Troy, she and Aegisthus killed Agamemnon, and Aegisthus became King of Mycenae. Orestes, the son of Agamemnon and Clytaemnestra, was spirited away to the kingdom of Phocis, where he formed a close friendship with the King's son Pylades and grew to manhood. His sister Electra remained behind, nursing vengeance against her father's murderer and usurper.

Orestes, at the bidding of Apollo's oracle at Delphi (in

Phocis), returned to Mycenae and, aided by Electra and his friend Pylades, killed Aegisthus and Clytaemnestra. The Eumenides, or Furies, pursued him all over the world, in retribution for his bloodguilt for killing his mother. Finally, he took refuge at the temple of Athena in Athens, and was acquitted by the Areopagus, the Athenian court on Mars Hill. The goddess Athena herself cast the deciding vote, when the jurors split. The Furies having been propitiated by being made tutelary spirits of Athens, the Areopagus became the court that dealt justly with murder, and Orestes returned to Mycenae.

The whole of this mythical background is mentioned repeatedly in the play. Euripides selects from it for this drama the portion dealing with the return of Orestes and the slaying of Aegisthus and Clytaemnestra. The author starts with the mythical material and fills it out with his own invention, in order to stress the character and motivations of the protagonists. He shows us what went on in the hearts of Electra and Orestes that made it possible for them to do these horrible deeds. And he shows us how they felt after the murders were committed. He centers our attention on the souls of the persons involved, rather than on abstract ideas of honor, duty, or justice. He offers us psychological realism, in the best sense of that term.

In Euripides' version, when Orestes returns he finds that Electra has been reduced to a lowly status by Aegisthus, who is her father's murderer and her mother's husband. He has forced Electra to marry a peasant, to avoid possible retaliation from a highborn husband or son of hers. As she first enters, with Orestes and his friend Pylades hiding in the background, she is indeed "hapless Electra," a princess who has fallen to menial tasks, ragged clothes, and filthy body. Her head is shaven, in mourning for her father. At first she expresses the modest aspiration to be a good wife and to do the household chores for the good man who, though forced on her, has avoided consummating their marriage in order not to stain her royal lineage and thus effect what Aegisthus desires. But soon we find that all she seeks is revenge on her father's murderers—both of them.

When Orestes comes forth to meet her and talk about these things, he does not reveal his identity, but pretends to be a messenger from Orestes (she does not recognize him, because they have not seen each other since they were children). She tells the "stranger" all about her present situation, including the intimate details of her unconsummated marriage. She tells also how her mother lives amid pomp and wealth, while Aegisthus pelts her father's monument with stones, taunting, "Where is thy son Orestes? Is he ever coming in his glory to defend thy tomb?" (p. 330a). All things, she tells the "stranger," call on Orestes to return and avenge his father. In response, Orestes expresses what may be a defense of tragedy.

> O God! how awful is thy story! Yes, there *is* a feeling, arising even from another's distress, that wrings the human heart. Say on, that when I know the loveless tale, which yet I needs must hear, I may carry it to thy brother. For pity, though it has no place in clownish natures, is inborn in the wise . . . (p. 329d)

The recognition scene occurs when Orestes' identity is made known by the old servant who spirited him away to Phocis. The old man recognizes Orestes as soon as he catches sight of him. He announces, "I see Orestes, Agamemnon's son, before me," and Orestes assures Electra that it is really he, "thy one and only champion" (p. 332b).

So far Euripides has presented the basic situation and motivations that impel Electra and Orestes to act. The rest of the play deals with their acts and how they react to them. Orestes soon learns that he has no friends left in Argos, and must accomplish his revenge alone, aided only by Pylades and Electra —who is especially eager to prepare her mother's death. "Thy work begins at once," she says enviously to Orestes, "thou hast drawn the first lot in the tragedy" (p. 333b). In a curious bit of dialogue, she steels her brother's heart for the deed he is to do, tells him that if he fails and dies, she will commit suicide. Hence, she urges, "show thyself a man" (p. 333c). He goes off to kill Aegisthus, while she sets the scene for her mother's murder.

Suspense mounts as cries are heard offstage, and Electra and the chorus of Argive country women wonder what is happening, whose are the cries. Then a messenger arrives to tell them that Orestes has accomplished his revenge. He has taken advantage of the gracious invitation of Aegisthus to partake in a religious sacrifice by hitting him with a cleaver as he was bending over the entrails of the sacrificial animal. There ensues a strange, terrible scene as Electra gloats over Aegisthus' corpse, taunts him for being the weak, junior partner in a marriage with a highborn woman, expresses disgust at his affairs with women and disdain for his desirability as a mate. Finally, she announces that justice has been done and he has received his deserts. To which the chorus responds

> Terrible alike his crime and your revenge; for mighty is the power of justice. (p. 335d)

Now it remains to kill Clytaemnestra, but Orestes balks at the murder of his own mother. The duty to avenge his father's murder clashes with his aversion for the curse of bloodguilt that will pursue him if he kills his mother. Even the authority of Apollo's oracle cannot make him believe it would be right to kill her. But the implacable and single-minded Electra holds him to the purpose they had agreed on, begging him not to turn coward, to be a man, and to do the deed that has to be done. Orestes reluctantly gives in to her.

> . . . 'tis an awful task I undertake; an awful deed I have to do; still if it is Heaven's will, be it so; I loathe and yet I love the enterprise. (p. 336a)

He and Pylades hide Aegisthus' corpse inside the house, and wait there in ambush as Clytaemnestra enters the scene.

One of the most dramatic moments in the play occurs here, as Clytaemnestra defends what she has done and Electra rejects her defense. Clytaemnestra lists two just grievances she had against Agamemnon—first, his sacrifice of their daughter Iphigenia, merely to help foolish Menelaus regain wanton Helen; and, second, his keeping the captive Trojan princess Cassandra as his mistress in the family house. Such shameless and humiliating behavior, she says, was the last straw and led to his death and to her alliance with his enemy Aegisthus, for his enemies were the only allies available to her. But Electra counters that long before Iphigenia was sacrificed, Clytaemnestra was prettying herself for eyes other than her husband's; that, indeed, she never wanted her husband to come home from the war. And actually she has slain a daughter and a son by forcing Electra and Orestes to endure the living death of ignominy and exile. If life is the payment for life, then Electra and Orestes may rightly slay Clytaemnestra for Agamemnon's murder, Electra argues.

Says Clytaemnestra to all this:

> Daughter, 'twas ever thy nature to love thy father. This too one finds; some sons cling to their father, others have a deeper affection for their mother. I will forgive thee, for myself am not so exceeding glad at the deed that I have done, my child. (p. 337a)

Electra has inveigled her mother to visit her on the pretext that she has recently borne a child, and Clytaemnestra now enters the house to make the customary sacrifice, as a favor to her daughter. Clytaemnestra's pleas for mercy are heard, and soon her corpse and that of Aegisthus are shown, and Orestes and Electra enter, stained with their mother's blood—and utterly horrified at what they have done.

Here is the psychological climax of the play. The brother and sister are sick with horror and guilt at the murder they have committed, however righteous the vengeance wrought. "This foul deed of blood," Orestes calls it. "I am the guilty cause," Electra admits. It was she who urged Orestes on, and held the sword firm when he flinched before his mother's pleading. Orestes observes wryly,

> Again thy fancy changes with the wind; for now thou thinkest aright, though not so formerly; an awful deed didst thou urge thy brother against his will to commit, dear sister. (p. 338a)

As Electra covers her mother's corpse, "both loved and loathed," the demigods Castor and Polydeuces intervene to settle the troubles of the cursed house of Atreus. (They are called the Dioscuri, meaning "the sons of Zeus." They are also brothers of Clytaemnestra and Helen, for their mother was Leda, to whom Zeus came in the form of a swan.) They pronounce Clytaemnestra's death righteous vengeance, but they judge the matricide to be an unrighteous act. Apollo's oracle gave false advice to Orestes, but what is done is done, and Orestes must fulfill the destiny ordained by Zeus. Here Orestes' fate is foretold, following the traditional myth; he must go into exile, pursued by the Furies, seek refuge in Athens, and be acquitted by a jury on Mars Hill. The Furies will go down into a cleft in the earth to found a new oracle, Orestes must wander until his doom is fulfilled, and Electra is to marry Pylades.

Fate, with an assist from Apollo's false oracle, has spun the plot—that is the Dioscuri's final word. They could not save their sister from her fate or her children from their guilty deed, but they will protect men whose lives are devoted to piety and justice. Electra and Orestes bid each other a last farewell. The Dioscuri fly away and the characters exit, as the chorus sings,

> Farewell! truly that mortal's is a happy lot, who can thus fare, unafflicted by any calamity. (p. 339c)

This is a complex play, far more difficult to interpret than the *Medea.* The first part of the play sets up a perfect melodrama, with the pitiable, wronged Electra and Orestes pitted against terrible murderers, adulterers, and despoilers—Clytaemnestra and Aegisthus. The stage is set for evil to be punished and justice to be done. But the way it is done and the effect that the doing of the deed has on the main characters involve a sudden jump to the chaotic, tangled, and ugly. Things are no longer neat and clean and logical. Aegisthus and Clytaemnestra do not appear as villainous characters, and Electra and Orestes appear in the worst possible light. The King and Queen are tricked and butchered at religious rites, made vulnerable by impulses of kindly courtesy and maternal solicitude. Justice, indeed, may have been done, but the concrete deed is most ignoble and foul. And, in the end, neither the queasy Orestes nor the seemingly strong-willed Electra can accept the terrible murder of their own mother.

Everything is awry, instead of righted—blood has shed blood ever since the curse on the house of Atreus started. Even the gods are wrong, and Apollo is the ultimate culprit, a fool if not a knave. There is a horrible gulf between the bright pictures of vengeance spawned by the imagination and the gore and horror of the actual deed. Orestes and Electra quail before the irremediable and unchangeable actuality of what they have done, and Orestes has to flee to human and humane justice before the avenging Furies. We realize that suffering has not ennobled or illuminated Orestes and Electra, that from the start Orestes has been mechanically acting out an abstract idea of vengeance, and that Electra has been a sick person, obsessed with vicious impulses, and not merely a wronged girl seeking righteous revenge.

V

In *Orestes,* Euripides continues the story begun in *Electra,* but here he introduces fresh and original material, instead of following either the old myths or Aeschylus' dramas. Euripides dramatizes events that he imagines took place between Clytaemnestra's murder and Orestes' flight from Argos.

As the play opens, it is the sixth day after Clytaemnestra's death. Electra is sitting in the palace at Argos (the capital of the province of Argos) beside the sickbed of Orestes. He lies there mad and befouled, not eating and not washing, passing through fits of madness and weeping in his saner moments. The city of Argos has declared him and Electra to be outlaws, and the assembly is meeting to vote on their death sentence. Menelaus has just returned from Troy, and has sent Helen and their daughter Hermione to the palace during the night, lest survivors of the men slain at Troy should see Helen and stone her. Now Electra awaits the arrival of Menelaus, the sole hope of safety for her and her brother in their desperate situation. She repeatedly puts the blame on Apollo and his wicked, lying oracle for what has happened to her and her brother.

When Orestes awakens, in a sane mood, Electra wipes the foam off his lips, pushes his matted hair back, and helps him to walk around. But suddenly he falls into one of his fits, sees the Furies, "those maidens with their bloodshot eyes and snaky hair . . . death's priestesses with glaring eyes, terrific goddesses" (p. 396c), and he picks up his bow and arrows to drive them away. (The Furies—also called the Eumenides, meaning "kindly ones," in an attempt to placate them—were fearful goddesses who punished crimes, especially those against kinfolk, and pre-eminently murder of parents by children. They were often portrayed as winged women with snakes twined in their hair and blood dripping from their eyes.)

Orestes becomes calm again and seeks to release Electra from her guilt by assuming sole responsibility for the murder. But then he puts the ultimate blame on Apollo.

'Tis Loxias [Apollo] I blame, for urging me on to do a deed most damned, encouraging me with words but no real help; for I am sure that, had I asked my father to his face whether I was to slay my mother, he would have implored me oft and earnestly by this beard never to plunge a murderer's sword into my mother's breast, since he would not thereby regain his life, whilst I, poor wretch, should be doomed to drain this cup of sorrow. (p. 396d)

After Electra leaves to get some rest, Menelaus enters, at long last home from Troy, victorious, with his beautiful wife regained. A strange and dramatic meeting occurs between him and Orestes, who falls at his uncle's knees, begging him for aid in his hour of need. This wonderful dialogue follows:

Men. Ye gods! what do I see? what death's-head greets my sight?

Or. Thou art right; I *am* dead through misery, though I still gaze upon the sun.

Men. How wild the look thy unkempt hair gives thee, poor wretch!

Or. 'Tis not my looks, but my deeds that torture me.

Men. How terribly thy tearless eyeballs glare!

Or. My body is vanished and gone, though my name hath not yet deserted me.

Men. Unsightly apparition, so different from what I expected!

Or. In me behold a man that hath slain his hapless mother.

Men. I have heard all; be chary of thy tale of woe.

Or. I will; but the deity is lavish of woe in my case.

Men. What ails thee? what is thy deadly sickness?

Or. My conscience; I know that I am guilty of an awful crime. (p. 397c-d)

Orestes tells Menelaus how his madness began on the night he buried his mother, and how the Eumenides—"Three maidens black as night I seem to see" (p. 398a)—pursue and torment him. He appeals to Menelaus to save him, in return for the aid his father Agamemnon gave to Menelaus in his time of need.

At this point another dramatic entrance and meeting occurs. Tyndareus, the father of Helen and Clytaemnestra (he, as well as Zeus, is accounted their father in the Greek stories), comes in, and is furious at the sight of Orestes, the murderer of his daughter. He inveighs against the evil of setting aside the law and taking revenge for murder. A deed like Orestes' only piles horror on horror, murder on murder, and brings divine punishment—witness Orestes' madness.

Orestes steps in to defend himself, as Jason and Clytaemnestra have done in the previous plays. He pleads that the murder of his mother is just retribution for her murder of his father. He also claims that he has done a public service for all Greece by striking a blow in defense of husbands against adulterous and murderous wives. Finally, he finds Apollo to be the guilty one.

> Find him guilty of the crime, slay him; his was the sin, not mine . . . Say not then that the deed was badly done, but unfortunately for me who did it. (p. 400a)

Tyndareus, infuriated by this kind of talk, goes off to plead with the citizens to sentence Orestes and Electra to death. He warns Menelaus not to aid them. Orestes' final plea to Menelaus is fruitless, for the latter is unwilling to stand up against the Argive populace. Orestes, disgusted by his flimsy excuses, berates him as a traitor and a weakling. He tells Pylades later

> Caution was the line he took—the usual policy of traitorous friends . . . he never was a warrior . . . (p. 401c)

Orestes now boldly decides to go to the council and plead his case. But he succeeds only in getting permission to commit suicide rather than to suffer death by stoning. He is nobly prepared to meet his death. He tells Electra to be quiet, when she bursts out into piteous and lengthy laments; that the best thing is to accept their allotted fate. But he relents and expresses an amazingly ardent love for her as they say their last farewells. (See p. 404c.)

At this point, where their suicide might bring a tragic close to the sad story of the house of Atreus, the play takes a sudden turn. Pylades suggests that they first harm Menelaus, who abandoned them to their fate, either by killing Helen or by burning the palace down, so that Menelaus will not profit by their fall. And Electra adds that they should take his daughter Hermione as hostage, in case Menelaus should try to avenge Helen's death. In an odd scene the three conspirators pray to

Agamemnon to aid them from beyond the grave, each claiming credit for Clytaemnestra's murder.

Or. I slew my mother—
Py. I held the sword—
El. 'Twas I that urged them on and set them free from fear—(p. 406b)

Events march quickly as Orestes and Pylades go in to kill Helen. We hear her cries for help, while Electra, on stage, calls out, "Cut, stab, and kill," to the two men. She sends Hermione into the house and shouts, "Hold her hard and fast; point a sword at her throat." But Helen, we learn, has escaped, vanishing from the room, through magic arts or divine intervention, just as she was about to be murdered. Now Menelaus appears, to rescue his daughter and the presumed corpse of his wife.

The excitement mounts as Orestes and Pylades appear on the roof, holding Hermione fast. Orestes proposes an impossible deal to Menelaus—the life of Hermione for a commutation of his and Electra's death sentence. Otherwise Hermione will be killed and the place will be burned down. Menelaus will then have nothing. As the anguished father curses and pleads, the sword is at Hermione's throat, and Orestes orders the palace to be set on fire.

Suddenly, in the midst of this chaos and passion, divine intervention occurs. Apollo appears in the clouds, with Helen at his side. (This appearance of a god is called an "epiphany," and occurs frequently in Greek stories and dramas.) Everything is solved. Apollo has saved Helen, at the command of Zeus, and now she will join her brothers Castor and Polydeuces in the sky. She was merely a divine means of solving the overpopulation problem by starting a war. Orestes is destined to a year's exile, a trial at the Areopagus that will acquit him, and marriage with Hermione (at whose throat he has his sword pointed). Reconciled with the people of Argos through Apollo's aid, Orestes will rule in Argos while Menelaus rules in Sparta. Pylades will marry Electra, as previously planned, and live happily ever after.

Good will and joy prevail, as Orestes praises Apollo (whose word, character, and good sense he had previously doubted);

Menelaus hails Helen and promises Hermione to Orestes; and Apollo commands, "Reconcile all strife." The god departs to bring Helen to the heavenly mansions, and the chorus hails "majestic Victory" as the play ends.

Like *Electra,* this is a very rich and complicated drama, not easily put into pat phrases or handled by theoretical concepts about the nature of tragedy. The episodes are packed with dramatic intensity and we mount steadily to a climax of passion and violence, when suddenly everything is settled in a spirit of peace and fellowship, and everyone is included in a happy ending. As in *Electra* our sympathies are enlisted for the doomed brother and sister, in their common suffering and madness, even though their suffering results from their terrible deed. We are reminded of the incitement to murder presented by their mother's adultery and slaying of their father, and of the ultimate responsibility of Apollo. The whole picture changes, however, just as Orestes is about to die nobly by his own hand. Suddenly, at the instigation of Pylades and Electra, Orestes decides to butcher two women, in order to pay back a man who has abandoned him in his hour of need. From that point on, we watch the actions and reactions of the characters with amazement, excitement, and interest, as events mount to a point where it takes divine intervention to set things right again.

VI

Would the staging of these plays add to what you get from a mere reading?

Aristotle claims that the tragic theme may be communicated and the tragic effect produced through reading the dialogue, choral lyrics, and stage directions. Most of the key actions in these plays—the murders and the attempted murders—take place off stage. Obviously, then, much of what occurs must be communicated through the dialogue, choruses, messengers, etc. Does it, however, make any difference in the dramatic effect to have the words spoken by persons, with physical movements, gestures, masks, etc.? Could you more easily feel the suspense and painful waiting if you were physically present with the actors at a theatrical performance? Would it help to see the chorus knocking on the barred doors in the *Medea,* Jason's reaction when he finds Medea has murdered the children, Orestes and Pylades on the rooftop on the point of murder and arson? Can the imagination alone do the work, as in epic narrative? Or are both imagination and enaction necessary for plays like these, both to communicate the tragic theme and to produce the tragic effect?

This brings us to two more points—the words and the music. The original plays are written in Greek verse. According to Aristotle, a certain kind of diction is necessary in tragedy. Do we lose anything by not having the same pattern and quality of word sounds that were present in the original? Is meaning transmitted by the material texture and placing of words, as well as by their logical sense? If so, can the original meaning be approximated or interpreted in translation into a very different language? Would this be better done here by poetry or by prose?

We do not have the ancient music for the choral lyrics. For the Greeks, music was of great importance in tragedy; indeed, originally, Greek tragedy was mostly choral singing. Are we missing as much in a Euripidean play without music as we would if we had only the libretto of a Wagnerian opera?

Do these plays conform to Aristotle's ideas about tragedy?

Aristotle said that a tragedy should show the fall from happiness to misery of a person above the average lot. He had a high opinion of Euripides as a tragic poet. Do these plays, however, fit Aristotle's recipe for tragedy? Are Medea, Electra, and Orestes ideal tragic heroes in Aristotle's sense?

Medea's fall from happiness has occurred before our play opens, and Euripides dramatizes her active response to her misery. She intensifies her misery by killing her children, but she achieves her purpose of revenge against Jason. Granted that the ending is terrible, is it unhappy, a fall from happiness, for the protagonist Medea?

Would Jason make a good tragic hero? If so, what events in

Jason's story might a playwright dramatize, and where would he begin and end his play? If Medea is a tragic heroine, what is her tragic flaw?

Electra and Orestes start out unhappy in the *Electra,* act to obtain a much-desired revenge, and end up more intensely unhappy than at the start, when they realize what they have done. The fall from happiness to misery has already occurred before the play began, just as in the *Medea.* Here again Euripides dramatizes the active response to suffering. But where Medea obtains a horrible fulfillment, here we have the new twist of a fall from an existing unhappiness (exile and degradation) into a deeper unhappiness (guilt and remorse). Do the highborn Orestes and Electra, from the famous house of Atreus, fulfill Aristotle's requirements for the tragic hero? What is the flaw in their case that brings them to doom?

Is the *Orestes* a tragedy at all? Things are all made neat and right in the end by the action of Apollo. Here is the happy ending all right, but would you, therefore, call this play a comedy? Would it be a tragedy if it ended with the murder of Hermione and the burning of the palace? Or, to fit Aristotle's formula, should it have ended with the suicide of Orestes and Electra? What flaw in the character of the two protagonists prevents this "proper" tragic ending? Is there a fall from nobility to meanness in Orestes? If so, is this a tragic fall or merely something sad and painful to witness?

Aristotle says that tragedy should arouse and purge emotions of pity and terror. Did you feel pity and terror as you read these plays? Is this emotional experience the main thing you got out of your reading, or are the feelings merely accompaniments of your awareness of the themes and meanings you encountered in the play? Is your pity and terror in reading tragedies a vicarious emotional release, as in reading adventure and murder thrillers, or is something much deeper and more lasting involved? What attitude toward and what understanding of human existence have you found in these plays?

If you were writing a formula for tragedy, based on these Euripidean dramas of suffering and action, how would your recipe differ from Aristotle's?

Do various improbabilities and inconsistencies make these plays unconvincing?

In the *Medea*, the King of Athens suddenly appears and vanishes after one short scene, never to appear in the action again. The only function of his appearance is to furnish Medea with a sure refuge after her coming horrible deeds. Is it probable that he should appear out of the blue just to help the play along? Does he have to appear in the action? Would it be better to have such things occur off stage and be communicated to us by messengers?

And why could not Medea take her boys along with her alive, instead of as corpses, when she flies off to Athens? If she has power to stay high in the air, out of Jason's reach, does she not have power to prevent any harm Creon's kin might intend against her boys? Aside from her motive of revenge against Jason, is it probable that she could not have saved the boys and taken them with her? Does this at all affect your belief in this scene, or is it just an inconsequential detail, not affecting the dramatic essence? Since Medea is a sorceress, possessed of magic powers, do you find her perch in the air believable? Would it be more or less believable on stage than in print?

What other inconsistencies and improbabilities have you noticed in these plays? Do they or do they not detract from your enjoyment and understanding?

Does the device of divine intervention detract from the tragic effect?

The *deus ex machina*, or "god from a machine," was literally that in ancient Greek drama. A god was brought on the scene through stage machinery to solve all difficulties and wind up the plot. Aristotle and others have criticized this device as a weak substitute for a resolution that should develop internally from the plot and characters.

We have two examples in these plays of the *deus ex machina*. In the *Electra*, the Dioscuri arrive from on high to comment on what has happened, to prophesy on the future, and to tell the protagonists what to do. In the *Orestes*, Apollo appears in the clouds to stop the imminent murder and arson and to reconcile all the warring elements that have brought the play to its violent climax.

Which of these divine interventions do you find the most wrenching and the most difficult to fit in with the preceding action of the play? What do you think was Euripides' intention in using this device in each of these cases? How else could he have ended these plays?

Does tragedy require sympathetic characters with whom we may identify?

It would be hard to find any lovable and admirable figures among the leading characters of these plays. The sympathy we have for their suffering at the start is usually alienated by the deeds they do before the play is over. Does this matter as far as the dramatic effect is concerned? Do we have to sympathize or identify with the main characters involved? Why are we held spellbound and so deeply moved by the words and deeds of Medea, Electra, and Orestes? In what do their solidity and their attraction for our hearts and understanding lie?

Does Euripides give us a psychological interpretation of the Greek myths?

We have seen how surely Euripides portrays human motivation and the response to action and suffering. Does he go further than this to a clinical analysis of unconscious psychological complexes, in the modern sense? For example, do Clytaemnestra's remark on daughters' love for their fathers and Orestes' proclamation of ardent love for Electra refer to incestuous feelings, or should we not go beyond the bare surface meaning of the dialogue in its context? Are the Furies merely projections of Orestes' madness? Is Euripides giving us a psychological interpretation of the avenging Furies, which never appear in this play, as they do in Aeschylus' *Eumenides*?

Do sudden reversals add to or detract from the dramatic effect in these plays?

Aristotle says that "peripeties" (sudden reversals), in which the opposite of what is expected happens, add richness to the dramatic effect. In the *Electra,* we have such a turn, when Electra and Orestes end up horrified at the murder of their mother. Does this involve "recognition" (of what they have done) as well as reversal? In the *Orestes,* just as Electra and Orestes are to commit suicide, they turn about and proceed to kidnaping, attempted murder, and arson. Most of the exciting action of the play occurs after this point. Is there any difference between the quality of the reversal in the two plays? Which is most effective dramatically?

SELF-TESTING QUESTIONS

The following questions are designed to help you test the thoroughness of your reading. Each question is to be answered by giving a page or pages of the reading assignment. Answers will be found on page 232 of this Reading Plan.

1 Who is Aegeus?

2 Who is the "lioness fiercer than Tyrrhene Scylla"?

3 Which character in *Electra* never speaks?

4 What reasons does Orestes suggest as to why Electra's husband does not consummate their marriage?

5 What is Orestes' attitude toward ancestry or class as the mark of virtue?

6 What ludicrous "clues" to Orestes' presence does the Old Man cite?

7 What weapon did Apollo give to Orestes to drive off the Furies?

8 Who warned Orestes when he murdered his mother that he was incurring an eternal curse?

9 What Athenian demagogue spoke against Orestes at the Argive assembly?

10 Who saves his life by prostrating himself before Orestes?

Third Reading

ARISTOPHANES

The Clouds, The Birds, The Lysistrata

Vol. 5, pp. 488–506, 542–563, 583–599

The Old Comedy of Athens—of which Aristophanes is the supreme representative—was an amazing combination of low humor and high ideals, of biting satire and delicate lyrics, of current concerns and transcendent fantasy. It combines the functions of our musical comedy, burlesque show, pantomime, social farce, and political commentary. There has never been anything like it.

The plays that we have selected were written during the Peloponnesian War, in which the fate of Athens was at stake. Yet Aristophanes delivers a biting social and political satire. He attacks the government, the generals, and popular morality without fear or favor. Nowadays we hear that the present critical hour for our country and our culture is no time for comedy, for social and political satire. But apparently Aristophanes and the Athenians felt differently about the appropriateness of criticism in a time of crisis.

The comedies we are to read here are no solemn

and scolding morality plays. Aristophanes subjects individuals, opinions, and attitudes to ridicule and caricature. Yet there is a spirit of geniality and humor which, however rough it gets at times, invites the victims to laugh along with the author and spectators.

In the first of our three plays, an old reprobate tries to avoid paying his debts by learning the tricks of argument taught by the new learning. In the second, a couple of Athenians flee from the civic corruption of Athens to the realm of the birds, in order to build an ideal city in the air. In the third, the women of Greece wage a peace campaign, and succeed in ending the Peloponnesian War by denying their husbands the joys of conjugal love.

Aristophanes, the Old Comedian, has a wonderful time with these themes. He employs all his gifts of imagination, caricature, and lyricism in these plays. He takes the most outrageous liberties with persons and properties, and is not above the crudest of jokes. We should have a wonderful time, too.

GUIDE TO

Third Reading

I

The word comedy is derived from two Greek words meaning "revel" and "song." Scholars believe that Greek comedy originated in the revels at the festivals for Dionysius, the god of wine and fertility. The revels consisted of the kind of unrestrained dancing, singing, and ribaldry that goes on nowadays at Mardi Gras festivals in Latin-American countries. Representations of the phallus—the male generative organ and symbol of fertility—were prominent in these activities. Aristotle, in the *Poetics,* says that comedy originated in "the phallic songs." (See Vol. 9, p. 683b.) As in the primitive rituals of other peoples, there was also a type of revel which consisted of the mimicking of animals. Scholars infer that the type of chorus found in *The Birds* (see also *The Wasps* and *The Frogs*) came from this aspect of the early Dionysiac revels.

We are not certain about the exact development of comedy, from the early revels to Aristophanes. Aristotle tells us that a decisive change occurred when general and impersonal plots were introduced to replace the personal invective and lampoons of which comedy had previously consisted. (See Vol. 9, p. 683d.) Personal lampoons, however, were an important element in the comedies of Aristophanes, and the objects of his caricature were often seated out in the audience watching their representations on the stage. (There is a story that Socrates stood up at the performance of *The Clouds* to let the audience judge how the mask of the stage Socrates compared with the face of the real Socrates.) And Aristophanes' comedies are not elaborately and neatly plotted, like the comedy of a later era. A typical Aristophanes comedy consists of a number of loosely connected episodes that develop a situation or problem presented at the start of the play. The dramatic scenes are usually not bound together in any logical sequence, but are characterized by a free imagination and spontaneity, something like the improvisations of a musician on a theme.

Scholars divide Greek comedy into three types: Old, Middle, and New. Aristophanes' plays are the sole surviving examples of the Old Comedy. Judging from his plays and from what little we know about other writers of his time, the Old Comedy combined the functions of our burlesque shows, comic operas, and journals of opinion. The Old Comedy furnished belly laughs, pratfalls, coarse jokes, and the kind of ridiculous impersonations that a W. C. Fields or a Sid Caesar would perform. But the Old Comedy was also a vigorous critic of the weaknesses of the leaders and people of Athens; it was the vehicle for social and political satire, and provided the audience with the kind of critical view of persons and events that we look for in newspaper cartoons, editorials, columns, and radio and TV commentaries.

Aristophanes wrote his plays in a time of crisis for the Athenian city-state. The traditional values and way of life were breaking down. Aristophanes thought that the new democracy was characterized by a corruption that was consuming the moral fiber of the people. He also opposed the new intellectualism, the skeptical and critical spirit that was promoted by the Sophists—teachers of rhetoric, logic, and other arts—and by writers like Euripides. (For his lampoons on Euripides, see *The Wasps* and *The Thesmophoriazusae.*) He was also bitterly opposed to imperialism and militarism. Most of his plays were written during the Peloponnesian War between the coalition of Greek city-states led by Athens and the coalition led by Sparta. (See Thucydides, *The Peloponnesian War,* Vol. 6, for a full description of this important conflict.) Aristophanes wrote three antiwar plays during the war (*The Lysistrata* is one of them), and many of his other plays contain uncomplimentary references to the political and military leaders of Athens. Yet, such was the spirit of unrestrained liberty for comic writers that, though the fate of Athens hung in the balance, Aristophanes was not punished and his plays were not banned.

Like Greek tragedy, the Old Comedy consists of both dramatic and lyric elements. In Aristophanes' plays, the set form and rhythms for the choral songs balance the free-and-easy meters of the dramatic episodes. For instance, where two choruses argue or converse with one another (as in *The Lysistrata*), their songs are of exactly the same length and beat. The choral songs also present the tender, delicate, fantastic elements in Aristophanes' plays, as well as the humorous and satirical aspects. One of the most important functions of the chorus in Aristophanes is the direct address to the spectators, called the parabasis ("step forward"). In the parabasis, the comic poet expresses his own opinions, sometimes commenting on the play, or appealing to the judges to give it the prize. References to the spectators and judges are frequent in Aristophanes' plays. (See the parabasis and the address to the judges in *The Clouds*, pp. 494d-496b, 502b-c.)

The actors in the Old Comedy wore masks—sometimes very grotesque ones—and "socks," that is, light shoes, in contrast to the heavy, high-heeled "buskins" of the tragic actors. Some of them wore obvious and abundantly padded representations of the phallus. The actors were all men, whether they took the roles of men or women. The chorus consisted of about twenty-four singers, who wore masks and strange costumes (especially when they represented animal life). As for stage mechanics, you will notice that, in *The Clouds*, Aristophanes uses the eccyclema, or "wheel-out," a device to show interior scenes, and the crane to swing an actor in the air. (See pp. 488a, 490c.)

We do not have the elements of "spectacle," music, and actual enactment which contributed so much to the effect of the Old Comedy. Most of the topical references are now obscure or unimportant. Yet, despite these obstacles, so great is the literary artistry of Aristophanes that these last surviving plays of the Old Comedy have an amazing power to communicate to modern readers. His keen wit, robust humor, and verbal acrobatics come through to us even in inadequate and bowdlerized translations. He shares this universal communicability with such comic writers as Rabelais and Fielding in our series of readings. A comic genius such as Aristophanes requires a combination of gifts and the power to unify them that is found only rarely in the history of literature. In our own time and language, James Joyce is perhaps the only important writer with something of the Aristophanic gift.

II

The Clouds was first produced at the Great Dionysiac festival in Athens in 432 B.C. It was a failure with the audience and judges, so Aristophanes rewrote it in the form which we now have. The author defends this play—"of all my plays . . . the wisest and the best"—in a choral song. (See pp. 494d-495c.)

The play is an attack on the new learning and the new spirit of critical inquiry which had developed in Greece in the fifth century B.C. Aristophanes here attacks both the old natural philosophers, who inquired into the nature and causes of the physical universe, and the "modern" teachers of rhetoric, politics, and mathematics—the so-called Sophists. He does so in defense of traditional morality and religion, for he holds that the new learning is subversive of the old values and beliefs. Aristophanes' attack is concentrated on the Sophists, who are accused of teaching young men how to win arguments with clever logic and rhetoric, to make the worse appear the better cause.

Now it happens that Plato, too, opposed the Sophists. And in such Platonic dialogues as *The Republic,* the *Gorgias, Protagoras,* and *Sophist* (see Vol. 7), Socrates appears as a vigorous and effective enemy of the Sophists. Yet in *The Clouds* he is portrayed as a typical Sophist in logical method and moral attitude. It is Socrates who is the main butt of Aristophanes' ridicule. The reason for this may be that Socrates—despite his opposition to the Sophists' ethical and religious views—also represented the spirit of critical inquiry that challenged traditional answers. He shared with the Sophists the question-and-answer method of argument for which he is so famous. Socrates was a familiar and controversial figure to the Athenian audience, and Aristophanes may have found it convenient to use him, justly or not, as the typical representative of the new learning. The original form of the play is said to have been much gentler and the revised version much rougher on both Socrates and the Sophists. Perhaps Aristophanes did this to please the crowd.

The protagonist of *The Clouds* is Strepsiades, an old gentleman who is deeply in debt because of the extravagances of his wife and his son Pheidippides, who is crazy about horses. The latter, with his passion for chariot racing, has practically ruined his father by the debts he has run up. "A galloping consumption caught my fortunes," comments the old man. A way out of his plight occurs to the father—he will enroll his son in the Phrontisterion ("Thinking-house"), run by Socrates in the house next door. There he will learn the Worse or Unjust Logic, which will enable him to defend his father for nonpayment of debts. But Pheidippides does not want to have anything to do with "Those palefaced, barefoot vagabonds," and lose his healthy outdoor color. So the old man cuts off all support from his son and enrolls in Socrates' school himself.

He finds various ridiculous subtleties being pursued by the students there, such as the question, "How many feet of its own a flea could jump" and whether "gnats/Hummed through their mouth, or backwards, through the tail?" He also learns that while Socrates was gazing open-mouthed studying the heavens a lizard defecated on him from the rooftop. Many disciples are pursuing their meditation in ridiculous postures and Socrates himself is suspended from a basket up in the air, in order to contemplate the heavens properly. Strepsiades is initiated into the school and Socrates invokes the Clouds, which appear as a chorus of goddesses.

The Clouds, Strepsiades learns, are the originators of rain, thunder, and lightning, and also the donors of the skills of argument and rhetoric. They are adored by the Sophists, false prophets, and windy poets, for these things of vapor and dew change shape and appear as whatever they please. Socrates informs the shocked Strepsiades that the Clouds are the only true gods, that they alone are responsible for the rain and thunder—not Zeus, for there is no Zeus. Socrates gives a natural explanation of thunder, in terms of digestive and excretory processes, suitable to Strepsiades' understanding. He ridicules the old man's belief that Zeus unleashes the thunder against perjurers.

Strepsiades is convinced and Socrates says,

> Now then you agree in rejecting with me
> the Gods you believed in when young,
> And *my* creed you'll embrace "I believe in wide space,
> in the Clouds, in the eloquent Tongue." (p. 493c-d)

As the Clouds offer him their aid, Strepsiades protests that he does not want to become a philosopher, but only to become a master of eloquence and sophistry so that he may best his creditors in the law courts. He wants to

> . . . appear without conscience or fear,
> Bold, hasty, and wise, a concocter of lies,
> A rattler to speak, a dodger, a sneak,
> A regular claw of the tables of law,
> A shuffler complete, well worn in deceit,
> A supple, unprincipled, troublesome cheat;
> A hang-dog accurst, a bore with the worst,
> In the tricks of the jury-courts thoroughly versed. (p. 494a)

Socrates finds the old man a dull student, with no memory and unable to grasp the simplest general notions. All Strepsiades wants is the specific practical skill necessary to cheat his creditors, not knowledge of harmony or grammar. In an uproarious scene, Socrates tries vainly to teach Strepsiades the gender of nouns, which is the furthest thing from the old man's mind. Ordered to lie on a bed and meditate, Strepsiades moans as the bedbugs bite him and concocts ridiculous devices to beat out his creditors. Socrates finally becomes disgusted and expels the old man from the school.

Still determined to make use of the new learning to cheat his creditors, the old man brings his son Pheidippides to Socrates' school—after first showing off his new knowledge that Zeus does not exist and that the feminine of "fowl" is "fowless." The old man pleads with Socrates to teach his son both the Better and the Worse Logics, so that he may make the worse the better cause—"Give him the knack of reasoning down all Justice" (p. 499b). Socrates leaves it to Pheidippides to judge for himself between the two Logics, which are impersonated by two actors in a scene in which each presents the argument for his own way.

Right Logic pleads for the old discipline which taught the youth of Athens the virtues of honor, truth, modesty, temperance, respect for elders, physical culture, and courage. Wrong Logic pleads that the new learning will give youth the ability to contradict the old rules and laws, to make the worse seem the better cause, and to argue oneself out of any difficulties a life of sensual pleasure may lead to.

> For take this chastity, young man:
> sift it inside and out:
> Count all the pleasures, all the joys,
> it bids you live without:
> No kind of dames, no kind of games,
> no laughing, feasting, drinking—
> Why, life itself is little worth
> without these joys, I'm thinking.
> Well, I must notice now the wants
> by Nature's self implanted;
> You love, seduce, you can't help that,
> you're caught, convicted. Granted.
> You're done for; you can't say one word:
> while you follow me
> Indulge your genius, laugh and quaff,
> hold nothing base to be.
> Why if you're in adultery caught,
> your pleas will still be ample:
> You've done no wrong, you'll say, and then
> bring Zeus as your example.
> He fell before the wondrous powers
> by Love and Beauty wielded:
> And how can you, the Mortal, stand,
> where He, the Immortal, yielded? (p. 501d)

Finally, Wrong Logic gets the better of Right Logic by getting the latter to admit that the lawyers, tragic poets, orators, and the very audience watching the play are proven adulterers—so why should a young man be sensitive about being the same? Right Logic admits himself defeated, and Socrates proceeds to educate Pheidippides to be "a splendid sophist."

It is the "Old-and-New day," the last day of the month, on which debts must be paid. Pheidippides, instructed in Wrong

Logic, proceeds to show his father that there can be no such day, both "old" and "new." Emboldened by this technicality, Strepsiades refuses to pay one creditor on the grounds that he has made a mistake about the gender of a word. He sends another packing because he is ignorant of the laws of nature and because interest is logically ridiculous.

The old man is in his glory. He has accomplished all he proposed. But his triumph is short-lived, for his son, too, has learned Wrong Logic. Pheidippides beats his father and then proceeds to demonstrate that it is right for a son to beat his father. When he wants to prove also that it is right to beat his mother, Strepsiades finally realizes that he has corrupted his son in his vicious desire to cheat his creditors. He proclaims himself a fool for having abandoned fair dealing and reverence for Zeus to follow Sophistic logic and scientific atheism.

As the play ends, the old man has begun to burn up the Thinking-house. To the outraged cries of Socrates and his disciples, the old man answers

> For with what aim did ye insult the Gods,
> And pry around the dwellings of the Moon?
> Strike, smite them, spare them not, for many reasons,
> *But most because they have blasphemed the Gods!* (p. 506d)

III

The Birds was first presented at the Great Dionysiac festival in 414 B.C., where it won the second prize. It was produced at the time of the ill-fated Sicilian expedition (described by Thucydides in Book VI of *The Peloponnesian War,* Vol. 6), and contains many topical references to its leaders and events. There are also allusions to the sacrilegious mutilation of the statues of the Hermae, on the eve of the expedition, which had shocked Athenians, and was, justly or not, ascribed to the notorious Alcibiades, one of the leaders of the expedition. Some interpreters have seen this play as an allegory on the Sicilian expedition; others as a satire on the shortcomings of Athenian democracy; and still others as an attempt by Aristophanes to create an image of a good and peaceful society—in protest against the war and civil corruption.

Whatever the worth of these interpretations, the value of

The Birds is by no means limited to its contemporary political relevance. Indeed, one commentator asserts that this work is more communicative—and less topically limited—for the modern reader than any other of Aristophanes' comedies. *The Birds* is a delightful comic extravaganza, with lilting, catching dialogue and choruses, and scenes of humor and burlesque that still retain their ability to elicit chuckles. We are fortunate to have this verse translation, which by its rhythms as well as its witty words does so much to carry over to us the spirit of the original—despite the lack of music, "props," costumes, and physical enactment.

As the play opens, Peisthetaerus and Euelpides, two elderly Athenians, are making their way to the palace of Epops, the Hoopoe, King of the birds (also called Tereus, after the ancient myth—see note 1, p. 542). They explain to the spectators why they are giving up their precious rights as Athenian citizens to go to the birds.

> Not that we hate our city, as not being
> A prosperous mighty city, free for all
> To spend their wealth in, paying fines and fees.
> Aye, the cicalas chirp upon the boughs
> One month, or two; but our Athenians chirp
> Over their lawsuits all their whole life long.
> That's why we are journeying on this journey now,
> Trudging along with basket, pot, and myrtles,
> To find some quiet easy-going spot,
> Where we may settle down, and dwell in peace.
> Tereus, the hoopoe, is our journey's aim,
> To learn if he, in any place he has flown to,
> Has seen the sort of city that we want. (p. 542d)

They tell Epops, when they meet him, that they want to be as free as the birds, and find "some city, soft/As a thick rug, to lay us down within." None of the cities Epops mentions is satisfactory to the two Athenians.

Peisthetaerus proposes a "grand scheme" to found a bird-state in the air, midway between the gods and men, and to levy a toll on both. Because of their strategic location, the birds can control the passage of the steam of savory sacrifices to the gods and can also ruin or save human crops. Hence the birds can be rulers of the universe.

Epops and his wife Procne, the nightingale, summon the birds to assemble to hear the new proposal. A chorus of twenty-four birds enters. Peisthetaerus enumerates some of them.

> Jay and turtle, lark and sedgebird,
> thyme-finch, ring-dove first, and then
> Rock-dove, stock-dove, cuckoo, falcon,
> fiery-crest, and willow wren,
> Lammergeyer, porphyrion, kestrel,
> waxwing, nuthatch, water-hen. (p. 546a)

Some of the most delightful lyrics in the play follow as Epops and the chorus discuss the new arrivals. The birds are incensed at the coming of these specimens of their ancient enemy, man, and are all set to tear them to pieces. Finally Epops gets them calmed down enough to listen to Peisthetaerus expound his proposal.

Peisthetaerus, in a full-dress oration, with a wreath in his hair, tells the birds that they were the original sovereigns of the universe, with a lineage far antedating that of Zeus. He summons up examples from the legends and myths of many peoples to show that birds were the original deities of mankind. Now they have fallen so low that they are hunted and trapped and eaten by men. The chorus responds to this sad tale by demanding how they can regain their lost glory and dominion.

Peisthetaerus gives them a detailed proposal to build a walled city between heaven and earth, to which men shall pay tribute (grain and insects) and render worship. The gods are to get no part of the sacrifices, nor have access to humans (especially women), until they agree to relinquish their sovereignty to the birds. And if men refuse honor and tribute, the birds will ruin their crops and herds, but if they agree, the birds will help them to attain wealth and health. The birds are completely won over and enter into a solemn pact with the two Athenians to "march on the Gods" and regain lost sovereignty.

The chorus sings the glories of the winged state, and conveys some notion of why Aristophanes has chosen the birdland for his ideal city.

> Ye men who are dimly existing below,
> who perish and fade as the leaf,

Pale, woebegone, shadowlike, spiritless folk,
 life feeble and wingless and brief,
Frail castings in clay, who are gone in a day,
 like a dream full of sorrow and sighing,
Come listen with care to the Birds of the air,
 the ageless, the deathless, who flying
In the joy and the freshness of Ether, are wont
 to muse upon wisdom undying. (p. 551b-c)

The chorus discourses on "things transcendental," on the first principles of the world. It tells of all the wonderful things birds do for man—aid him to win love, to tell the seasons, to foretell the future (birds were used for omens in ancient Greece, and Aristophanes makes a play here on the Greek word for "bird" which is the same as the word for "omen"). Then they shift to a lighter note, calling the spectators to a life of ease and pleasure, which will be theirs if they live like the birdies do.

All that here is reckoned shameful,
 all that here the laws condemn,
With the birds is right and proper,
 you may do it all with them. (p. 552b)

Father-beating (echo of *The Clouds*) is one of the many acts forbidden in human society that one can get away with in birdland. Also among the conveniences of the winged state, the chorus tells the spectators, is that one can speedily leave the theater to eat, relieve oneself, or make love and still be able to return in time to see the end of the play.

At this point Peisthetaerus and Euelpides return, newly equipped with wings they have just grown in order to consort properly with their allies. The next step is to give the city "Some grand big name." Peisthetaerus comes up with the name "Cloudcuckoobury" (or "Cloudcuckootown" or "Cloudcuckooland"). The fighting cock is chosen as official guardian of the new state, and the birds proceed to build the protective wall. Meanwhile a priest comes to perform the initial sacrifice to the new gods, the birds. Peisthetaerus loses patience with his long-winded, endless prayer and finishes the sacrifice himself.

Now enters a string of cranks and quacks attracted by the erection of the city in the air: a windy and corny poet, a phony prophet, a land surveyor, an inspector general, a statute seller hawking new laws. Peisthetaerus gets rid of all of them. He treats only the poet gently, buying his departure with some badly needed clothes. The others get abuse and blows to hasten their exit from the new state. These are scenes in the tradition of Athenian comedy and American burlesque.

The first divine trespasser into the precincts of the new city is Iris, the messenger of the gods. She is amazed and shocked to find that she needs a "stork-pass" in order to enter the realm of the birds. She says that Zeus has sent her on a mission to mankind to bid them send up the savor of sacrifices to the gods. Peisthetaerus challenges her:

Pe. What do you say? What Gods?
Ir. What Gods? To us, the Gods in Heaven, of course.
Pe. (*with supreme contempt*) What, are *you* Gods?
Ir. What other Gods exist?
Pe. Birds are now Gods to men; and men must slay
Victims to them; and not, by Zeus, to Zeus. (p. 558a)

He sends her packing back to Olympus.

Now a herald returns from earth to inform Peisthetaerus that mankind has gone "bird-mad."

Why, till ye built this city in the air,
All men had gone Laconian-mad; they went
Long-haired, half-starved, unwashed, Socratified,
With scytales in their hands; but O the change!
They are all bird-mad now, and imitate
The birds, and joy to do whate'er birds do.
Soon as they rise from bed at early dawn,
They settle down on laws, as we on lawns,
And then they brood upon their leaves and leaflets,
And feed their fill upon a crop of statutes. (p. 558b-c)

All men want wings now, and Peisthetaerus orders a batch of wings to be gathered—suited to singing, prophetic, and aquatic birds to fit men's varied tastes—so that men may lead the good birdlife. Sings the chorus,

Here is Wisdom, and Wit, and each exquisite
Grace,
And here the unruffled, benevolent face
Of Quiet, and loving Desire. (p. 558d)

Now Cloudcuckoobury is beset with human visitors. The first is a father-beater, who is in love with the bird law that a youngster may beat his father, but he is quite put out by another bird law that the full-grown son must support his father. Then we get another windy poet who pleads for wings that he may soar high "And pluck poetic fancies from the clouds." Despite Peisthetaerus' protest, he sings a song which is so awful that Peisthetaerus beats him and drives him away. Next comes a sycophant—something like an income-tax informer—whose job is to snitch on the property holders in the island colonies. He wants wings in order to serve his writs speedily and despoil the accused men of their estates. The informer is not impressed by Peisthetaerus' idea that talk gives men wings:

> Through talk the mind flutters and soars aloft,
> And all the man takes wing. (p. 560a)

Peisthetaerus chases the informer off stage with a whip.

The last of the visitors is the famous demigod Prometheus, who earned Zeus's enmity for bringing man the gift of fire and the arts. Prometheus conceals himself under an umbrella so that Zeus will not see him. "All's up with Zeus," is Prometheus' message. Imports of savory steam have been completely cut off since Cloudcuckooland was built and burnt offerings stopped. Unrest has developed among the barbarian gods (the "Triballians"), who threaten to revolt if Zeus does not see to it that the markets are well stocked with savory smells. Prometheus advises Peisthetaerus not to make peace unless Zeus restores rule to the birds and gives him Miss Sovereignty to wife. She is the fine girl who keeps the store for Zeus. She keeps the thunderbolts, wise counsel, good laws—*everything* indeed. Marry the girl, advises Prometheus, and "*you'll* have *everything*."

In the final scene of the play, an embassy arrives from Olympus consisting of the sea-god Poseidon, the hero Heracles, and a Triballian god—"the uncouthest God I ever came across" says Poseidon.

> . . . O Democracy,
> What will you bring us to at last, I wonder,
> If voting Gods elect a clown like this! (p. 561c)

The gods try to get the attention of Peisthetaerus, who is engaged in roasting some birds that have been executed for revolting against the people's party in birdland. Peisthetaerus insists on rule being restored to the birds and on his marriage to Miss Sovereignty as the only acceptable peace terms. Poseidon refuses, but Heracles (whom the comic poets always satirized as a glutton) is anxious to get at the roast fowl. "Let's not fight over a woman," he says in effect. The embassy votes and the Triballian's barbarous gibberish is taken for assent, so with hungry Heracles in favor, the ayes have it, two to one. The birds have won.

The play ends with the chorus singing a wedding hymn at the marriage of Peisthetaerus and Miss Sovereignty.

> All that was Zeus's of old
> Now is our hero's alone;
> Sovereignty, fair to behold,
> Partner of Zeus on his throne,
> Now is forever his own.
> Hymen, O Hymenaeus! (p. 563c)

IV

Of Aristophanes' plays, *The Lysistrata* is probably the best known to modern readers. Gilbert Seldes' modern translation was warmly received by American playgoers in the 1930's. The play was first produced in 411 B.C., shortly after the disastrous failure of the Athenians' Sicilian expedition and their enemy Sparta's alliance with Persia. It is the last of the three antiwar plays written by Aristophanes during the Peloponnesian War. The first was *The Acharnians,* originally produced in 425 B.C., and the second was *The Peace,* first produced in 421 B.C. When *The Lysistrata* was first performed the war was in its twenty-first year, and the Athenians were sick of it. Aristophanes expressed his own and his fellow Athenians' dark mood in this wonderful, imaginative, bawdy fiction on how to obtain the long-desired peace. (See Book VIII of Thucydides' *History of the Peloponnesian War* in Vol. 6 for a historical discussion of this period.)

The plot and development of *The Lysistrata* is very simple, compared with *The Birds,* with its many episodes and characters. The women of the warring Greek cities band together to end the war by denying sexual love to their menfolk until they declare peace. At this point the fun begins, and we watch the development and denouement of this basic situation. Will the women be able to hold fast to their no-loving campaign? Will the men endure their deprivations and go on fighting, or will they give in? Just imagine the comic as well as the painful consequences of this daring plot of womankind!

As the play opens, Lysistrata, the leader of the Athenian women, has convened a conference in Athens of the representatives of the women of the warring Greek city-states. She proposes that the women force their men to make peace by denying them sexual love.

> O ladies! sisters! if we really mean
> To make the men make Peace, there's but one way . . .
> We must abstain—each—from the joys of
> Love. (p. 584d)

At first the women recoil in horror from such a suggestion, but Lysistrata convinces them that with their feminine fripperies and charms they can secure the peace they all long for.

> For if we women will but sit at home,
> Powdered and trimmed, clad in our daintiest lawn,
> Employing all our charms, and all our arts
> To win men's love, and when we've won it, then
> Repel them, firmly, till they end the war,
> We'll soon get Peace again, be sure of that. (p. 585a)

The assembled lady representatives take a solemn oath to abstain from the joys of love until peace is obtained. The non-Athenian women leave to organize the no-loving campaign in their home cities. The Athenian women, under Lysistrata's lead, wage a two-front campaign against their men. In addition to denying them sexual love, they also seize the Acropolis, which contains the treasury, and thus the means to finance continuance of the war. The outraged Athenian men thus find themselves stricken both in their private boudoirs and in the national treasury.

The battle for the Acropolis gives Aristophanes an opportunity to stage a comical scene between a chorus of old women and a chorus of old men. Much contempt and vituperation is exchanged between the elderly representatives of the warring sexes. The old men, who are veterans of former wars, appeal to Euripides as an authority for their low opinion of women. The war veterans, however, are no match for the old ladies who conquer them by pouring down hot water on their heads. The women also vanquish a squad of Scythian archers, who were the policemen of ancient Athens. The police are led by a magistrate, who is one of the newly appointed Directors of Public Safety. Despite his low opinion of women, the turn of events forces him into a discussion with Lysistrata.

In this debate scene—so typical of Greek plays—the magistrate takes the position that "War is the care and business of men," while Lysistrata takes the view that war is the concern of women, and, moreover, that they would be better managers of the political community than the men. She tells how the women in the past have been silenced and told to stick to their knitting when they have remarked on the stupid blunders which men have perpetrated in military and political affairs. But now the women have revolted in order to save the state, and a reversal of the traditional roles is in order.

> What! you unfortunate, shall we not then,
> Then, when we see you perplexed and incompetent,
> shall we not tender advice to the State?
> So when aloud in the streets and the thoroughfares
> sadly we heard you bewailing of late,
> "Is there a Man to defend and deliver us?"
> "No," says another, "there's none in the land";
> Then by the Women assembled in conference
> jointly a great Revolution was planned,
> Hellas to save from her grief and perplexity.
> Where is the use of a longer delay?
> Shift for the future our parts and our characters;
> you, as the women, in silence obey;
> We, as the men, will harangue and provide for you;
> then shall the State be triumphant again,
> Then shall we do what is best for the citizens. (p. 589d)

She points to the nimble dexterity with which women disentangle a knotted skein of thread and the thoroughness with which they clean a fleece as ideal experience for the kind of work that has to be done in politics. Here is how she puts the analogy between preparing the fleece and securing the common good.

> First, in the washing-tub
> plunge it, and scour it, and cleanse it from grease,
> Purging away all the filth and the nastiness;
> then on the table expand it and lay,
> Beating out all that is worthless and mischievous,
> picking the burrs and the thistles away.
> Next, for the clubs, the cabals, and the coteries,
> banding unrighteously, office to win,
> Treat them as clots in the wool, and dissever them,
> lopping the heads that are forming therein.
> Then you should card it and comb it, and mingle it,
> all in one Basket of love and of unity,
> Citizens, visitors, strangers, and sojourners,
> all the entire, undivided community.
> Know you a fellow in debt to the Treasury?
> Mingle him merrily in with the rest.
> Also remember the cities, our colonies,
> outlying states in the east and the west,
> Scattered about to a distance surrounding us,
> these are our shreds and our fragments of wool;
> These to one mighty political aggregate
> tenderly, carefully, gather and pull,
> Twining them all in one thread of good fellowship;
> thence a magnificent bobbin to spin,
> Weaving a garment of comfort and dignity,
> worthily wrapping the People therein. (p. 590c-d)

The women end the discussion by dressing the magistrate up in graveclothes, and they tell him to drop dead. He runs off, terribly offended, to show his fellow magistrates what these lady radicals have done to him. The chorus of women take on the chorus of men in another pitched battle and are apparently victorious.

At the end of several days, however, Lysistrata finds it hard to keep the upper hand over the men, for her forces in the Acropolis are unable to stand the deprivation of their husbands' caresses. The girls are trying to sneak home on all sorts of pretexts. There are various household chores that need to be done, they plead. But Lysistrata encourages them to bear up for just a while longer in this war of attrition, in which the other side is suffering just as much or more.

One of the funniest scenes in the play occurs now, as Cinesias, a deprived husband, tries to persuade his wife Myrrhina to return to his arms. He even brings their little child along as a lure to bring her down from the Acropolis. Myrrhina, under Lysistrata's orders, goes down to him to enflame his ardor but leave him unsatisfied. Says Lysistrata,

> . . . 'tis yours to roast and bother him well;
> Coaxing, yet coy: enticing, fooling him,
> Going all lengths, save what our Oath forbids. (p. 593d)

Myrrhina drives the poor fellow mad with frustrated desire, as she fusses about the proper place to lie down, then about a mattress, next a pillow, than a blanket, and so on, until she finally leaves him, still unsatisfied, urging him to be sure to vote for peace.

The campaign of this ancient League of Women Voters has been successful outside of Athens too. A herald comes from Sparta to tell of the sad state of the Spartan menfolk, and returns with Athenian proposals to call a peace conference at once. The manly warriors of the Greek city-states must admit defeat and give in to the women on their own terms. Sings the men's chorus,

> That was quite a true opinion
> which a wise man gave about you,
> We can't live with such tormentors,
> no, by Zeus, nor yet without you. (p. 596b)

The climax of the play comes with the great reconciliation scene, in which Lysistrata scolds both sides and presents reasons why they should be friends.

> And now, dear friends, I wish to chide you both,
> That ye, all of one blood, all brethren sprinkling
> The selfsame altars from the selfsame laver,
> At Pylae, Pytho, and Olympia, ay
> And many others which 'twere long to name,
> That ye, Hellenes—with barbarian foes
> Armed, looking on—fight and destroy Hellenes! (p. 597b)

She reminds both the Spartans and the Athenians how each had come to the other's aid at critical occasions in the past.

> Such friends aforetime, helping each the other,
> What is it makes you fight and bicker now?
> Why can't ye come to terms? Why can't ye, hey? (p. 597c)

When the two sides start bickering about the peace terms and territories, an Athenian points out that there is only one thing that the men want—and that is to go to bed with their wives. This sensible observation puts an end to the palavering, and the women serve a banquet at the Acropolis, where the ambassadors exchange pledges of peace. The play ends with the Spartan and Athenian envoys dancing with their wives "in grateful honour to the Gods." The chorus calls on the gods "to witness the peace and the harmony . . . which divine Aphrodite [the goddess of love] has made." On this note Aristophanes' play about the women's peace campaign ends. For another version of women in politics, see Aristophanes' play *The Ecclesiazusae* ("Women in Parliament").

V

Are Aristophanes' plays indecent? Should they be censored?

The jokes and allusions that give offense to some modern readers are of two types—scatological (dealing with the excremental functions) and sexual. In the latter it is particularly the references to the phallus or sexual deviations that offend. Our translation has eliminated practically all the phallic and perverted references and most of the scatological ones. Of course, it is impossible to eliminate the theme and scenes of *The Lysistrata,* but the obvious evidence of the male plight that appears in the original has been deleted here. Yet there is still enough of the scatological and sexual left to raise questions in many minds.

The defense that has been made of Aristophanes is that his jokes fitted in with the tastes of his time, and that, moreover, many of the allusions were proper and even religious in an art derived from the Dionysiac revels. Also, it is pointed out that, like Shakespeare in Elizabethan England, he was a theater man playing to the crowd and throwing in many coarse passages just to please the common people—it was good "box office." Again, it is pointed out that respectable women and children were not permitted to attend theatrical performances, so that delicate and budding sensibilities might not be offended.

Do you think that Aristophanes has to be defended at all? Are his coarse allusions and jesting harmful to moral judgment and action? Are they healthy or sickening? Do you find them humorous or not? Would the plays be just as good and true to Aristophanes' personal flavor if the coarseness were eliminated completely? Or, if you approve of Aristophanes' scatological and phallic references, would you want to keep them unexpurgated both in the text and in the performance? Could a modern audience stomach Aristophanes unexpurgated? Do you know of any contemporary plays where such allusions and jokes are made? Is direct reference to the excremental and sexual functions always offensive in theatrical performances?

Is it right for the poet to take sides in political questions?

One of the bewildering things about Greek Old Comedy is the mixture of political satire with low farce. When we go to the theater, especially when we go to see a comedy, most of us expect to be entertained. The appearance of serious political questions seems to be out of place. And if the poet takes sides, that would seem to alienate a good part of the audience. Did the war party or democrats of ancient Athens find Aristophanes' satirical attacks on them enjoyable theatrical entertainment?

One answer we might give is that entertainment and politics are not mutually exclusive. Indeed, many persons think that politics, especially democratic politics, furnishes an infinite source of merriment. There is undoubtedly a good deal of this kind of light entertainment in Aristophanes, where everybody gets enjoyment out of the joking at the foibles of public officials and their electors—even those who are the butt of the joke. The musical comedy *Of Thee I Sing* in the 1930's was this kind of political entertainment, at which the president, vice-president, and Supreme Court of the United States, as well as the voters, could have a wonderful time watching themselves being made fun of. (A performance in Washington, D.C., of this musical comedy duplicated the situation that occurred in Athens when one of Aristophanes' political satires—also a musical comedy—was being performed.)

But anyone who reads these plays carefully will realize that Aristophanes is not merely playing the role of an amused spectator at the comedy of political life. He is obviously deadly serious and deeply concerned about demagoguery, civic corruption, and imperialism. In such plays as *The Knights*, Aristophanes attacked Cleon, the leader of the popular war party. The result was a series of judicial attacks by the powerful Cleon, attempting to deprive Aristophanes of his Athenian citizenship, by trying to prove that the poet was not born in Athens. But the courts did not take away Aristophanes' citizenship nor were his plays ever banned, no matter how much they went counter to public opinion. There were no restraints on freedom of expression in the Greek comic theater. In such plays as *The Birds*, Aristophanes even makes fun of the gods. Apparently the Greek people were able to appreciate the biting satire on their foibles and politics by this old conservative who opposed their ways and views.

For a contemporary analogy, let us look to the late Bertolt Brecht, who was a comic dramatist with Communist convictions. His works, including the musical comedy the *Threepenny Opera,* combine wit, lyrics, and political satire. Their target is the iniquity and corruption which Brecht finds characteristic of bourgeois capitalist society. His plays are good "theater," and he is regarded by many critics as one of the greatest dramatic writers of the twentieth century.

Assuming that you are firmly opposed to Communist ideas and practices and generally in favor of the capitalistic system, would you go to see the kind of plays Brecht wrote? Would you enjoy the political satire as well as the music and wit? Is it proper to perform such plays in our society? Should the right of such plays to be performed be upheld even in a time of war with a Communist enemy? Should antiwar plays be permitted in wartime? Or should the theater stay out of politics entirely, in war or in peace?

Would it be better in The Clouds *to have Pheidippides cheat the creditors, rather than Strepsiades?*

The old man is too stupid to learn the New Learning, so he sends Pheidippides to Socrates' school to master the art of false reasoning. Why, then, does not Aristophanes have the young man bilk the creditors after he has attained the requisite skill? Would it be more logical, in keeping with the previous action, to do it this way? First, you would have Pheidippides cheat the creditors, then you would have him beat the old man—both actions based on the same false reasoning. Or is it funnier to have the old man pick up a few new tricks from the son and then be beaten after he has fended off his creditors? Suppose you were the director of the play, how would you stage the final scenes?

Is it inconsistent for Aristophanes to preach reverence for Zeus in The Clouds *and to make fun of the gods in* The Birds?

In *The Clouds,* Aristophanes ridicules putting natural phenomena in the place of the gods. He sees a connection between moral corruption and lack of reverence for the supernatural. In *The Birds,* he has sport with the gods and the sacrifices with which men propititate them. Is he being irreverent? Is he going too far, from the viewpoint of Greek religion, to ridicule the gods as well as men? Sören Kierkegaard, the nineteenth-century Danish religious philosopher, said that a sense of humor was necessary for a religious man. Is this true or is humor out of place in religion? Is Aristophanes poking fun at man's religious attitudes, practices, and beliefs, or at the gods?

Is it of any significance that Zeus does not appear in the play? How do you think the Greek audience reacted to Aristophanes' spoofing—with shock or enjoyment? Would it be possible to stage an American play poking fun at God, the prophets, saints, and apostles?

Is The Lysistrata *subversive?*

When *The Lysistrata* was first produced, Athens was in a critical military situation. It had suffered terrible defeats, the enemy was being strengthened by alliances, and the Athenian people were tired of the war. What result could *The Lysistrata* have except to weaken whatever will to resist and carry on there still was in Athens? How could the authorities permit this play to be staged? Does the fact that this play is a comic fantasy make any difference? Does that make it easier to take than a serious antiwar play? Or does a play like *The Lysistrata* act as a safety valve, allowing the people as well as the playwright to let off the steam built up by the pressure of sacrifice and deprivation? Would you be in favor of allowing *The Lysistrata* to be staged in the United States during wartime?

Is The Lysistrata *indecent?*

The Lysistrata deals frankly and explicitly with the physical aspect of conjugal love. In it, women deliberately evoke and frustrate their husbands' desire in order to end the war. One scene shows a woman tantalizing her husband as they prepare to go to bed, and all the preparations for the sexual act are shown on the stage. Would it be outrageous to public propriety to have such a scene enacted on the stage nowadays? Are the references to the female titillation and the male frustration indecent? Does it make any difference that this play deals with wedded love instead of illicit romance? Or does that make it even worse? Does *The Lysistrata* encourage immorality or incontinence? Is any public presentation or discussion of sexual matters wrong? Or does propriety depend on the manner and tone of the presentation? Do you think *The Lysistrata* is too indecent for public performance? If so, why? If not, why not?

SELF-TESTING QUESTIONS

The following questions are designed to help you test the thoroughness of your reading. Each question is to be answered by giving a page or pages of the reading assignment. Answers will be found on page 232 of this Reading Plan.

1 Why is war harder on women than on men?

2 Which of the birds does Euelpides fall into a passion about?

3 What good would it do Strepsiades to lock up the moon in a box?

4 What is the ritual for the women's oath in *The Lysistrata?*

5 Who is "the giant" whom Aristophanes floored "in his hour of pride"?

6 Which of the birds is a kinsman of Peisthetaerus and Euelpides?

7 In what respect is Euripides "wise and knowing"?

8 What is the feminine of "trough"?

9 What is the call of the hoopoe?

10 Why is it more convenient to worship the birds than the gods?

Fourth Reading

VIRGIL

The Aeneid

Vol. 13, pp. 101–379

Virgil's *Aeneid* stands midway between the Homeric epics and Dante's *Divine Comedy*. Its middle position is not merely historical but also literary. For Virgil's *Aeneid* was a deliberate attempt to reproduce in his own time and tongue the grandeur of the Homeric epics. And during the centuries of the eclipse of Greco-Roman culture, Virgil's name was revered, and this work helped to conserve and transmit the precious legacy of the ancient world. It was Virgil who was the great inspiration and exemplar for Dante when he came to write the *Divine Comedy*. Virgil has a supreme place among the shapers of the imagination of the Western world, equaled only by Homer and Dante.

The *Aeneid* is an amazing combination of myth, legend, and history, of poetic fiction and religious prophecy, of the sensitive rendition of personal feeling and the grandiose glorification of a political system. It is the story of the resurrection of a people from utter defeat and despair, through many frustrations and sufferings, to become the founders of a great world empire. It is the story of their heroic leader, who is appointed by heaven to achieve this mission, and does so even when it conflicts with his personal feelings and inclinations. It is the story of love—between man and wife, lover and mistress (it contains one of the most passionate love stories in world literature), parents and children, and comrades-in-arms. And it is also the story of the invisible, unseen, supernatural realm of the gods and the dead, with philosophical and theological overtones.

For twenty centuries, readers have enjoyed the *Aeneid*, for its style as well as its story, for its manner as well as its matter. Virgil's stately, gracious, and elegant rhetoric was one of the glories of the Latin language. It influenced the style of Western writers down through the ages and helped to shape the syntax of many modern languages. Its allusive imagery, symbolic richness, and epigrammatic conciseness have delighted readers who enjoy the fine points of style and the well-turned phrase, as well as an absorbing story and a serious theme.

GUIDE TO

Fourth Reading

I

Publius Vergilius Maro—whom we call Vergil or Virgil in English—was born in 70 B.C. on a farm in northern Italy. The great singer of the glory of Rome came from a region that was not in the sphere of Roman citizenship. Virgil's strong sense of a common Italian nationality is manifest in the *Aeneid.* He was born in a time of severe crisis for the Roman state. A century of revolution and civil wars, as well as of new conquests abroad, ended in the assumption of power by Augustus, Virgil's friend and sponsor. The first forty years of Virgil's life were the last forty years of the Roman Republic. During this century of crisis, military leaders, such as Julius Caesar, Pompey, and Mark Antony, assumed political power and fought among themselves for supremacy. Augustus, Caesar's adopted heir, became the first Roman emperor, although he did not assume that title, and claimed only to be the restorer of the Roman Republic.

"Peace and order" were the watchwords of the new regime. The famous "Roman peace" was enforced over large areas of Europe, Asia, and Africa by Roman soldiers and administrators. A large and efficient governmental machine was created to administer the affairs of Rome, Italy, and the Empire. Augustus also actively sponsored the development of Roman literature. Aided by his friend and adviser, the wealthy Maecenas, he supported and encouraged notable writers, including Virgil and Horace, and promoted one of the great eras in Roman literature. To counterbalance these favorable auspices, there was considerable censorship and restriction on what a writer could or could not say. Augustus banished the poet Ovid from Rome for life because he was offended by one of his poems. In addition to negative restrictions, poets were subject to the positive requirements of treating certain themes glorifying Rome's past and present, her divine mission to rule the world, and Augustus' reign and family.

It was not mere servility, however, that prompted Virgil to write the *Aeneid.* It had long been the ambition of Roman writers to equal the Greek writers in every type of literature, and especially to rival Homer's epics. More than a century before Virgil was born, the poet Ennius had written a national epic in Homeric meters about the glories of Rome, from mythical times to his own day. Virgil's first work was the *Eclogues,* pastoral poems in imitation of the *Idylls* of the Greek poet *Theocritus.* His next work was the *Georgics,* a didactic (instructive) poem on farming, modeled in form on the *Works and Days* of the Greek poet Hesiod and in thought on the Roman poet Lucretius' work *On the Nature of Things.* (See Vol. 12.) Finally he wrote the great epic—about the glory of the Roman nation—that he had long aimed to write.

This work, the *Aeneid,* took the rest of his life—about eleven years. He considered it unfinished—unpolished and unrevised—at the time he died. One of his letters indicates that he considered the poem a failure. Indeed, it was his final request that it be destroyed. But Augustus, who was naturally interested in the subject of the poem and had heard part of it read by Virgil himself, overruled the poet's wishes and had it published after his death. Thus this work's important role in world literature is due to an emperor's command. In this case at least, politics served culture.

Virgil's task was to write a national epic that would link the heroic age of the Homeric poems to the history of Rome and the present Augustan age. He found the proper material in ancient Roman legends or fables, according to which the Trojan Prince, Aeneas, who is one of the characters in Homer's *Iliad* (see Vol. 4, pp. 31-33 and pp. 143-145), led a remnant of Trojans to Italy and became the progenitor of the founders of Rome. Virgil found the "scriptural" basis for Aeneas' survival, and that of the Trojan remnant in these words of Neptune in the *Iliad:*

"... It is fated, moreover, that he should escape, and that the race of Dardanus, whom Jove loved above all the sons born to him of mortal women, shall not perish utterly without seed or sign. For now indeed has Jove hated the blood of Priam, while Aeneas shall reign over the Trojans, he and his children's children that shall be born hereafter." (Vol. 4, p. 145b)

And he found a basis in legend and previous literature for the story that Aeneas founded a city in Latium, from which Rome originated. The legend was taken seriously in the ancient world, as is indicated by the request of a Greek city in the third century B.C. for aid from Rome on the grounds that it was the only Greek state that had not warred against Troy. Similarly, in the *Aeneid,* Virgil considers a Roman general's destruction of Argos and Mycenae as revenge for Troy. (See p. 233b.) Stesichorus, a Greek poet of the seventh and sixth centuries B.C., wrote what was probably the first literary treatment of the Aeneas legend in his *Sack of Troy*. Roman historians and poets before Virgil, such as Ennius, accepted the legend.

Thus Virgil found the bare bones of his story ready at hand in well-known legends and literature. But the conception and the literary execution of the *Aeneid* is the work of his own poetic genius. He originated a magnificently organized and sonorous work, whose lines have remained in men's minds and echoed in their ears for nearly two thousand years. The *Aeneid* is the work of a superb literary craftsman, of a conscious and sophisticated artist, who deliberately contrived this epic poem. It is impossible in translation to reproduce Virgil's mastery of sound effects, his verbal "music," but even in translation we are able to appreciate his use of allusions, his symbolic images, his elegant and stately mode, and the conciseness with which he packs a world of meaning into a phrase or sentence. Tennyson called Virgil's verse "the stateliest measure ever moulded by the lips of man." And Dante said that Virgil taught him all he knew about poetic style.

II

The *Aeneid* is divided into twelve "books." The first six books tell of the wanderings of Aeneas and his men from Troy to Latium (an ancient country in central Italy, the seat of the Latin people and language, and the land where the original site of Rome was located). The last six books tell of the war in Latium between the Trojans and Italians.

The work opens with a "proem," or preface (extending to the third line on p. 104), which states the subject of the *Aeneid* and the underlying cause of the action that is to take place. Here is the subject, told in the first ten lines of our translation:

> Of arms I sing, and of the man who first
> From Trojan shores beneath the ban of fate
> To Italy and coasts Lavinian came,
> Much tossed about on land and ocean he
> By violence of the gods above, to sate
> Relentless Juno's ever-rankling ire,
> In war, too, much enduring, till what time
> A city he might found him, and bear safe
> His gods to Latium, whence the Latin race,
> And Alba's sires, and lofty-towering Rome. (p. 103a)

The proem goes on to tell us that a third city is involved—Carthage, favored by the goddess Juno, and intended by her to be a world empire, but destined to be overthrown by the Trojans' descendants, the world-conquering Romans. Moved by old grudges against the Trojans, as well as by apprehension about their posterity, Juno decides to make things hard for them.

> Fired with these thoughts besides, the Trojan few,
> 'Scaped from the Danai and Achilles fell,
> Still must she keep upon wide ocean tossed
> Aloof from Latium; and for many a year
> They roamed, fate-driven, through all the circling seas:
> So vast the toil to found the Roman race. (pp. 103b–104a)

After the proem, the action of the *Aeneid* begins. The Trojan fleet has just sailed from Sicily, on its way to Latium, toward which the Trojans have been voyaging for seven years. (See p. 123b.) Spiteful Juno has Aeolus, the lord of the winds, stir up a storm that scatters the Trojan fleet and nearly destoys it. However, Neptune, the god of the sea and sponsor of Troy (see pp. 141b, 147a), quiets the waters, and the battered remnant of the Trojan fleet is able to land on the coast of Libya. Meanwhile, in heaven, Venus, the mother of Aeneas, protests to Jupiter against what has happened to the Trojans.

THE VOYAGES OF AENEAS
Arx Monoeci (Monaco)
Ilva (Elba)
CORSICA
SARDINIA
ETRURIA
UMBRIA
LATIUM
TROJAN CAMP
Lavinium
C. GARGANUS
APULIA
CAMPANIA
Cumae
Neapolis (Napoli Naples)
Capreae
Tarentum
Aeolian Is.
Lipara
Lacinium
Scylaceum
Caulonia
Drepanum
CYCLOPS' HARBOUR
Thapsus
Ortygia
Helorus
Gela
Camarina
Pachynus
Carthage
Melita (Malta)
MEDITERRANEAN SEA
THE WAR IN LATIUM
L. Vulsinensis
Tiberis
Nar
Nursia
Amiternum
Graviscae
L. Sabatinus
Nersae
Agylla (Caere)
Lacus Fucinus
Pallanteum (Roma)
Tibur
Anio
Praeneste
Alba Longa
Lavinium
Ardea
Privernum
Laurentum
Circeii
Anxur
Caieta
Capua
Cumae
Sarnus
Baiae
Phaeacia (Corfu)
Buthrotum
EPIRUS
THESSALY
MT. OLYMPUS
Leucas
Leucate
Actium
Calydon
Thebes
Samë
Ithaca
Zacynthus
Strophades Is.
ARCADIA
Malea
Cythera
Euboea
Thasos
Athos
Lemnos
AEGEAN SEA
Samothrace
MYSIA
Rhoeteum
Troy
MT. IDA
Antandros
Lesbos
LYDIA
Smyrna
Chios
Claros
Myconos
Delos
Donysa
Olearos
Naxos
Rhodes
Pergamea
CRETE
MT. IDA
MT. DICTE

Jupiter reassures her that the destiny he has promised to Aeneas and his people shall come to pass. He utters the main prophecy of the work, linking the Trojans to the future of Rome, all the way down to Virgil's time.

"Truce, Cytherea, to thy fears, and know
Unshaken stand thy children's destinies:
Lavinium's city and predestined walls
Thou shalt behold, and in thine arms up-bear
High-souled Aeneas to the stars of heaven;
Nor hath my purpose warped me. This thy son—
For I, to ease thy gnawing care, will speak,
From fate's dark roll her inmost secrets wring—
Shall wage a mighty war in Italy,
Crush the proud folk, and for his warriors found
A city and a system, till the third
Summer hath seen him lord in Latium,
Three winters o'er the vanquished Rutules sped.
But young Ascanius, newly now surnamed
Iulus—Ilus was he while enthroned
Stood Ilium's State—shall compass in his reign
Thirty great cycles with revolving months,
And from Lavinium shift his empire's seat,
And Alba Longa's ramparts rear with power:
Here now shall reign full thrice a hundred years
Great Hector's line, till Ilia, royal maid
And priestess, shall twin offspring bear to Mars,
Their sire; then glorying in the tawny hide
Of the she-wolf, his nurse, shall Romulus
Take up the nation, build the war-god's town,
And call them Romans after his own name.
For these nor goals of power, nor times I fix—
Grant them a boundless sway. Fierce Juno too,
Who now with terror scares earth, sea, and heaven,
Shall turn to kinder counsels, and with me
Cherish the Romans, masters of the world,
The toga'd nation. So hath heaven decreed.
A time shall come with gliding lustres, when
The house of Assaracus to her yoke shall bow
Phthia and famed Mycenae, and bear sway
O'er conquered Argos. From that glorious line
Of Troy descending, Caesar shall be born,
Destined to bound with ocean his domain,
As with the stars his glory, Julius,
A name bequeathed from great Iulus. Him,

> Laden with eastern spoils, shalt thou one day
> Hold safe in heaven: to him too prayers shall rise.
> Then wars shall cease, the rugged times grow mild;
> Hoar Faith, and Vesta, and Quirinus then
> Yoked with his brother Remus, shall give laws;
> Grim-knit with bolts of iron, War's temple-gates
> Shut fast shall be, while hellish Rage within
> High on a grisly pile of arms, his hands
> Brass-bound behind him with a hundred knots,
> Shall roar terrific from blood-boltered mouth." (pp. 110a-111a)

Notice how this prophecy connects ancient legends and fables with actual history, the events of this story with Augustan Rome and an ideal future state. Aeneas is linked with Augustus through Aeneas' son Ascanius, or Iulus, from whom the Julian gens (clan)—to which Caesar and Augustus belonged—claimed descent. His is also the ancestor of Romulus, the legendary founder of Rome, through his descendant Ilia, and Lavinium, the city he founds, is associated with Rome through Alba Longa, the city of which Rome was traditionally believed to be a colony. Notice also, despite the detailed forecast of events, how grandly, even grandiloquently, *open* the prophecy is. Rome is to be an empire *without end;* no limits are set to it in time or space. And it is to preside over a time when there will be no more war and men will be ruled by religion and law alone.

Many allusions in the prophecy are conveyed through names or epithets. "Cytherea" is an epithet for Venus and refers to the island of Cythera, which was bound up with her legend and her worship in ancient Greece. "Assaracus" was an ancient king of Troy and the great-grandfather of Aeneas. "Quirinus" is the term for Romulus after he became a god, and the reference to Remus, Romulus' brother, refers to the strife between the two brothers in which Remus was killed. "Vesta" refers to the goddess of the hearth and alludes to the legend that Aeneas brought her eternal fire from Troy to Lavinium, along with the Penates, or household gods, both of the family and of the state. For these allusions we need a good classical dictionary. We also need a good English dictionary for the odd phrase "Nor hath my purpose warped me," which means simply "I have not changed my mind," or "My will has not changed."

Readers should apply this method of careful interpretation to all the important passages in the work. (For a discussion of the prophecies in the *Aeneid,* see Section IV below.)

Aeneas and his men (including the crews of the other ships, which have safely landed) find refuge at the nearby city of Carthage, newly founded by Phoenicians from Tyre under Queen Dido. She, too, has been forced to flee her native land, and hence feels sympathy with the Trojans, as well as admiration for their world-famed valor. She extends generous and gracious hospitality to them. At a banquet she gives in their honor, Aeneas tells of his seven years of wandering, as Ulysses told the Phaeacians of his journey in the *Odyssey.* Aeneas' story takes up Books II and III of the *Aeneid.*

He gives a vivid, graphic account of the fall of Troy—of the ill-fated entry of the wooden horse and of the emergence of the Greeks from it to butcher the Trojans and pillage Troy. There are many terrible and poignant moments. An apparition of the slain Trojan hero Hector bids Aeneas leave Troy, carrying its household gods to the faraway city he is destined to found. Aeneas witnesses the brutal slaying of old King Priam at his own altar. Aeneas is about to kill Helen in revenge for all Troy's woes when his mother, Venus, appears to dissuade him, pointing out that Helen is not to blame, and that it is the gods who have brought Troy low. In one of the most touching and memorable scenes in the *Aeneid,* he rescues his family from the burning and dying city, taking his old, paralyzed father, Anchises, on his back, and leading his son, Ascanius (Iulus) by the hand, while his wife, Creüsa, and the servants follow behind.

The old man, mounted on his son's back, carries the household gods, and the procession make its way out of the horror-filled, flaming city. But when they arrive at their destination, they find that Creüsa is missing, and Aeneas, mad with grief, returns to Troy. He runs up and down the streets, exposing himself to detection and death, with anguished cries of "Creüsa!" Suddenly her shade appears to tell him not to weep for her, for divine fate has decreed her death and his survival, so that he may fulfill a great destiny and marry another woman where the river Tiber flows. His attempts to embrace her are baffled, and she vanishes frustratingly into empty air. On his return to the family group, he finds a great throng of Trojan refugees, ready to go into exile anywhere that he will lead them. He takes a last look at Troy, which is beyond hope of rescue now, and then heads for the mountains.

Aeneas tells how the Trojan remnant built a fleet and set out for the unknown land to which destiny had called them. They made several false starts, first settling in Thrace and then in Crete, until Aeneas learned in a vision that their appointed destination was Italy, the land of their ancestors. In the Strophades Islands, they fought off the foul Harpies—half-birds and half-women. At Buthrotum, they found a second Troy, ruled by the Trojan prince and seer Helenus, who received them warmly, prophesied their safe arrival in Italy, and instructed them on the proper course to take. In Sicily, they ran into the Cyclops and rescued a comrade of Ulysses who had been left behind in the ogre's cave. They then sailed along the Sicilian coast to Drepanum, where Aeneas' father died—"Snatched from these mighty perils all in vain," laments Aeneas. Finally they set sail for Italy once more, but, says Aeneas to Dido, "heaven drave me to your shores." Thus ends Prince Aeneas' tale of his wanderings.

Book IV tells the great romantic love story of this work—the "ill-starred" love of Dido for Aeneas. His solicitous mother, Venus, has her other son, Cupid, inflame Dido with passionate love for Aeneas, in order to forestall any trickery on the part of Juno or the Carthaginians. Dido betrays her vows of constant fidelity to her late husband and neglects her royal duties. The torrid affair becomes an open scandal, and rumors of it spread throughout Libya. News of it also reaches Olympus, and Jupiter dispatches Mercury at once to admonish Aeneas to quit dallying in Carthage, and to set off for his own appointed kingdom in Italy. Aeneas bows to the voice of heaven and secretly prepares to depart. He delays telling Dido of his departure, but she, with the acuteness of a woman in love, senses his purpose and denounces it. She points out that her love for him has deprived her of political security and of her good name, and she pleads with him to stay, at least until he has given her a son as a replica of himself. Aeneas, held by the divine command, conceals his own pain at losing her. He tells her that his destiny is not his own and that he must go where he is directed by higher powers: "Not self-impelled steer I for Italy" (p. 177a). Dido, enraged, berates him as a false and hardhearted man, who cloaks his perfidy behind supposed divine mandates, and she curses his future life.

> "... I keep thee not,
> Nor would rebut thy words; go, with the winds
> Chase Italy, seek realms beyond the wave.
> I hope indeed that on the mid-sea rocks,
> If aught the good powers can, thy lips will drain
> The cup of suffering, and oft cry aloud
> On Dido's name: with murky firebrands I
> Will follow thee, though far, and, when cold death
> Has severed soul and limbs, in every place
> My shade shall haunt thee. O graceless, thou shalt rue it,
> And I shall hear thereof, yea, for the tale
> Will reach me, even among the nether dead." (p. 177b)

When a final plea to Aeneas to delay his departure fails, Dido, still in love with him, decides that suicide is the only way out for her—to "end sorrow with the sword" (p. 182a). At the sight of the Trojan fleet sailing she is again enraged at Aeneas and invokes a curse of suffering and sorrow against him to the end of his days. She prays for eternal enmity between her people and his, pointing to the future wars between Carthage and Rome.

> "... And ye, O Tyrians, the whole stock and race
> Dog with your hate for ever; to my dust
> This boon bequeath ye. Let there be no love,
> No league between the nations. O arise,
> Unknown avenger, from my tomb, to chase
> With fire and sword the Dardan settlers, now,
> Hereafter, whensoe'er the strength is given.
> Betwixt them, shore with shore, billow with wave,
> And host with host, I call down enmity;
> Be they themselves, and their sons' sons at war!"
> (p. 184b; see also p. 302a)

(The "unknown avenger" probably refers to the Carthaginian general Hannibal.) Dido has had a funeral pyre erected bearing Aeneas' arms and garments and the bed where they have known love. After a last fond look at these "Relics once dear," she takes her life with the Trojan sword that was a gift of Aeneas, uttering the hope that the giver will be haunted by the sight of the flames of her funeral pyre as he sails away. The Trojans, well out to sea, see the fire, and guess uneasily the terrible fate that "outraged love's fierce anguish" had led a "frantic woman" to (p. 187a).

Again the Trojans are foiled in their attempt to reach Italy, for a storm pushes them back to Sicily, where they are welcomed by King Acestes, himself of Trojan parentage. Book V deals with the events in Sicily. The Trojans hold a festival in honor of the first anniversary of Anchises' death, which combines solemn sacrificial rites and athletic contests, like those described in Book VIII of the *Odyssey*. Virgil gives us graphic and exciting accounts of a ship race, a foot race, a boxing match, an archery contest, and a cavalry exhibition by the Trojan boys. But now again, at a moment of festive happiness, the Trojans suffer a sudden reversal of fortune. The spiteful Juno inspires the Trojan women with an aversion to further wandering and with a fit of hysterical passion that results in their burning the fleet. Jupiter aids Aeneas by sending down a rainstorm that saves all but four of the ships. Anchises' ghost advises Aeneas to leave a colony of Trojans behind in Sicily and to proceed to Italy with his best men. But before he engages in the conquest of Latium he is to come down to Hades to visit his father who now dwells in the Elysian Fields, the abode of the blest.

As the Trojan fleet sails for Italy, Venus arranges with Neptune to give it a safe voyage, at the cost of one Trojan lost at sea. This turns out to be Palinurus, the pilot of Aeneas' ship, who is drugged by the god of sleep and flung overboard, the tiller still in his hands. This scene, taking place in darkness, is one of the most haunting and evocative in the work, as Sleep comes seeking Palinurus, bearing doom to the innocent and trusting helmsman. Aeneas says in elegy:

> "O all too trustful of the smiling face
> Of sky and ocean, on an unknown shore,
> And naked, Palinurus, thou wilt lie." (p. 210a)

Book VI tells of Aeneas' descent to Hades. As the book opens, the Trojans finally reach Italy, anchoring off Cumae. Here Aeneas consults the Sibyl, or prophetess of Apollo, who, in a state of mantic possession, transmits the oracle's prophecy of terrible wars in Latium, occasioned by a foreign bride. The Sibyl agrees to guide Aeneas to Hades if he will first pluck the golden bough that is hidden in a nearby grove. Aeneas leads a search party and succeeds in finding the golden bough and bringing it to the Sibyl, who thereupon leads him down to Hades.

At the river Acheron, which the dead souls must cross, Aeneas meets Palinurus, who must wait for a hundred years with the souls of the unburied, until he can cross. The ferryman Charon refuses to take Aeneas across because he is alive, but the golden bough forces him to give in. On the other side of the river, the Sibyl drugs the monstrous watchdog Cerberus and she and Aeneas enter Hades. Here they see first the souls of infants, the unjustly executed, and suicides. A little farther on, in the Mourning Fields, they meet the souls of those who died from love—among them, Dido of Carthage. Aeneas, weeping, greets her lovingly and tells her how sad he is to have, unwillingly, been her "doomsman." But Dido ignores him, and turns away to seek her first husband, who echoes her grief and "gives her love for love" (p. 223b). Next, among the shades of the great warriors, he meets the horribly mangled figure of the son of Priam who had married Helen after his brother Paris' death, only to be betrayed by her into the hands of the Greeks and to be butchered in the bedchamber on the night Troy fell.

Aeneas and the Sibyl come to the crossroads where one fork leads to Tartarus, the abode of the dammed, and the other to Elysium, the abode of the blest. The prophetess explains to Aeneas that those who have committed sins that were not expiated on earth must suffer terrible punishments in Tartarus, which teaches the lesson: "learn justice, and spurn not the gods" (p. 227b). Aeneas and his guide enter Elysium, where great heroes, priests, bards, and donors of the arts live in bliss. Here Aeneas meets his loving and joyful father, and again, as with Creüsa's ghost, his embraces vainly clasp empty air. A vast throng of souls are clustered at the river Lethe, drinking the waters of forgetfulness, so that they may live in the body again. Anchises explains to Aeneas that men's souls, which are the creation of a world-indwelling Spirit, must go through a period of purgation after death to rid them of the stains incurred during their imprisonment in the body.

The souls in Elysium, after they have been utterly purified to nothing "But sense aethereal and pure spirit-fire" (p. 231a), during a cycle that lasts a thousand years, are called by God to drink the waters of forgetfulness so that they may ascend to earth with the desire to be born again. Anchises points out to Aeneas in the vast throng at the riverside his glorious descendants of mixed Trojan and Italian stock—including Romulus, Julius Caesar, Augustus, and the latter's adopted son and intended heir, Marcellus. There is a story that Augustus wept when he heard Virgil read this passage about the beloved youth who died before his glory could be accomplished.

The whole of Anchises' speech extols the glory of Rome. (See pp. 231a-234b.) He points with pride to the Roman achievement, as compared with that of peoples more adept in the arts and sciences—meaning the Greeks.

> "... Others the breathing brass shall softlier mould,
> I doubt not, draw the lineaments of life
> From marble, at the bar plead better, trace
> With rod the courses of the sky, or tell
> The rise of stars: remember, Roman, thou,
> To rule the nations as their master: these
> Thine arts shall be, to engraft the law of peace,
> Forbear the conquered, and war down the proud."
> (pp. 233b-234a)

Book VI ends with the strange image of the gates of horn and ivory, which has intrigued readers over the centuries:

> There are twin gates of Sleep, whereof the one
> Of horn is rumoured, and real spirits thereby

> Win easy outlet; and one finished fair
> Of gleaming ivory, but false dreams are thence
> Sent by the Manes to the world above.
> There with these words Anchises, following forth
> His son and eke the Sibyl, sees them pass
> Out at the ivory gate. . . (p. 235a)

III

Books VII-XII of the *Aeneid* tell of the war in Latium, prophesied many times in the first half of the work. A vast panorama of individuals, peoples, battles, and councils is unrolled. Aeneas remains the great hero—"true" and "good"—with Juno still working against him, Venus for him, and Jupiter assuring the fulfillment of the decreed destiny. A great counterhero appears in the person of Turnus, the Rutulian prince, "a new Achilles," magnificent in prowess and valor. But whereas the old Achilles killed the Trojan prince Hector, this time the Trojan prince Aeneas kills the new Achilles. Another new character is the poignant King Latinus of Latium, who desires to carry out the will of the divine oracle and marry his daughter to Aeneas, but is foiled by the intervention of Juno, who arouses his people and Turnus to war against the Trojans. Unable to subdue the god-aroused fury of the people, the old man relinquishes royal power and immures himself in his palace. (Virgil himself forgets this in the later books, and talks as if the King were responsible for the war, but this is a lapse probably due to the unfinished state of the work.)

A remarkable reversal of ancient enmities occurs when Aeneas makes a firm alliance with the Greek (Arcadian) king Evander, who rules Pallanteum, the future site of Rome. Evander, too, has his poignant moment, when the corpse of his beloved only son, Pallas, is brought back from the battle and he laments the deafness of the gods to whom he prayed for his son's safety, and the horror of his dragging out his empty life as a "son-surviving sire" who has lived too long. Other touching instances of the love of father for son are that of Aeneas for his pride and joy Ascanius (Iulus) and that of the enemy tyrant Mezentius for his son Lausus. There is also the love of mother for son, shown in the terrible lamentations of Euryalus' mother, when she sees his severed head brutally held up on an enemy spear, and she prays with all her heart for her own death. Similar genuine devotion and grief are shown by the nymph Juturna for her brother Turnus.

Let us now follow the sequence of events that make up this literary "spectacular." After Aeneas returns from Hades, he sails from Cumae to the mouth of the Tiber, where all the prophesied signs appear to announce that this is the appointed site of the Trojans' new city. He is welcomed by King Latinus as the prophesied foreign hero who is to wed his daughter and bring fame to the Latin race. Juno is furious at the Trojans' good fortune, and although she cannot swerve inevitable destiny from its course, she is able to unloose terrible havoc and carnage before Aeneas gains his destined rule over Latium. "If powerless to bend heaven, I'll stir up hell," she says (p. 244b).

She sends down the horrible Allecto, the Fury of war and wrath, who stirs the Latin queen, Amata, to hysterical passion against her daughter's marriage to Aeneas, and arouses the previously intended son-in-law, Turnus, to furious indignation, so that he summons his Rutulian people to war against the Trojans. Allecto also arranges an accident that sets up a fight between the local peasants and the Trojan soldiers, so that the Latins clamor for war. The King refuses to have any hand in a war against the Trojans, in defiance of the divine oracles, but Juno herself performs the royal ritual of opening up the Gates of War to symbolize the beginning of the conflict. Forces gather from various Italian peoples and cities, under the leadership of Turnus, to push the Trojans out of Italy.

Aeneas, advised by the god of the Tiber, arranges an alliance with the Arcadian king Evander, an old enemy of the Italians. He also arranges an alliance with the Etruscans, who are angry at the Rutulians and who believe that Aeneas is the foreigner prophesied to lead them. Venus also brings aid to her son—a wondrous suit of armor made by Vulcan, including a shield upon which is portrayed the history of the Rome to be, from Ascanius to Augustus—"The fame and fortunes of his sons to be" (pp. 275b-278b).

While Aeneas is absent making alliances, Turnus besieges the Trojan camp. His attempt to burn the Trojan ships is foiled when Neptune turns them into sea-goddesses. But the stouthearted Turnus is not daunted by the divine intervention, for now the Trojan access to the sea is cut off, and he relies on his "counter-fates" and his determined valor to overcome the seemingly favored Trojans. A heroic Trojan effort to get through the enemy lines at night to contact Aeneas fails, and the next morning the first great battle of the war takes place, as the Rutulians attack the Trojan camp. In the terrible confusion of conflict, the tide turns first to one side, then to the other. Turnus, locked inside the Trojan gates, has to jump into the Tiber to escape.

Even the gods are perturbed over the new conflict. Jupiter demands to know why the forbidden conflict between Trojans and Italians has taken place. Venus complains to Jupiter of the trials of the Trojans, besieged again in a new Troy, to which they have gone in obedience to his command, and she fears he intends a new disaster for the Trojans. Juno replies scornfully that the suffering of the Trojans is the fault of Aeneas alone, his invasion of Italy parallels Paris' rape of Helen, and the Trojans rightfully suffer for the misdeeds of their princes. Jupiter ends the council by declaring his impartiality.

> "... Each shall his own sowing reap—
> Or toil or triumph: Jupiter is king
> Alike for all. The fates will find a way." (p. 305a)

The Trojans are hard pressed by their besiegers. But Aeneas, leading a fleet of Etruscan ships, comes to the rescue. Despite Turnus' efforts to prevent it, Aeneas succeeds in disembarking the reinforcements, and a tremendous battle ensues. Turnus kills Pallas, the son of Evander, and Aeneas is foiled by Juno's intervention from killing Turnus in return. She constructs a phantom of Aeneas to lure Turnus off the battlefield.

Aeneas grants the Latins a truce to bury their dead. The Latins in council debate the issues of war and peace, and many of them, horrified by the senseless slaughter, wish to sue for peace. One of them, in accordance with a suggestion of

Aeneas, proposes that Turnus fight Aeneas man-to-man for the hand of the princess Lavinia. Turnus is scornful of civilian chatter and confident that the fortunes of war may change, but he asserts his readiness to duel Aeneas, if the common good requires it. He trusts his own valor and is willing to leave it to heaven to judge between him and Aeneas.

But at this moment the report arrives that the Trojans are advancing on the city, and Turnus rushes to lead the defense, scorning the councilors who "sit praising peace, / While they [the Trojans] rush armed on empire" (p. 340b). While he prepares an ambush for the Trojan infantry, the warrior-maiden Camilla—a romantic, Amazon-like figure, the chaste and valorous favorite of Diana—leads the Italians against the Trojans in a tremendous cavalry battle. When she is slain, the Italians fall back to the city, and Turnus—seeing that the Latins are too dejected to offer further resistance—offers to settle the conflict by hand-to-hand combat with Aeneas.

> ". . . I go to meet him. Bring the holy rites,
> Sire, and rehearse the treaty. Or will I
> To Tartarus hurl this Dardan runagate
> From Asia—let the Latins sit and see—
> With my sole arm our common shame rebut;
> Or let him hold us as his thralls of war,
> And take to bride Lavinia." (p. 354a-b)

He rejects the King's proposal that he stand aside and let the peace be made without risk to his own life. "Suffer me / To pledge my life for honour," he says (p. 355a). And to the Queen, who pledges suicide should he be slain, he says, ". . . Turnus is not free / To bid death tarry" (p. 356a). Then he rouses himself to terrible fury in preparation for the duel to the death, and Aeneas does the same.

At the sacred rites beforehand, Aeneas and the King swear to abide by the result of the duel and the terms now agreed upon. Aeneas promises that the Trojans will leave Italy permanently if he is beaten, and that if he wins, the Italians will be treated as equals and brothers of the Trojans, and Latinus will remain as king.

> ". . . Nor shall Italian at my bidding bow
> To Teucrian, nor list I to reign; let both,

> Unconquered, beneath equal laws unite
> In everlasting bonds of amity.
> My gods I'll give them, and my sacred things;
> The sword Latinus, as my sire, must sway,
> And, as my sire, the daily round of State . . ." (p. 359a)

While Aeneas and Latinus are pledging perpetual peace, Turnus' sister, the nymph Juturna, acting for Juno, stirs up the Rutulian soldiers to shame at seeing their leader sacrifice his life while they look on. Somebody throws a spear, the solemn truce is broken, and the fighting begins all over again.

In the melee, the unarmed and unarmored Aeneas is badly wounded by an arrow, but he is healed suddenly by a miraculous drug sent by Venus. His attempt to close with Turnus is frustrated by Juturna, who drives her brother's chariot so that he and Aeneas never meet. Now Aeneas wheels and attacks the city, which he considers the very center of aggression and treaty breaking. The Queen, seeing the commotion and the Trojan attack, thinks Turnus has been slain, and hangs herself. The King, stunned by the fate of his wife and his city, walks in torn garments, "Soiling his white hair with unsightly dust" (p. 370a).

Turnus finally realizes that the charioteer is his sister in disguise, and he begs her to let him go to meet his fate and escape dishonor. To save the city from destruction, Turnus calls on his Rutulians to desist from fighting and to let the duel with Aeneas decide the day. Aeneas comes down immediately from the city walls and joins combat with Turnus. Up in heaven, Jupiter holds the scales of doom or victory for the two contenders. Turnus has bad luck as a borrowed sword shatters in his hand, and he is left with a bladeless hilt. He runs over the field searching for his own sword, with Aeneas in pursuit, relentlessly tailing him five times around the field.

> . . . for not light
> The prize they seek, nor trivial; the heart's blood
> And very life of Turnus are at stake. (p. 374a-b)

Juturna aids Turnus to recover his sword, while Venus helps Aeneas to get his spear loose from the ground. So the two are poised for the final moment, one with sword, one with spear.

Meanwhile, in heaven, Jupiter lays down the law to his

spouse, Juno, who through Juturna has been delaying the destined end. "The bound is reached," he warns her, "further venture I forbid." For

> ". . . Heaven claims Aeneas a tutelary god,
> Fate lifts him to the stars. . . ." (p. 375a)

Juno agrees to what cannot be otherwise, but secures a final favor for her Latins, when the peace and marriage are arranged.

> ". . . bid them not put by
> The native name of Latins, nor become
> Trojans, or pass for Teucrians on men's lips,
> Nor alien speech assume, nor altered garb.
> Let Latium, and let Alban kings endure
> For ages; be there still a Roman stock,
> Strong with Italian valour. Troy is fallen,
> And, name with nation, let the fallen lie." (p. 376a)

This settled, Jupiter sends one of the Furies down as a sign to Turnus and Juturna that the end is at hand. Turnus is terrified as the Fury appears in the form of a small bird.

> A strange
> And fearful numbness loosed his limbs; his hair
> Stood stiff with horror, the voice stuck in his throat. (p. 377a)

Juturna, grief stricken, wishes she were mortal now so that she could join her doomed brother in the underworld. Sobbing, she disappears under her sacred pool.

To Aeneas' taunts to come out and fight, Turnus replies manfully,

> "Thy fiery words, fierce man,
> Affright me not; the gods and adverse Jove
> Affright me." (pp. 377b-378a)

When he tries to hurl a huge stone at Aeneas, he is paralyzed and reduced to a dreamlike impotence by the Fury's spell. Aeneas brings down his befuddled and faltering foe with one throw of the spear. Turnus acknowledges himself vanquished and at the victor's mercy, and he begs Aeneas for the magnanimous gift of life, now that he has won all. Aeneas is half minded to grant this ultimate request, when he sees "the fatal badge" of Pallas' sword belt hanging as a trophy from Turnus' shoulder. Aeneas, in furious revenge and sorrow, renders the death stroke to Turnus for Pallas. "Pallas deals this blow," he tells Turnus.

> Then the warrior's limbs
> Grow chilled and slackened, and the spirit flies
> Moaning indignant to the shades below. (p. 379a-b)

So ends Virgil's *Aeneid.*

IV

Early Christian writers were so struck by the prophetic quality of Virgil's writings that they called him "the Prophet of the Gentiles." Let us glance briefly at the nature and content of Virgil's prophecies.

If we look at Virgil's *Fourth Eclogue* (pp. 14-15), we may grasp quickly in this earlier work the character of the prophecies in the *Aeneid.* The eclogue foretells the imminent return of the golden age when there shall be no more war, all lands will have abundance, and there will be an end of fear. A new "golden race" of men will appear and a baby boy shall "Reign o'er a world at peace," where the sheep need not fear the lion, and poisonous snakes and plants will die out—in "the coming time" that is now at hand. This poem has often been called the "messianic" eclogue, and early Christian interpreters saw in it an unconscious prophecy of the coming of Christ.

The general points of resemblance with the prophecies in the *Aeneid* are obvious. A time of peace, order, virtue, and perfect bliss is anticipated. It is imminent—for history moves in cycles that recur—and now "the last age" of the old cycle has come and gone, and the world is on the verge of a new era which will be the golden age: "the majestic roll / Of circling centuries begins anew."

This is the time when Saturn reigns. Saturn was the Italian god of agriculture, who, according to legend, had in early times been a king at the site of Rome, and had taught the people the arts of civilized life and given them laws. His time was a golden age of abundance, so that Italy was anciently known as *Saturnia,* the land of plenty. In Book VIII of the *Aeneid,* King Evander tells of the ancient time when Saturn gave to Latium "the golden years" before a baser age came in, full of war and avarice, and "The land of Saturn cast her name away" (pp. 267b-268a). It is the return to an age such as this that Virgil prophesies, and he links this mythical prehistory with the actual history of Rome, emblazoned on Aeneas' shield, and with the present Augustan age. Augustus is the new Saturn. In Book IX, Apollo hails Ascanius (Iulus) as the prince of the coming world peace, for under his descendants all wars shall be abolished. (See p. 296a-b.) In Book VI, Anchises points to

> "... Caesar Augustus, a god's son, who shall
> The golden age rebuild through Latian fields
> Once ruled by Saturn ..." (p. 232a)

Thus Virgil prophesies the return of a golden age. It is at hand. It will emerge inevitably in the cyclical recurrence of good and evil ages. But in the proclamation of an empire *without end,* unlimited in time and space, there seems to be the definite hope that the new peace, order, and plenty will be perpetual.

V

Is Aeneas a heroic character?

Some readers object to Virgil's portrait of Aeneas as too goody-goody (in the poem, he is constantly called "the good" or "the true"), as passive, obedient, docile, with all his actions initiated by the gods, constantly reinforced by their support, always responsive to their orders, and ultimately winning out through their intervention and the unfair hamstringing of his opponent. Is this the way Aeneas strikes you? Is Turnus a nobler character than Aeneas—a man who is doomed, in spite of his virtue, by the will of the gods? Does Aeneas have any virtues that Turnus lacks? Is pious obedience a fitting characteristic for the hero of a work like the *Aeneid?* Or must the hero of such a work be truly heroic—a man whose actions spring out of his essential nature? Would Turnus make a good tragic hero? If so, what would be his tragic flaw?

Does the Aeneid's *political and nationalistic slant detract from its literary value?*

Many critics feel that the *Aeneid* is defective as a representation of human life, as compared with works like Homer's, because the exigencies of political purposes and actual history override the requirements of poetic fiction. The American poet and critic Mark Van Doren complains that the chief characters and events of the *Aeneid* are always represented as having a political or national significance in the future, so that their full meaning is not to be found in the present, in the characters and events of the story, but outside of it.

Do you agree that the historical or political function is primary in Virgil's work? If so, do you think it has a good or bad effect, as far as literary power and effectiveness are concerned? Does the linking of the story of Aeneas with the history of Rome add to or detract from your appreciation of the *Aeneid*? Do the characters and events of the *Aeneid* seem less real to you than those of the *Odyssey*? Who is more real to you as a concrete, individual person—Aeneas or Ulysses? Can you point to passages in the *Aeneid* that are impressively personal and real, and not rendered abstract by political and historical reference?

Do you think the use of epic poetry to glorify a nation is good or bad for literature? What would be a good theme for an American national epic? Who would your legendary or historical hero be?

Is Aeneas' treatment of Dido like Jason's desertion of Medea?

Aeneas' treatment of Dido may remind us of Jason's desertion of Medea. Leaving aside Medea's magic power to wreak revenge, are there any differences between the two cases? Or is Aeneas rather like Ulysses, who leaves Circe after a pleasant year to make his way home?

What is it that makes Aeneas decide to leave Dido? Do you think more or less of Aeneas because of this choice? How do you think Virgil wants us to think of it? Does Virgil take sides?

He tells us that Aeneas was in love with Dido and was pained to leave her. Do you think Aeneas really loved Dido? As much as his dead wife, Cerüsa? As much as his future land and race?

What does Virgil mean to indicate to us when he tells us that Dido in Hades ignored Aeneas for "her first lord" who "Echoes her grief, and gives her love for love" (p. 223b)? Is Dido a fit heroine for tragedy? If so, what is her tragic flaw?

How does the Aeneid *compare with the Bible as a religious work?*

Obviously the *Aeneid* is a religious as well as a national poem. It tells of the working out of divine will in the history of a people. Prophecy, purgation through suffering, the intransigent advance of the elected remnant of a nation—the sustaining power of Providence—all these elements are not only broadly religious but resemble central themes in the Bible, particularly in the Old Testament.

Leaving aside the Greco-Roman mode of imagining a plurality of divine powers and the traditional notion of the divine inspiration or authorship of the Bible, are there any essential differences between the biblical and Virgilian prophecies? Is the inflexible, unchanging Fate of the *Aeneid* the same as the Divine Providence of the Bible? Do both works have the notion that history moves in recurrent cycles? In what way does the end envisaged by biblical prophecy resemble that proclaimed in the *Aeneid* and in what way does it differ? In what respects do Moses and Aeneas differ as leaders of their people to the Promised Land? What is the content of the promise in each case? In what respect are the Christian and Virgilian notions of Hell the same, and in what respect different?

Does divine intervention detract from the plausibility and effect of the story?

Does the constant intervention of the gods in human thought and action detract from the reality of the story? Does divine interference make the scenes seem like charades and the characters like puppets? Or do you forget about the divine intervention, accept it as a conventional way of presenting human motivations, and concentrate on the human characters and story?

For instance, does it detract from the impact of Dido's love that she has been inflamed by Venus, instead of spontaneously feeling passion for Aeneas, or do you forget this as you read the story? Does it matter to you that it is one of the Furies that arouses Turnus to furious indignation at having his intended bride given to Aeneas, instead of his anger being his own natural response?

What of the divine paralysis of Turnus' faculties at the crucial point in his duel with Aeneas? Does this handicap impair the portrait of Aeneas' heroic valor and prowess and make the duel pointless? Or do you accept it as the inevitable conclusion of this drama, in which the will of heaven ultimately decides the course of events? Does divine intervention make for good drama?

Why does Aeneas depart from Hades through the ivory gate of false dreams?

Virgil's image of the gates of horn and ivory is rich in all kinds of possible meanings, and is all the more suggestive because the poet does not spell out its meaning. Do Aeneas and the Sibyl depart through the ivory gate because they are not really shades of the dead? Or is Virgil hinting to us that his story of Hades is purely imaginary? Or is he suggesting some other meaning or cluster of meanings?

What does the symbol of "the golden bough" indicate earlier in Book VI? Why does the bough have magic potency?

SELF-TESTING QUESTIONS

The following questions are designed to help you test the thoroughness of your reading. Each question is to be answered by giving a page or pages of the reading assignment. Answers will be found on page 232 of this Reading Plan.

1 What historical and legendary events are portrayed in the "fane" (temple) of Juno at Carthage?

2 Who is King Iarbas, and what is his role in the story?

3 How does Euryalus win the foot race at the funeral games?

4 What legendary events are portrayed on the gate of Apollo's temple at Cumae?

5 What dreadful aspects of human existence does Aeneas meet before the entrance to Hades?

6 Who is Deiphobus, and what is his story?

7 What is the meaning of the "eating of the tables"?

8 What is the meaning of the Arcadian rites for Hercules?

9 Where does Virgil refer to his home province?

10 For what vice does Turnus' brother-in-law taunt the "Phrygians" (Trojans)?

Fifth Reading

DANTE

The Divine Comedy

Vol. 21

Dante is the great successor of the ancient epic poets, Homer and Virgil. Poised on the verge of the modern era, he created in the *Divine Comedy* a new and unique work that included the cultural legacy of the ancient and medieval worlds. It is a tremendous work that no reader can fully grasp in a single reading. Dante takes in almost everything—art, literature, history, legend, religion, philosophy, politics, and the nature of man, the world, and God. Yet he welds all this disparate material into a unified whole, through his imaginative genius.

For Dante is above all a poet, one of the greatest that ever lived. And only a very great poet, who possessed the power to create a coherent world of the imagination, could have written the *Divine Comedy*. This work, which takes man's ultimate destiny as its theme, is filled with memorable characters, impressive and touching incidents, magnificent symbolism, and lovely language. Its philosophical and religious message is expressed in the form of a story that is inseparable from the message. What Dante has to say cannot be grasped without reading his story with care and understanding.

The story is a remarkable one, in which the author is the chief character, and historical persons play their parts along with characters from legend and myth. Virgil, the author of our last reading, is here, and so is Homer, as well as the characters in their works. What a host of heroes and villains, biblical patriarchs and prophets, Greek philosophers and poets, medieval philosophers and mystics, and the prelates and politicians of Dante's time—all in one work!

This story and these characters express the traditional Christian theme of sin-repentance-redemption. Dante's journey begins in Hell and ends in the presence of God at the summit of Paradise. Dante dedicated himself to rendering concrete the Christian view of man's spiritual nature and destiny, to giving it shape and body and color and voice. He also wanted his work to be a literary masterpiece worthy to stand beside the creations of the great poets of the past. He succeeded beyond measure and left to us a magnificent work of the imagination based on the Christian vision of reality.

GUIDE TO

Fifth Reading

I

The *Divine Comedy* is called "divine" because of its wondrous artistry as well as for its sacred theme. The original title was simply *The Comedy of Dante Alighieri.* It is called a "comedy" because it has a happy ending—redemption.

Dante's work was novel in many ways. It was written in Italian, the tongue of the common people, instead of in Latin, the traditional language of scholars and writers. The author made himself a character in the story, indeed, the protagonist. Virgil, with all his sense of the present moment, had not done that, nor had any other great epic poet. Actual persons, living and dead, appear in Dante's work, which combines the fictional and the real in a unique way. Dante uses historical persons as characters in his fictional story to express spiritual and moral truths that transcend history and fiction.

For this "comedy" is deadly serious. Dante aims at moral edification by appealing to the minds and hearts of his readers through his poetic fiction—"to put into verse things difficult to think." He stated his moral intention in a letter to his patron, where he said that the real subject of the work is man's freedom of choice and his responsibility for his moral attainments or failings.

> The subject of the whole work, taken merely in its *literal* sense, is the state of souls after death, considered simply as a fact. But if the work is understood in its allegorical intention, the subject of it is man, according as, by his deserts and demerits in the use of his free will, he is justly open to rewards and punishments.

Dante forewarns us not to take his work merely as a story of the afterlife. The *Divine Comedy* is a human comedy, and its

subject is man as a moral being. Dante tells us to seek for the underlying meanings and not to be satisfied with the surface story.

The *Divine Comedy* is an allegory. Its words and characters and events are symbolic. They stand for something other than their immediate, literal meaning. But Dante's work is not mere and simple allegory in which characters are personified virtues, vices, abstractions, or types. In John Bunyan's *Pilgrim's Progress,* the names of characters and places signal clearly what they represent—Christian, Evangelist, Mr. Worldly Wiseman, Giant Despair, the Slough of Despond, the Valley of Humiliation, Vanity Fair. In Spenser's *Faerie Queene,* the characters and places also represent particular virtues and vices, but the Faerie Queene represents both Queen Elizabeth I and Glory, and there are oblique references to historical events in Elizabeth's reign. In the *Divine Comedy,* characters and events have a multiplicity of meanings—historical, fictional, moral, and spiritual. Persons and things are to be taken both literally and symbolically.

Virgil, for instance, is the Roman poet who wrote the *Aeneid.* He is also a fictional character in this story and the representative of natural wisdom and virtue. Beatrice is the Florentine girl whom Dante loved and lost. She is also a fictional character in Dante's work, with an important role in the story, and she represents supernatural wisdom or revealed truth. And so with Bonaventura, Bernard, Thomas Aquinas, and dozens of other characters in the *Divine Comedy.* Many levels of meaning are contained all at once in a single incident or person in Dante's work. All the levels are expressed together and we can take them in all together as we read the story.

Sometimes Dante uses the simpler type of allegory, as in the three beasts at the beginning of the work, which represent certain vices that impede Dante's journey to salvation. In the masques or pageants in Purgatory, there is a simple one-to-one relationship between the things or persons and what they represent (the chariot is the Church, the pole is the Cross, the Griffon is the two natures of Christ, etc.). But usually there is a multiplicity of senses in Dante's words and persons and

events, and they take on deeper and deeper meaning as we see their connection with the whole story. The *Divine Comedy* is a coherent structure, where all the parts and details hang together. The meanings and their connection, however, are to be grasped through our reading and imagination and appreciation, not through external glossaries, dictionaries, footnotes, guidebooks, and maps—helpful though these may be. A good allegory conveys much more than any explanation of it can. Our suggestions and hints here are just that—hints and indications of a multiplicity of meanings by suggesting one likely meaning. Dante himself breaks off from conveying the meaning through the story alone and gives us hints at meanings and sometimes tells us about the plan of one of the sections of his poem and his imagined world.

Dante's work is arranged quantitatively in a rigid pattern. He allowed himself exactly one hundred "cantos," or chapters, to tell his story. The three "canticles," or sections—*Hell, Purgatory,* and *Paradise*—are almost identical in length, with thirty-four cantos allotted to Hell and thirty-three to each of the other two sections. The cantos are numbered anew at the beginning of each section. The original work was written in a fixed verse pattern, *terza rima,* in which the verses are three lines long, and the second line of a verse rhymes with the first and third lines of the next verse. Since our translation is in prose, we need not go further into the verse scheme, except to note that it imposed fixed limits within which Dante expressed all the feeling, insight, and imagination he had to convey.

The world of Dante's work has a definite topography. Each of the realms with which the three canticles deal is divided into ten levels. Each realm has three primary levels, which are further subdivided into seven levels; to these are added two fringe levels and an upper level apart from the other nine levels. Thus there are ten levels in all—on a scheme of three, divided into seven, plus two, plus one. Hell, for example, has three primary divisions for the vices of Incontinence, Violence or Brutishness, and Fraud or Malice. Incontinence is further divided into four types and Fraud into two; thus, including Violence, which remains undivided, there are seven levels of vice. The Christian Dante added two levels, above and below Incontinence, for the unbaptized and the heretics; and he added a tenth level above the other nine for the indecisive fence-sitters. This division into ten main levels is complicated by a further subdivision of the three lowest circles of Hell. Purgatory and Paradise are more regularly arranged and adhere closely to the 3-7-2-1 scheme. The charts at the end of the book will help you to follow Dante on his journey. (See pp. 159-163.)

The *Divine Comedy* also has a definite chronology. The action begins on the night before Good Friday in the year 1300, and ends on Thursday evening. It takes exactly seven days. The sun is at the spring equinox, and the moon is full. The year is the exact mid-point of the biblical life span for Dante, since he was born in 1265. Also significant in this story of sin and redemption is the start of the action at Eastertide. Dante enters Hell on the evening of Good Friday and emerges at dawn of Easter Sunday. The general parallel with Christ's Passion and Resurrection seems clear. Perhaps there is also a more specific parallel with the story of Christ's descent into Hell on Good Friday and His rising on Easter Sunday.

II

Hell is the most familiar part of the *Divine Comedy* to the average reader. Later writers have referred to it and many artists have painted scenes from it. There is a fascination about the scenes of horror so vividly evoked by Dante, and the vices portrayed remind us of our own, of people we know, or of those we read about in the newspapers. However, we should not become so fascinated that we forget that *Hell* is only the prelude to this work, and that it takes its full meaning only within the whole, with Dante's arrival at the summit of Paradise.

The *Divine Comedy* begins with these famous lines:

> Midway upon the journey of our life I found myself in a dark wood, where the right way was lost. (p. 1a)

Frightened and confused by the dark and tangled wood,

Dante tries to find his way back to the right way from which he has strayed. He attempts to climb a hill whose summit is lit by the rising sun, but three wild animals—a leopard, a lion, and a wolf—prevent him. He appeals for aid to a passing figure which turns out to be the shade of Virgil, Dante's revered master in the poetic art. Virgil tells Dante that he will guide him out of the dark wood by a way that leads through Hell and Purgatory to Paradise. Indeed, Virgil has been commissioned to guide Dante by Beatrice, who descended to Limbo to make this request, prompted by the Virgin Mary and her messenger Lucia.

Let us try to interpret the most likely meanings expressed in these first cantos. The "midway" of Dante's life journey is age thirty-five, in the year when this poem is set. The "dark wood" is probably sin or error, and the "right way" is that of Christian faith. The hill probably represents the ascent to felicity and may be the same as Mount Purgatory, which Dante ascends later. But Virgil tells him it is impossible to ascend it directly; first he must go through Hell. We may take this to mean that the way of repentance must include suffering. The rising sun may stand for God or the divine light. The three beasts are variously interpreted. The leopard may stand for concupiscence, luxury, fleshly and material temptation; and the lion may stand for pride, the wolf for avarice. The beasts may also represent the three primary divisions of Hell—Incontinence, Violence, and Fraud. They may further have a political significance representing the three powers Dante loathed—Florence, France, and the Papacy. Virgil, the poetic spokesman for the Roman Empire, predicts a "hound" that will save Italy from the "wolf." We do not know whether Dante had any definite person in mind as the political savior, but the "wolf" seems to be the Papacy, whose political ambitions Dante bitterly opposed.

The listing of possible interpretations above shows the various levels of meaning that may be conveyed in any passage in the *Divine Comedy*. The more meanings we grasp, the more rewarding and enjoyable our reading will be. But we need not grasp all the possible meanings at first. The essential tone and direction of the opening cantos is conveyed by the literal story itself and by the deft, sure, and sensitive language in which it is expressed. And once we know, as we do from the beginning, that this is a story about the movement from sin through repentance to redemption, the graphic and concrete details take on fuller and deeper meaning. We know from our own experience that all the dark and tangled woods men get lost in and the wild beasts they encounter are not material substances outside of them. When we realize this, a whole world of meanings opens up to us, which becomes more and more evident as we read through the whole poem.

Let us now glance at the main incidents in Dante's journey through Hell and get a clear picture of the way Hell is arranged. Over the entrance gate to Hell are inscribed these doleful words:

> "Through me is the way into the woeful city; through me is the way into the eternal woe; through me is the way among the lost people. Justice moved my lofty maker: the divine Power, the supreme Wisdom and the primal Love made me. Before me were no things created, save eternal, and I eternal last. Leave every hope, ye who enter!" (p. 4a-b)

Hell is the creation of divine power, wisdom, love—and justice. It is the eternal dwelling place of "the woeful people, who have lost the good of the understanding," who are utterly cut off from God, the ultimate truth and good.

After Dante and Virgil pass through the gate, they enter a transitional zone or anteroom, before Hell proper (as in the *Aeneid*). This is reserved for the pathetic souls who decided neither for nor against God, the indecisive neutralists who are rejected by both Heaven and Hell. They now run perpetually after a whirling banner, as unstable as their weathercock minds. Beyond them are the river Acheron and the boatman Charon, who ferries the damned souls across to Hell proper. They are billeted there in lower and darker and narrower regions, according to the seriousness of their sins. Hell is cone shaped (see p. 159), and Dante and Virgil travel down toward the apex, toward blackest sin, toward Lucifer.

The first level is Limbo, the place of the unbaptized in Christendom and of the virtuous pagans, whose one defect was not to have known the Christian revelation. Their only punishment is to be cut off perpetually from hope of Heaven, to long eternally for God's presence. Limbo is a peaceful and pleasant place, fit for the good and great men of old. Here dwell Homer, Socrates, Plato, and Aristotle.

Just below Limbo come the four levels of Incontinence, in order of increasing seriousness—sexual lust, gluttony, hoarding or spending, and wrath. Dido and other great lovers in literature and history come first. Their sins are lesser because they spring from normal desires and interest in or tenderness toward others. The touching story of Paolo and Francesca, who gave way to their desire when they were reading a love story together, brings out the nature of this sin in a concrete and touching way. The punishment for those who surrendered to stormy passions is to be whirled about eternally by a dark and howling storm. The gluttons, in the level below, wallow in the mire, mauled by the monstrous dog Cerberus, who is as ravenous and brutish as their appetites were. The wrathful wage savage attacks on one another or lie sullenly mired in black mud for all eternity. The punishment usually fits the crime in Dante's Hell. Often it is similar to the sin, but now it is experienced as eternal torment, without hope of escape.

All these sinners dwell in Upper Hell, reserved for the lesser of the three main divisions of sin. The sins of incontinence are rooted in human weakness, self-indulgence, overgrasping for good things. Nether Hell is reserved for the really vicious and malicious sins of violence and fraud. To get there, Dante and Virgil cross the river Styx, and need the aid of an angel from Heaven to get inside. Nether Hell, called the City of Dis (Pluto), is surrounded by walls red-hot from the eternal fire inside. It is guarded by the fallen angels who rebelled against God; and they are aided by the Furies (guilty conscience) and the Medusa-head that turns people to stone (despair). Dante is terrified by these baleful figures.

The first level inside Dis is reserved for the heretics, who lie burning eternally in red-hot sealed tombs. Like Limbo in Upper Hell, this special Christian level is above and apart from the other circles of Lower Hell. It is here that Virgil explains to Dante the plan of Hell. (See Canto XI, pp. 15a-

16b.) All of the sins of Lower Hell aim at injury, to others or to oneself, but since fraud is a peculiarly human sin, it is placed lower than violence. The latter is divided into three levels of increasing viciousness and torment, as violence has been committed against neighbors, oneself, or God. Violence against God includes not only blasphemy and atheism, but also the rejection or destruction of nature and art, as in sodomy or usury—since nature is God's creation and art (including industry and agriculture) is derived from it. Fraud is divided into two levels—the higher for those who swindle or betray people in general, the lower for those who deceive their kin and friends.

The first of the three levels of violence is a river of boiling blood, in which are immersed those who harmed their neighbors. The second is a pathless wood of gnarled and sterile trees, which contain the souls of suicides. The third is an arid desert, under a constant rain of flakes of fire, the place of the blasphemers, sodomites, and usurers.

An odd scene occurs before the two poets descend to the levels of Fraud. Virgil throws Dante's waist cord into a gulf and brings forth the monster Geryon, the symbol of Fraud. Dante says he had originally intended to catch the leopard with his waist cord. Mounted on the monster's back, Dante and Virgil descend to the first of the two levels of Fraud. It is composed of ten concentric valleys or trenches, called Malebolge—"the evil valleys"—in which are punished those who have committed fraud in general. The valleys in descending order contain (1) panderers and seducers, (2) flatterers, (3) simoniacs—sellers of holy rites and offices, (4) sorcerers and diviners, (5) barrators—sellers of public offices and favors, (6) hypocrites, (7) thieves, (8) perverse counselors, (9) sowers of division—religious, civil, and familial, (10) falsifiers of things, deeds, and words.

The giant Antaeus picks up Dante and Virgil and sets them down in the lower level of Fraud—the lowest level of Hell—where those who committed fraud against intimates are punished. It is divided into four concentric rings on the frozen river or lake Cocytus, at the bottom of Hell, the point farthest removed from light and warmth. The four rings from the outermost to the center are the abode of traitors to kindred, country, guests, and masters. In the center of the inner ring is Satan, with three faces, symbolizing impotence, ignorance, and hate—the opposite of the divine qualities of power, wisdom, and love, a kind of anti-Trinity.

Dante and Virgil climb down Satan's body, holding on to his shaggy hair, until they pass through the center of the earth and follow a path that brings them to the surface again at dawn of Easter Day.

III

Purgatory is an essential part of the *Divine Comedy.* It belongs between *Hell* and *Paradise,* just as repentance does between sin and redemption in the Christian scheme of things. This section may be easier for the reader to grasp than the preceding one, because Dante's Purgatory is much more neatly and systematically arranged than his Hell.

Purgatory is a mountain with ten levels, ledges, or cornices (not a layer cake, as in the chart on p. 161). It is an arduous mountain climb that Dante and Virgil must undertake. Purgatory has three main divisions—Lower, Middle, and Upper—corresponding to the sins of perverted, defective, and excessive love. The three divisions are further subdivided into seven levels, corresponding to the seven deadly sins—pride, envy, wrath, sloth, avarice, gluttony, and lust. Again there is a preliminary zone, Ante-Purgatory, which has two levels—one for excommunicants and one for last-minute penitents. Between Ante-Purgatory and Purgatory proper is Peter's Gate, which has three steps—contrition, confession, and satisfaction. At the top of the mountain is the earthly Paradise, which was lost by the first man, and is now the tenth level of Purgatory.

The island on which the mountain of Purgatory stands is situated at the antipodes of Jerusalem. Dante and Virgil reach it immediately after leaving Hell, and find it guarded by Cato, the old Roman censor, symbol of the moral virtues. His face is lit by four holy stars in the sky, which represent the four cardinal moral virtues—prudence, temperance, fortitude, and justice. Following Cato's instructions, Virgil washes the stains of Hell off Dante's face with purgatorial dew and girds him with a smooth and pliant reed—"the humble plant"—probably representing humility.

> The dawn was vanquishing the matin hour, which was flying before it, so that from afar I discerned the trembling of the sea. We went along over the solitary plain like a man who turns to the road which he has lost, and, till he find it, seems to himself to go in vain. When we were where the dew contends with the sun, and, through being in a place where there is shade, is little dispersed, my Master softly placed both his hands outspread upon the grass; whereon I, who was aware of his intent, stretched toward him my tearful cheeks: then he wholly uncovered on me that color which hell had concealed.
>
> We came, then, to the desert shore which never saw man navigate its waters who afterwards had experience of return. Here he girt me, even as pleased the other. O marvel! that such as he culled the humble plant, such it instantly sprang up again there whence he had plucked it. (p. 54b–c)

The two wayfarers see a shipment of souls come in on a vessel powered by the wings of an angel, who has steered it from the Tiber (standing for the Roman Catholic Church) to Purgatory. The souls sing a psalm on Israel's exodus from Egypt, symbolizing their redemption from earthly corruption. Then the two poets start the climb up Purgatory with the newly arrived souls.

On the first ledge are the excommunicated, who repented in their hearts but not in time to be received back into the Church. They must remain in Ante-Purgatory for thirty times the period of their rebellion. On the second ledge are the tardy penitents who waited until the last moment, due to laziness, busyness, or sudden death, to express repentance for their sins. They must remain in Ante-Purgatory for a period equal to their lives on earth, before they can enter Purgatory proper. Those who have neglected their spiritual destiny because of preoccupation with earthly business—represented here by kings and emperors—dwell in a beautiful valley.

It is here that Dante sees the four stars of the natural virtues replaced by the three stars of the theological virtues—faith, hope, and charity. Here, too, he sees the ancient "adversary" of man, the snake—perhaps the same one that tempted Eve—

driven away by two angels, clad in green, the color of hope. And here he has his first night's sleep and dreams the first of the three significant dreams that mark his journey through Purgatory. He dreams he is borne up to heaven by an eagle, only to waken at Peter's Gate, to find from Virgil that he has actually been borne up to the entrance of Purgatory proper by Lucia, one of the three heavenly ladies interested in Dante. She represents illuminating grace whose aid is extended to the flesh-and-blood wayfarer. Now occurs one of the great transition scenes of the *Divine Comedy*, the crossing of the threshold into Purgatory proper, where man's salvation begins. (See Canto X.)

At the entrance gate sits an angel, dressed in the ashen garments of penitence, a naked sword in his hand. Dante and Virgil mount up the three steps of contrition, confession, and satisfaction, and Dante begs humbly on his knees for the angel to open the gate. The angel inscribes seven P's on Dante's forehead for the seven deadly sins (*peccati*, in Italian), and says: "See that thou wash those wounds when thou art within." Two keys, one of gold and one of silver, are required to unlock the gate. These are apparently the keys of the kingdom given to Peter to bind or unloose from sins. (There are different interpretations of what each key stands for.) The angel tells Dante, "Enter, but I give you warning that whoso looks backward returns outside." As the gate swings open Dante seems to hear the liturgical hymn in praise of God: *Te Deum laudamus.*

With some difficulty the two wayfarers make their way through a cleft in the rock to a wide ledge that runs all the way around the mountain. This is the place where the stain of the sin of pride is wiped away. A crowd of penitents approaches, each bearing huge stones, bent double under their heavy burden, eyes on the ground, chanting the Lord's Prayer—for those left on earth, not for themselves. They must go round and round the ledge until they are completely purified of pride. One of them was arrogant with pride of ancient and noble ancestry, another was vainglorious about his artistic powers, still another devoted himself to political power. Now they know that in the aspect of eternity, worldly renown is mere wind. On the cliff face are sculpted great examples of humility, while on the pavement are engraved notorious examples of pride.

An angel wipes away the "P" of pride from Dante's forehead with a gentle touch of the wings, and guides the two wayfarers to an easy pass to the next ledge. As they leave the ledge of pride, they hear the first beatitude, "Blessed are the poor in spirit," beautifully sung. Dante feels remarkably light and rested now. Virgil tells him that this will be increasingly the case as he goes upward and drops the other "P's."

If we look closely at what occurs on the first ledge of Purgatory proper, we will discern a pattern that is followed on the other six ledges before the summit is attained. On each ledge a penance is undergone that is appropriate to the particular sin, until the stain is wiped away. The penitents are goaded to virtue and hindered from sin by extraordinary examples—seen, heard, or envisioned. The goads to virtue always start with an example from the life of the Virgin Mary. The penitents chant prayers, selected from the Psalms or the liturgy, except in the case of sloth—perhaps because activity is prayer here. Also, one of the beatitudes from the Sermon on the Mount is pronounced, usually by the angel who wipes off the "P" for the particular sin and directs the two poets to the next ledge. It may be helpful to the reader to note the penance, examples, prayer, and blessing in each case, in order to judge their appropriateness.

On the second ledge huddle the envious, dressed in sackcloth, their eyes sewed up with wire to shut out the sight of the goodness they once viewed with envy. Virgil explains to Dante that envy excludes fellowship, because it is directed to earthly goods, of which each gets a smaller part, the more there are to share. Lovers of the infinite Good, however, have all the more to share, the more lovers of the Good there are to share with. Dante is too dull to understand this, so Virgil tells him to wait for Beatrice to explain it later.

On the third ledge stumble the wrathful through a thick smoke that blinds them here as their wrath did below. Their prayer is to the Lamb of God and the beatitude is "Blessed are the peacemakers, who are without evil anger." The two poets mount the stairway to the next level, but remain at the top step, to spend the night, for it is the rule on Purgatory that there can be no movement at night. It is here at this midway point that Virgil explains to Dante the plan of Purgatory. (See Cantos XVII-XVIII.)

> "Neither Creator nor creature," he began, "my son, was ever without love, either natural, or of the mind, and this thou knowest. The natural is always without error; but the other may err either through an evil object, or through little, or through too much vigor. While love is directed on the primal goods, and with due measure on the secondary, it cannot be the cause of ill-delight. But when it is bent to evil, or runs to good with more zeal, or with less, than it ought, against the Creator his own creature is working. Hence thou canst comprehend that love is of necessity the seed in you of every virtue, and of every action that deserves punishment. . . ." (p. 79b-c)

The arrangement of Purgatory accords with the various distortions of love. In Lower Purgatory, the sins of the love of harm to other men are repented. In Middle and Upper Purgatory, penitence is made for too little or too much love for what is good. Man's errors in love, as compared with the perfect order of nature, are explained by his unique quality of free will, which makes sin and responsibility possible. (See also the discourse on free will in Canto XVI, p. 77c-d.)

Dante is wakened from his nap by a host of the slothful who now come running at great speed, motivated by "good will and right love," who cry out prime examples of zeal and ardor and such mottoes as "Swift, swift, that time be not lost by little love." Their present fervor redeems their previous dilatoriness and lukewarmness. Now they are "so full of will to move" that they cannot stop. Here right and intense activity by itself seems to be the form of prayer.

It is on this night, his second on the mountain, that Dante has his second dream. An ugly hag turns into a beautiful siren as he gazes on her and she almost puts him into a state of enchantment. But a holy lady appears and rips her garments to show her ugliness, and Dante wakes with the smell of the foul odor coming from the hag, to hear Virgil calling to him to ascend to the fifth level. Virgil explains to the troubled Dante that the Siren is the old sorceress, because of whom the souls in Upper Purgatory do penance, but concentration on eternal things protects one from her baleful charms.

On the fifth level lie the avaricious, prostrated in the dust, sighing the Psalmist's words, "My soul cleaveth unto the dust." Pope Adrian V, converted from avarice only in the last month of his life, explains to Dante what the penance means.

> ". . . Even as our eye, fixed upon earthly things, was not lifted on high, so justice here has sunk it to earth. As avarice quenched our love for every good, whereby our working was lost, so justice here holds us close, bound and captive in feet and hands; and, so long as it shall be the pleasure of the just Lord, so long shall we stay immovable and outstretched." (p. 82d)

When Dante kneels reverently to him, Adrian tells him this is out of place here, for there are no offices or sacraments in Heaven. Dante proceeds, cursing the "wolf" of avarice that makes more souls its prey than any other "beast." He finds on this ledge a representative of political as well as ecclesiastical avarice—Hugh Capet, founder of the great French dynasty, which in Dante's time held sway in many lands, and made conquests in Italy. Capet proclaims the seizure and death in captivity of Pope Boniface VIII to be the foulest deed of his dynasty. Dante condemned Boniface bitterly for his personal character and corrupt practices, but still regarded him as the Vicar of Christ. Hence, the Capet who ordered the deed is called "Pontius Pilate."

An earthquake that shakes Mount Purgatory, accompanied by a chorus of "Glory to God in the highest," signals the purging of a soul from avarice. This turns out to be the soul of Statius, a first-century Roman poet, who explains that the mountain shakes when a purged soul feels itself pure and of its own free will moves to a higher ledge—the will to ascend is itself the proof of purgation, and the whole mountain celebrates it. (Statius' sin was not avarice, but its opposite, twin vice, prodigality.) This pagan poet has reached Purgatory because he was converted to Christianity through reading Virgil's *Fourth Eclogue*. (See Guide to the Fourth Reading, Section IV.)

"Thou first didst direct me on the way toward Parnassus to drink in its grots, and then, on the way to God, thou didst enlighten me. Thou didst like him, who goes by night, and carries the light behind him, and profits not himself, but makes the persons following him wise, when thou saidst, 'The world is renewed; Justice returns, and the primeval time of man, and a new progeny descends from heaven.' Through thee I became a poet, through thee a Christian. But in order that thou mayst better see that which I outline, I will stretch my hand to color it. Already was the whole world teeming with the true belief, sown by the messengers of the eternal realm; and thy words just mentioned were so in harmony with the new preachers, that I adopted the practice of visiting them. Then they came to seem to me so holy, that, when Domitian persecuted them, their lamentations were not without my tears. And so long as I remained in yonder world, I succored them; and their upright customs made me scorn all other sects. And before I had led the Greeks to the rivers of Thebes in my verse, I received baptism; but through fear I was a secret Christian, for a long while making show of paganism: and this lukewarmness made me circle round the fourth circle, longer than to the fourth century . . ." (p. 87b-c)

Statius joins Dante and Virgil in their ascent. On the sixth level, where gluttony is repented, the emaciated penitents are tantalized and frustrated by ripe and luscious fruit, hanging on branches that are out of reach. One of them explains,

". . . All this folk who sing weeping, because of following their appetite beyond measure, are here in hunger and in thirst making themselves holy again. The odor which issues from the fruit and from the spray which is spread over the verdure, kindles in us desire to eat and drink. And not once only, as we circle this floor, is our pain renewed; I say pain, and ought to say solace, for that will leads us to the tree, which led Christ with joy to say: 'Eli,' when with his blood he delivered us." (pp. 88d-89a)

And the beatitude is this,

"Blessed are they whom so much grace illumines, that the love of taste kindles not too great desire in their breasts, hungering always so much as is right." (p. 91b)

On the seventh and last ledge, the penitents are purified from lust by fire, the fitting "cure" and "diet" for their "wound." One group of penitents goes in the regular direction around the mountain, and represents normal, heterosexual love. Another goes in the reverse or perverse direction, and represents homosexual love (here called "sodomite" and "hermaphrodite").

Dante is terrified when it becomes necessary to go through

the fire to get to the staircase that leads to the earthly Paradise. A touching scene ensues, which brings out fully the guiding and supporting role of Virgil. The ancient master reassures Dante that the fire will not destroy him. He tells him to dip his hand in the flame to test it, if he is doubtful. When Dante refuses to budge, Virgil summons up the name of Beatrice, who awaits Dante beyond the flames. Dante's obduracy is softened at the mention of the beloved name. Virgil says, "How? do we want to stay on this side?" and smiles at him as at a child who is being coaxed with an apple. Virgil goes in first, with Dante in between him and Statius, who brings up the rear. The fire is so hot that Dante says he could have thrown himself into boiling glass to cool off. But Virgil constantly summons up the vision of Beatrice. I "seem already to see her eyes," he says. Thus they experience the ultimate trial of the human soul on its path to the summit of Purgatory.

The three poets pass the third night on the staircase, where Dante has his third dream—about Leah and Rachel, who represent the active and the contemplative life, respectively. Virgil announces that since Dante has passed through the purging fire, he no longer needs Virgil's guidance (i.e., the guidance of natural wisdom and virtue). Virgil says that Dante is now his own king and bishop.

"The temporal fire and the eternal thou hast seen, Son, and art come to a place where of myself I discern no farther. I have brought thee here with understanding and with art; thine own pleasure take thou henceforward for guide: forth art thou from the steep ways, forth art thou from the narrow. See there the sun, which is shining on thy front; see the young grass, the flowers, and the shrubs, which here the earth of itself alone produces. Until the beautiful eyes come rejoicing, which weeping made me come to thee, thou canst sit down and thou canst go among them. Expect no more or word or sign from me. Free, upright, and sound is thine own will, and it would be wrong not to act according to its choice; wherefore thee over thyself I crown and mitre." (pp. 95d-96a)

The three poets make their way through the divine forest, the sacred wood, of the earthly Paradise. They encounter Matilda, the guardian spirit of Eden, who represents the active life in the state of innocence, before man's fall. Eden is a place of perfectly clear water, bird songs, and sweet breezes. As

Dante proceeds he encounters a sacred pageant representing the seven gifts of the Holy Spirit, the twenty-four books of the Old Testament, the four gospels of the New Testament, the two natures of Christ, the three theological virtues, and the four cardinal virtues.

As the triumphal chariot (the Church) bearing Beatrice (Revelation) comes abreast of Dante, a thunderclap is heard, hallelujahs resound, and flowers are strewn to welcome the heavenly lady. Dante is smitten by the old flame of love that he has had since he was a boy. When he turns to confide in Virgil, he finds his beloved master gone, and he weeps for the first time since the angel wiped the stains and tears of Hell from his face. Beatrice bids him to cease weeping and brings him to a contrite realization of why he had to make this journey through Hell and Purgatory. (See Cantos XXX-XXXI.) This is a noble and impressive passage, important for an understanding of the whole work.

Beatrice rebukes Dante for having betrayed the high promise that was indicated of him by nature and by grace. As soon as she departed for another life, she says,

> ". . . he turned his steps along a way not true, following false images of good, which pay no promise in full. Nor did it avail me to obtain inspirations with which, both in dream and otherwise, I called him back; so little did he heed them. So low he fell that all means for his salvation were already short, save showing him the lost people. For this I visited the gate of the dead, and to him, who has conducted him up hither, my prayers were borne with weeping. The high decree of God would be broken, if Lethe should be passed, and such viand should be tasted, without some scot of repentance which may pour forth tears." (p. 100d)

Beatrice draws from Dante a tearful confession of his guilt at having deserted the pursuit of ultimate good for lesser things. He was mature enough, she observes, not to be sidetracked from eternal aspirations by "some young girl or other vanity of so brief a use." Dante is so overcome by remorse that he faints dead away. He is restored by Matilda, who immerses him in the waters of forgetfulness of the river Lethe. The four cardinal virtues, represented by four ladies or nymphs, lead Dante to Beatrice, and they plead for him with Beatrice, begging her to reveal her inner beauty or wisdom. Dante gazes on Beatrice entranced, and is temporarily blinded by her splendor.

Canto XXXII adds further and deeper meaning, as the pageant proceeds toward the sun, until it reaches the tree of knowledge where Adam lost his original innocence. Here the Griffon, symbol of the two natures of Christ (the second Adam), binds the chariot pole (symbol of the Cross) to the tree, from which, according to legend, it came. The bare tree, withered by the original sin, now blooms luxuriously, symbolizing Christ's redemption, and the color of the blossoms is purple, symbolizing the Empire under which it occurred. Dante falls into a deep sleep, and when he awakens he finds that the Griffon (Christ) has ascended above, while Beatrice (Revelation) remains seated by the chariot (the Church), under the freshly blooming tree. Urged on by her, he watches the history of the Church unfold in allegorical incidents—from the early pagan persecutions (the bird of Jove), the heresies (the fox), and Constantine's patronage (the eagle) down through the schism (the dragon), the corruption of the Papacy (the harlot), and domination by political power (the giant).

Beatrice prophesies that an imperial deliverer will come to abolish ecclesiastical corruption and the political domination of the Church. She chides Dante for the inadequacy of his philosophical knowledge to comprehend the mysteries which she wishes to reveal to him. He, having been washed in the waters of forgetfulness, cannot remember ever having been unfaithful to her. Now Matilda takes him to drink of the waters of Eunoë—"the memory of good"—so that he may see his past as good. Dante tells the reader that he has used up all the space allotted for this "second canticle" and ends his Purgatory on this high note:

> I returned from the most holy wave, reanimate, even as new plants renewed with new foliage, pure and disposed to mount unto the stars. (p. 105d)

IV

Paradise is the culmination of the *Divine Comedy*. It is the ultimate goal of Dante's descent through Hell, and his ascent from Purgatory. Paradise—the abode of perfect faith, hope, and love—is the exact opposite of Hell, which is characterized by an utter absence of these virtues. Now joy, peace, and light prevail, while there gloom, pain, and darkness reigned. Dante summons up all his poetic power and imagery to convey what ultimate redemption is like.

Paradise follows the plan of ten levels, with three main divisions and a tenth level above and beyond the other nine. Dante takes the Ptolemaic picture of the universe, which was accepted in his time, as the pattern for Paradise. In this scheme, the earth is at the center, with seven planets—the moon, Mercury, Venus, the sun, Mars, Jupiter, and Saturn. Beyond the planets are the fixed stars and the Primum Mobile (the first mover), the source of all cosmic motion, according to Aristotle's notion of the universe. (See the Sixth Reading in the Reading Plan *Foundations of Science and Mathematics,* for a full account of the Ptolemaic universe.)

Dante takes this ancient scientific scheme of nine spheres or heavens, adds a tenth sphere beyond time and space, and interprets all of the spheres in a moral and spiritual sense. The seven planetary heavens, in ascending order, are associated with incomplete virtue, earthly virtues, and the four cardinal virtues, thus:

1. Moon—inconstant virtue
2. Mercury—ambition
3. Venus—earthly love
4. Sun—prudence
5. Mars—fortitude
6. Jupiter—justice
7. Saturn—temperance

The eighth heaven of the fixed stars is the place of redeemed human souls. The ninth heaven, or Primum Mobile, is the abode of the angels. The tenth heaven, the Empyrean, is the ultimate place of God, angels, and redeemed souls; it is the eternal present beyond space and time where God is known immediately. The three main divisions are located physically on the infrasolar, solar, and suprasolar planes, corresponding morally to the near virtues, prudence, and the other three cardinal virtues. The two fringe levels are the fixed stars and the Primum Mobile, and the Empyrean is the level above and apart from the rest.

Beatrice points out to Dante that we are not to take these physical levels of the heavenly ascent literally. They merely indicate grades of spiritual grace. All the inhabitants of Paradise, from the Seraphim on down, occupy the highest heaven together, though being touched in higher or lower degree by the eternal breath. Paradise is the realm of divine love, which descends on all the inhabitants, though differing in degree according to their spiritual level. Hell, on the contrary, is characterized by the absence of love, and Purgatory by imperfect love. Creation must inevitably strive upward from the states of absent and defective love to the state of perfect love—the ultimate end and resting place.

Piccarda, the nun who was forced to be unfaithful to her vows, occupies the lowest level of Heaven—in Heaven for her intention, in the lowest level for incomplete performance. She accepts the divine will and order and does not resent her low place, for blessedness is to be at one with God's will, and every place in Heaven is Paradise—to be with God. To Dante's question whether she does not desire a higher place, she replies

"Brother, virtue of charity quiets our will, and makes us wish only for that which we have, and quickens not our thirst for aught else. If we desired to be more on high, our desires would be discordant with the will of Him who assigns us here, which thou wilt see is not possible in these circles, if to exist in charity is here of necessity, and if thou dost well consider its nature. Nay, it is the essence of this blessed existence to hold itself within the divine will, whereby our wills themselves are made one. So that as we are, from seat to seat throughout this realm, to all the realm is pleasing, as to the King who inwills us with His will; and His will is our peace; it is that sea whereunto everything is moving which It creates and which nature makes."

Then was it clear to me, how everywhere in Heaven is Paradise, even if the grace of the Supreme Good does not there rain down in one measure. (p. 110a-b)

Let us now glance at some of the main emphases and events in Dante's ascent to the Empyrean. One thing that stands out is the high value that Dante put on the state and law. He puts

Justinian, the great Emperor and codifier of Roman law, in the sphere of Mercury, or earthly ambition, and just rulers—both Christian and pagan—in the sphere of Jupiter, or justice. Dante held that the State and the Church were both divinely instituted, with powers bestowed directly by God; the former to care for man's temporal concerns, the latter for his spiritual concerns. Neither, he held, is to usurp the place of the other. In the work, Beatrice informs him that man has failed to attain Eden because of the corruptions and usurpations of both Church and State, and she prophesies a coming purification and right relation between the two divinely instituted powers.

Dante is rather surprised to find the pagan kings Ripheus of Troy and Trajan of Rome high in the heavens, but Beatrice informs him that some pagans may have received Divine Revelation and have been saved. No man can presume to know God's will and whom He has or has not saved. We recall that Cato stood guard at the foot of Purgatory and that Statius accompanied Dante all the way to Eden.

Also to be noted is the high place that Dante assigns to contemplation and the mystical or spiritualist type of religious life. Midway in the planetary heavens, in the sphere of the sun (symbol of the divine light), he puts Thomas Aquinas and Bonaventura. Aquinas represents the intellectual type of theology, and Bonaventura the spiritual or mystical type. They are placed on an equal plane, and the two clashing types of thought are here reconciled in a spirit of gentle courtesy and love. Going further, Dante inserts the figure of Joachim of Flora, an extreme spiritualist, who preached the imminent advent of a new age in which the institutions and disciplines of the visible Church would be absorbed into the contemplative perfection of the spiritual Church. Although the historical Bonaventura bitterly opposed Joachim, the Bonaventura of Dante's poem eulogizes him. (See p. 125a.) Dante saw both Joachim and Bonaventura as typical advocates of contemplation and spirituality—and he agreed with Joachim's view that the Church should be spiritualized and desecularized.

In Saturn, the highest of the planetary heavens, Dante meets Benedict, founder of the famous monastic order at Monte Cassino, who extols the contemplative way to God. In the Empyrean, the heaven of the heavens, above all the rest, Bernard of Clairvaux, the great contemplative and mystical monk, replaces Beatrice as Dante's guide. (See Canto XXXI.) Revealed knowledge gives way to immediate vision. Dante's son Pietro says in his commentary on the *Divine Comedy:*

He [Dante] pretends that he is abandoned by Beatrice. The metaphor is that we cannot see and know God through theology, but through grace and contemplation. Hence, through St. Bernard, that is, through contemplation, he obtains from the Virgin the privilege of seeing such things as cannot be apprehended through the written word.

The poem ends with a moment of mystical vision in which the poet sees the whole of things in its essential order. Although he cannot keep that vision in his earthly form, his desire and will are now permanently at one with that primal love which moves them now as it moves all things.

O Light Eternal, that sole abidest in Thyself, sole understandest Thyself, and, by Thyself understood and understanding, lovest and smilest on Thyself! That circle, which appeared in Thee generated as a reflected light, being awhile surveyed by my eyes, seemed to me depicted with our effigy within itself, of its own very color; wherefore my sight was wholly set upon it. As is the geometer who wholly applies himself to measure the circle, and finds not by thinking that principle of which he is in need, such was I at that new sight. I wished to see how the image was conformed to the circle, and how it has its place therein; but my own wings were not for this, had it not been that my mind was smitten by a flash in which its wish came.

To the high fantasy here power failed; but now my desire and my will were revolved, like a wheel which is moved evenly, by the Love which moves the sun and the other stars. (p. 157c-d)

For a fuller discussion of the *Paradise,* see the Seventh Reading in the Reading Plan *Religion and Theology.*

V

Does appreciation of the Divine Comedy *require acceptance of the Christian view of things?*

Suppose a reader rejects the idea of a creating and redeeming God, the reality and redeeming quality of Christ's Incarnation and Passion, and the Hell-Purgatory-Paradise scheme of the afterlife, as well as the efficacy of church sacraments and moral discipline for man's eternal existence. What can such a reader admire or affirm in Dante's work?

Obviously, there are all kinds of literary qualities in the *Divine Comedy* that may be appreciated apart from its basic view of man's nature and destiny. The spareness, the tenderness, the irony, the allusions and understatements that convey so much, the deft turns of phrase, the art and architecture of the whole work, the subtle and indirect way in which character traits or basic insights are conveyed—all these may be admired by a reader who rejects Dante's theology. He may hate what Dante says but love the way he says it. But is this disjunction between meaning and art possible with Dante?

If not, just what can a non-Christian admirer of Dante affirm, and how can he affirm it? Could he understand the *Divine Comedy* merely in a this-worldly sense, as dealing with man's moral development and experience, with the perils and struggles and journeys of the soul in this life? Does Dante explicitly allow for this as one possible interpretation? How does Dante himself handle the ancient pagan beliefs and myths? Why does he put the pagan giants at the bottom of the Christian Hell?

Is the Divine Comedy *inspired by a spirit of revenge and cruelty?*

Many readers claim that they have been utterly repelled by the spirit of cruel vindictiveness which they find in this work. Do you find any justification for this reaction? Would it apply to the whole work or only to parts of it? Would you say it would be more true of *Hell* than of *Paradise*? Are the place and condition of the sinners in Hell merely matters of external coercion? How did the sinners get to the place and state called Hell, and what do their sufferings have in common with their sins? Is the concept of absolutely lost and irredeemable souls compatible with the Christian notion of an all-powerful and all-loving God? Dante has also been charged with putting his enemies in Hell and his friends in Paradise or on the way there. After reading the work, and checking the footnotes, do you find any substance in this charge? Dante was very hostile to the Papacy of his time. Where does he put the popes in his imaginary afterworld?

What is the difference between the penances of Purgatory and the pains of Hell?

It seems that some of the same sins are repented in Purgatory that are punished in Hell. Why, then, are some sinners placed in Hell, without hope of Heaven, while others are put in Purgatory for the same sins? What is the distinction of function and aim between the penance of Purgatory and the punishment of Hell? What does penance accomplish? What is the difference in attitude toward their respective pains between the penitent in Purgatory and the lost soul in Hell?

What is the serpent doing in Paradise?

It seems rather strange to find the symbol of sin in Paradise. What is it doing there? Is it a reminder of the past or of present temptation? Is the temptation to sin still possible in Paradise? Does Dante mean that the inclination to sin is still lurking even where the human soul has started on its arduous path of purgation? What other possible meanings are there in this startling appearance of the snake in Paradise?

Why does Dante's waist cord pull up the monster of Fraud?

Dante says he had originally intended to catch the leopard with his waist cord. The leopard apparently symbolizes lust or incontinence. What does the waist cord symbolize? It may have something to do with monastic costume. Perhaps it stands for chastity or monastic vows in general. (The Franciscan friars wear a cord with three knots, for poverty, chastity, and obedience.) Some interpreters think it may refer to something in Dante's own life—that he had intended or prepared to enter holy orders. But then what does this have to do with the monster Fraud "that infects all the world"? What does Dante mean to suggest here—that monastic vows lead to hypocrisy or that the failure to adhere to them leads to fraud? Or does this symbol have anything to do with Dante's animus against the Papacy? Does Dante have a certain meaning or set of meanings in mind, or is this just a poetic conceit of his?

What kind of hero is Dante?

What kind of character does Dante make of himself in the *Divine Comedy?* Is he a paragon of virtue or more on the ordinary human scale with quite a few weaknesses? Would you say Dante is bold and determined or timid and indecisive as a character in this work? Which is his greatest weakness or sin, as he himself confesses in Purgatory? Does Dante's terror and reluctance to go through the fire in Purgatory make him more or less sympathetic to you as the hero of this story? Do the various moral and spiritual failings of Dante make this journey through the three realms that of Everyman, of "one of us"? Dante is not above praising himself as one of the great poets of the world. He has the five great ancient poets in Limbo appoint him their equal, and he puts words of the most high-flown praise of his poetry in the mouth of another character. Does this offend you or not? Do you consider Dante conceited and self-important? Can you think of any contemporary artists and writers of stature who blow their own horns?

SELF-TESTING QUESTIONS

The following questions are designed to help you test the thoroughness of your reading. Each question is to be answered by giving a page or pages of the reading assignment. Answers will be found on page 232 of this Reading Plan.

1 Whom does Dante address, "O courteous Mantuan soul!"?

2 What is the suggested interpretation for the "noble castle" and the "seven gates" in Limbo?

3 What were the final voyage and fate of Ulysses?

4 Why does Dante think Virgil has deserted him as they start the climb up Purgatory?

5 How does Virgil defend his assertion in the *Aeneid* that prayers are not efficacious?

6 Why is it impossible to ascend Purgatory at night?

7 What is the prayer of the envious in Purgatory?

8 What character from the *Aeneid* is an example of the sin of anger in Purgatory?

9 What characters from the *Aeneid* are examples of the sin of sloth in Purgatory?

10 Who are the examples of chastity in Purgatory?

Sixth Reading

CHAUCER

The Canterbury Tales

Vol. 22, pp. 159–550

Geoffrey Chaucer was the first great poet in the English language. The greatest work of this father of English poetry was the *Canterbury Tales*, one of the most enjoyable, genial, and broadly human works in Western literature. Here are represented the knights, squires, clergy, merchants, craftsmen, artisans, farmers, housewives, and other persons of low and high degree who made up fourteenth-century English society. And they are presented not as mere social types, but as unique characters who are individualized down to their fingertips and the very warts on their noses. At the same time they bear universal human traits. Chaucer gives us a fourteenth-century England in miniature, a universal human comedy, and unforgettable individual characters.

This breadth of human characters and social types is matched by a breadth in the material and manner of the stories told. Here are bawdy stories that will make you roar or blush or both, delicate tales of chivalry and romantic love, classic animal fables and ancient legends charmingly retold, scandalous tales of clerical corruption, together with edifying tales of spiritual devotion. And the style varies from the coarsest and most common street idiom to the most elegant and mock-elegant niceties. No English poet besides Shakespeare equals Chaucer in this quality of breadth.

This work is also remarkable for its combination of a general narrative with a number of smaller stories enclosed within it—like a long novel, in which the main characters tell a series of short stories or novelettes, with each story related to the character of the particular storyteller. As we go down the road with Chaucer's Canterbury pilgrims, we see them and hear their stories at the same time. The little stories are related to the big story. The storytellers and the stories illuminate one another in a unified whole that holds our interest from the beginning to the end.

GUIDE TO

Sixth Reading

I

Chaucer, like Dante, wrote his great poetic masterpiece in the vernacular of his place and time. As Dante worked with the Tuscan dialect of fourteenth-century Italy, Chaucer worked with the East Midlands dialect of fourteenth-century England. In each case, the dialect of the poet became the standard speech of the country. Chaucer's English eventually became "the King's English."

Early English literature was written in Anglo-Saxon, a Teutonic language, closer to modern Dutch than to modern English. This language is called "Old English." After the Norman Conquest in 1066, Norman French became the language of the ruling classes and of most literature. Gradually, Anglo-Saxon and Norman French grew together into one language, resembling modern English. This language is called "Middle English." The period of Middle English literature is roughly from 1150 to 1500. Chaucer was the greatest poet of this period. Besides Chaucer's works, the most notable writings were *Sir Gawain and the Green Knight,* an alliterative romance of perfect chivalry, and *The Vision of Piers Plowman,* a long spiritual allegory on religious corruption and purification.

Chaucer was a man of wide learning, well read in Latin, French, and Italian, as well as in his own language. Even a cursory reading of the *Canterbury Tales* reveals his knowledge of contemporary science and of ancient and foreign literatures. He was a skilled practitioner in Italian and French verse forms, the translator of famous works in French poetry and Latin prose, and an enthusiastic admirer of the Italian Renaissance. He knew intimately the works of Dante, Petrarch, and Boccaccio. His duties as a diplomat gave him firsthand experience of French and Italian culture. (See Biographical Note, p. v.)

In view of this substantial professional literary background and competence, it is amazing to find that until the last century Chaucer was regarded as an early, rough, rather prosaic versifier. For about three hundred years, his stature as a writer was based solely on his magnificent ability to tell a story and create characters. The reason for this misunderstanding was that English pronunciation changed markedly in the century after Chaucer's death, and the right way to read his verse was lost. Ignorant copyists who emended his writings did a great deal to make a proper reading impossible. Modern scholarship has succeeded in reproducing the original text of Chaucer and enabled us to appreciate his remarkable metrical power. Since the verse form of the *Canterbury Tales* is one of the basic rhythms in English poetry, it is important that we should know something about it.

The *Canterbury Tales* are written in a style that combines the bluff English of Chaucer's day with the elegant rhythm which he had learned from French poetry. The basic verse form of this work is the "heroic couplet," which was of French origin, and later became the favorite verse form of English epic poetry. The heroic couplet is a pair of lines, each having five accented syllables, with the end syllables rhyming. Thus, at the beginning of the work we read, in the modern translation:

> Wȟen Ápȓil wíth hȋs shówȇrs swéet wȋth frúit
> Tȟe droúght ȏf Márch hȃs piérced ȗntó tȟe róot (p. 159c)

As our accent markings indicate, an unaccented syllable is regularly followed by an accented one. The unaccented syllable is indicated by a ∨ and the accented one by a ⁄ . A pattern of stress is called a "foot," roughly corresponding to a "measure" in music, and this particular pattern—an unaccented followed by an accented syllable—is called an "iambic foot," or an "iamb." There are five of these "feet" in each line here. Hence the meter or rhythm of the heroic couplet is called "iambic pentameter" (five iambic measures, or feet).

If we look at Chaucer's original text, however, we will soon see that in actual poetic practice, things are not so simple and mechanical.

> Whan that Aprille with his shoures sote
> The droghte of Marche hath perced to the rote, (p. 159a)

If we are uninstructed in reading Chaucerian verse, it seems to us that there are eight syllables in the first line and nine in the second, unlike the ten syllables that we would regularly expect. Actually, there are more than ten syllables in each line, for Chaucer's couplets should be read with full sound value given to each syllable, including the pronunciation of the final *e, es,* and *ed.* Thus, in the example above, the rhyme is *so-tuh* and *ro-tuh.* And an exact marking of the meter would look like this:

> Whán thǎt Áprillě wíth hǐs shóurěs sótě
> Thě dróghtě ǒf Márchě hǎth pércěd tó thě rótě,

Thus we have an extra syllable in the first line and two extra syllables in the second line—but, since the extra syllables are not accented, the basic five-stress pattern holds.

If you read on, you will find that very few of Chaucer's lines fit the regular ten-syllable, iambic pentameter pattern. The reason for this variation is that Chaucer is a real poet, with a keen sense for the sound and impression of verse, not a hack working by rote. Perfect regularity of the iambic pentameter pattern would result in a singsong monotone that would soon make you drowsy. Chaucer varies the basic pattern slightly but frequently, just as we do in conversational speech. Sometimes he omits the unaccented syllable and starts a line with an accented one, or he may have two unaccented syllables before the accent. Both of these variations appear above. You may find others as you go through the work. They indicate deftness, not sloppiness, in writing verse. All good poets vary the basic metrical pattern they are using.

Other verse forms besides the heroic couplet are occasionally used in the *Canterbury Tales.* The tales of the prioress and the lawyer are written in "rhyme royal" (also called Chaucerian heptastich), stanzas composed of seven lines of iambic pentameter, with this rhyme scheme—*ababbcc.* This means that these lines rhyme with one another: the first and third; the second, fourth and fifth; and the last two. Chaucer also used this verse form in *Troilus and Cressida.* (See pp. 1-155.) The *Monk's Tale* is written in eight-line stanzas in iambic hexameter (six-foot lines), with the rhyme scheme *ababbcbc.* This verse form, called "alexandrine," is of French origin. The *Tale of Melibeus* and the *Parson's Tale* are written in prose.

II

There are many wonderful, enthralling, and amusing stories in the *Canterbury Tales.* But the best story of all, and the one most characteristic of this work, is the story told in the *Prologue* and in the transitional prologues and conversations between the tales. These introductory and joining pieces are not just a convenient scaffolding or platform, a mere excuse to get the real stories on the stage. On the contrary, it is these joining pieces that hold the work together and give it its particular substance and pungency. It is these pieces that convey the main characters and events of the work, and very often the point of telling a particular tale lies in something that has occurred in one of these pieces. A true appreciation of the *Canterbury Tales* requires a thorough reading of the *Prologue* to the work and the prologues to the tales.

The *Prologue* to the work sets the stage and introduces the characters. It is a remarkable piece of writing that gives us both an epitome of the *Canterbury Tales* and a microcosm of fourteenth-century England. For Chaucer's characters, whom we meet here, include typical soldiers, clergymen, businessmen, craftsmen, farmers, and housewives of the period. They are typical and yet so individualized that we may forget their social status, but we cannot forget their individual personalities and characteristics. Chaucer presents them to us so vividly that they seem like real persons whom we have come to know.

The *Prologue* begins in the Tabard Inn at Southwark. Here meets a group of some thirty pilgrims on their way to the shrine of Thomas à Becket, the martyred Archbishop of Canterbury. Chaucer—who, like Dante, puts himself into the story—is one of them, and he promises to tell us all about them. They comprise a knight, a squire (his son), and the knight's yeoman

(servant); a prioress, a nun (her chaplain), three priests, a monk, a clerk (theological scholar), a parson (parish priest), a summoner (for the ecclesiastical courts), and a pardoner (seller of papal pardons and indulgences); also a man of law (barrister), a physician, a shipman (sea captain), a franklin (country gentleman or freeholder), a merchant, a miller, a cook, a reeve (steward), a manciple (victualer), a plowman, and five master craftsmen or burgesses—a haberdasher, a carpenter, a weaver, a dyer, and an arras (tapestry) maker, as well as the Wife of Bath. Chaucer says that there were twenty-nine pilgrims in all (including himself). The three priests are never referred to again, and apparently are reduced to the "nun's priest." (See p. 499.) Two other persons, a canon and his yeoman, join the party while they are on the road.

Chaucer begins his character presentations with the knight, a paragon of chivalry and courtesy, who despite his military fame

> . . . bore himself as meekly as a maid.
> He never yet had any vileness said,
> In all his life, to whatsoever wight.
> He was a truly perfect, gentle knight. (p. 160a)

("Gentle" here means wellborn. See the discussion of "gentility" in the *Wife of Bath's Tale,* pp. 274b-275d.)

Chaucer notes acutely that the old warhorse's tunic has been "Sadly discoloured by his habergeon" (coat of mail). His son, the squire, though, has his "locks well curled, as if they'd laid in press," and is all "Prinked out" to attract a lady's favor. The young squire is quite a blade.

> He could make songs and words thereto indite,
> Joust, and dance too, as well as sketch and write.
> So hot he loved that, while night told her tale,
> He slept no more than does a nightingale.

But, adds Chaucer, in closing his description:

> Courteous he, and humble, willing and able,
> And carved before his father at the table. (p. 160b)

The prioress, like the knight, is a model of perfect form and courtesy, but here Chaucer conveys the impression that she is

working at it, deliberately copying the appearance of virtue. She intones the divine services "through her nose, becomingly," speaks fluent French as she has been taught at an English school, and has also learned impeccable table manners.

> At table she had been well taught withal,
> And never from her lips let morsels fall,
> Nor dipped her fingers deep in sauce, but ate
> With so much care the food upon her plate
> That never driblet fell upon her breast.
> In courtesy she had delight and zest.
> Her upper lip was always wiped so clean
> That in her cup was no iota seen
> Of grease, when she had drunk her draught of wine.
> Becomingly she reached for meat to dine.

But Chaucer adds,

> She was at pains to counterfeit the look
> Of courtliness, and stately manners took,
> And would be held worthy of reverence. (p. 161c-d)

However, she is a nice, pleasant, friendly person, softhearted and full of pity for even a trapped mouse. She is properly and neatly dressed. Chaucer hints at her size thus—"she was not undergrown."

Over against the gentle prioress, Chaucer sets the manly monk, who is interested only in hunting (called "venery" here). Not for him is observance of the strict monastic rules, or "mad" studying of books in a cloister cell, or fatiguing himself with labor on the land. His way is to ride to the hounds, day and night, and wear fine clothes, and be well fed.

> And smooth as one anointed was his face.
> Fat was this lord, he stood in goodly case.
> . . . .
> His boots were soft; his horse of great estate.
> Now certainly he was a fine prelate:
> He was not pale as some poor wasted ghost.
> A fat swan loved he best of any roast. (p. 162b)

There is also the friar, the greatest beggar in his order, who can get alms even from a needy, barefoot widow. He finds the best "pickings" among the publicans and sinners and avoids sick lepers and other "such poverty-stricken curs." He is an

easy man in allotting penitence to sinners requesting absolution, for he counts cold, hard cash above tears and prayers. He gives little knickknacks to the young women, plays deftly on the rote (a stringed instrument like the lute), is a champion ballad singer, a strong man, and helps to settle disputes on arbitration days. After listing all these attainments, Chaucer adds the little note of idiosyncrasy that makes us remember him.

> He lisped a little, out of wantonness,
> To make his English soft upon his tongue;
> And in his harping, after he had sung,
> His two eyes twinkled in his head as bright
> As do the stars within the frosty night. (p. 163d)

There is also the clerk, who is interested in nothing but study, and spends what little money he can obtain on books.

> Of study took he utmost care and heed.
> Not one word spoke he more than was his need;
> And that was said in fullest reverence
> And short and quick and full of high good sense.
> Pregnant of moral virtue was his speech;
> And gladly would he learn and gladly teach. (p. 164b)

And there is the country parson, who is learned, holy, and good. His one thought is to serve his parishioners and give them a living example of what he preaches. "He was a shepherd and not mercenary"—not like those who sublet their parishes to others in order to find easier posts in London.

> He had no thirst for pomp or reverence,
> Nor made himself a special, spiced conscience,
> But Christ's own lore, and His apostles' twelve
> He taught, but first he followed it himselve. (p. 168a)

There are also those two odd functionaries of the medieval Church, the summoner and the pardoner. The summoner was the man who summoned people to the ecclesiastical court to be tried for their sins—something like our court bailiffs. This one is so ugly that he scares the children, he gets drunk on strong, red wine, and then talks only in the few phrases of Latin he has learned. He questions the efficacy of the archdeacon's curse, and says a man can be punished only in his purse. Chaucer reprimands him for this blasphemous cynicism, but nevertheless finds him

> . . . a noble rascal, and a kind;
> A better comrade 'twould be hard to find. (p. 170b)

Chaucer has quite a bit of fun in describing the pardoner, who has official papal sanction to sell pardons for sins (pardoners might be laymen as well as priests). His wallet (traveling bag) is "Stuffed full of pardons brought from Rome all hot." It also contains supposed relics of the Virgin's veil, St. Peter's sail, and other dubious items with which he duped parsons and other gullible folk out of their money. Nevertheless, he is a proficient churchman.

> Well could he read a lesson or a story,
> But best of all he sang an offertory; (p. 171d)

Only then did he preach and appeal to the congregation for funds. Again Chaucer goes into the details of appearance and the idiosyncratic mark.

> This pardoner had hair as yellow as wax,
> But lank it hung as does a strike of flax;
> In wisps hung down such locks as he'd on head,
> And with them he his shoulders overspread;
> But thin they dropped, and stringy, one by one.
> . . . .
> As shiny eyes he had as has a hare.
> . . . .
> A voice he had that bleated like a goat. (p. 171c)

Among the "civilians" is the pompous, self-important, opinionated merchant whose name, despite all his self-asserted worth, Chaucer is unable to recall; the physician, who along with his colleagues, the druggists, grows rich from his profession; the miller—a giant of a man, a teller of bawdy stories, and a bagpipe player—who cheats his customers flagrantly. There is also the pious plowman who loves God and his neighbor, and is industrious, and helpful to all, without thought of reward; and the worthy reeve, the efficient and honest overseer of his master's estate, rich in his own right. And last, but certainly not least, is the redoubtable housewife from Bath who has had "five churched husbands . . . / Not counting other company in youth," but is now deaf and gap toothed, buxom and broad-bottomed, wearing a wimple and a broad hat, scarlet hose and soft new shoes, "And on her feet a pair of sharpened spurs."

The host (the innkeeper), a very genial man, suggests to the pilgrims that they while away their long journey with story-telling.

> "... And well I know, as you go on your way,
> You'll tell good tales and shape yourselves to play;
> For truly there's no mirth nor comfort, none,
> Riding the roads as dumb as is a stone ..." (p. 172b)

He proposes that each pilgrim tell two stories on the way to Canterbury and two on the way home, with the best story-teller getting a free supper at the others' expense. He himself will ride along with the pilgrims and be their guide. Those who will not comply with the rules shall have to pay for all the purchases along the way. The pilgrims agree, appoint the host their governor and judge, whom they will obey in all things, and after setting the price of the prize supper, they go to bed. The next morning, on the road, they draw "cuts" to see who shall start first. The knight draws the first cut and tells the first story.

> HERE ENDETH THE PROLOGUE OF THIS
> BOOK; AND HERE BEGINNETH THE FIRST
> TALE, WHICH IS THE KNIGHT'S TALE (p. 174)

III

Before we consider the tales the pilgrims tell, let us glance at what goes on between them along the road to occasion the various stories. This we learn in the prologues and transitional conversations. For instance, after the knight has told his tale, the miller, who is quite drunk, insists on telling a bawdy story of how a young scholar tricked a carpenter so that he might enjoy the latter's wife. The reeve feels personally offended because he was once a carpenter himself, and therefore retaliates in kind—"It's lawful to meet force with force." He tells a ribald story, too—in the miller's "own boor's language"—about how two young theological students pay back a cheating miller by making love to his wife and daughter. Similarly, the merchant complains about the misery of being married to his awful wife, and then proceeds to tell the story of how a young wife cuckolded her old husband and was so wily that she convinced him that what he saw with his own eyes did not take place. And the shipman is so anxious to ward off a dour sermon by the parson that he pushes in with another story of the resourcefulness of a woman when threatened by the revelation of her infidelity.

The war between the sexes occupies the minds of many of the pilgrims. After the merchant's tale of cuckoldry, the host laments *his* awful wife and miserable marriage. Indeed, he confesses, "I am sore sorry that to her I'm wed." This quite matches the merchant's

> ". . . I'd never another time fall in the snare.
> We wedded men in sorrow live, and care . . ." (p. 318b)

The women, too, have a spokesman, a very doughty one, too—the good wife of Bath, a staunch defender of the joys of marriage and the sovereignty of women. We shall take up her defense of marriage and women separately below. Note that the shipman's tale starts from the woman's point of view—"He moot [must] *us* clothe, and he moot *us* arraye"—about that fool, the husband, who must always pay. (See p. 383b.) Perhaps Chaucer originally intended the shipman's tale for the wife of Bath and then changed his mind.

As we have seen, the host is no distant, impartial judge. He is always eager to comment on a story, to praise nobility and lament vice, and let loose his salty observations on womankind —or woman unkind. But, above all, he is the master of ceremonies, intent on keeping the show going, inviting each to tell us his story in turn. When things get too serious or too dull, he sees to it that the next stories are "merry" ones. Eager to avoid a sermon, he silences the reeve's lamentation on the enduring pangs of lust and gets the old man to tell his ribald tale of the cockolded miller. After the physician's tale of the poor maiden who has her father kill her to save her from the clutches of the wicked judge, the host begs for a "merry" tale to cure his sadness. When Chaucer himself, in the story, tells a story that purposely burlesques the long-winded, tedious, detailed romances of chivalry, the host begs him to stop long before he has finished.

> "No more of this, for God's high dignity!"
> Exclaimed our host, "For you, sir, do make me
> So weary with your vulgar foolishness
> That, as may God so truly my soul bless,
> My two ears ache from all your worthless speech;
> Now may such rhymes the devil have, and each!
> This sort of thing is doggerel," said he. (p. 400b)

He heartily agrees when the knight stops the monk's long and sad account of notable falls of men, from Adam down to present times. Says the host to the monk,

> ". . . I pray you heartily tell us something else,
> For truly, but for clinking of the bells
> That from your bridle hang on either side,
> By Heaven's king, Who for us all has died,
> I should, ere this, have fallen down for sleep,
> Although the mud had never been so deep;
> Then had your story all been told in vain . . ."

And when the monk refuses, the host begs the nun's priest,

> ". . . Tell us a thing to make our hearts all glad . . ." (p. 449d)

Yet at the end of the work, the parson has the last word, and, after firmly refusing to tell any "foolish fable," he delivers a long homily on the seven deadly sins and the means of penitence for each of them. Possibly Chaucer wanted to end his work on a pious and solemn note, or perhaps he did not have time to work the parson's sermon into a real story.

IV

The good wife of Bath is undoubtedly the best remembered of all the pilgrims in the *Canterbury Tales*. This respectable and redoubtable lady who has buried "five churched husbands," after enjoying them very well, and is well versed in "the old, old dance" of love, is certainly an unforgettable character. Male readers may flinch a bit before this formidable woman, and perhaps regard her as too much for any one man to handle, and the ladies may blush before her frank description of her married life—or lives. But she remains in the readers' minds long after they have put this book down. Her memorable presence is conveyed to us through her prologue, one of the most masterly pieces of writing in the *Canterbury Tales*. It is a story in itself, one of the meatiest and most vivid in the whole work.

"This," she says in effect, "is the story of my life"—and the "this" here is marriage, living with a man. She claims the authority of an experience that began when she was twelve, and she looks forward to continuing and broadening her experience. She is not ashamed but proud of having had five husbands, and the whole prologue is a justification for the married state as well as a claim to the rightful sovereignty of the wife over the husband. Far from being disturbed by the biblical passages against women who have many husbands, she cites the scriptural injunctions to increase and multiply, and to marry rather than burn—as well as the example of the patriarchs and King Solomon, with their many wives. God never commanded virginity, she points out, and she argues that marriage is a divine vocation too, though perhaps a lower and more common one than celibacy. She has been made for the married state and its acts—perfect holiness is not for her. The "barley bread" of conjugal love is good too, even though it is not the "purest white wheat-seed" of virginity.

She argues that God gave us our genital organs for the express purpose of making love, as well as for the needs of internal hygiene. It is through them that man pays his debt to his wife, and she, for one, is willing and eager to see to it that he makes his payments as often as he likes. Moreover, the husband's body belongs to the wife. This note of possession and domination disturbs the pardoner, who interrupts to say that if this is what marriage is like, he is going to postpone getting married. The good wife warns him that before she is through he will hear far more of the tribulations of marriage, in which women like her are "the whip."

Then she proceeds to the tale of her five husbands. The first three were good, and the last two were "bad." The three good ones were rich but old, and not strong enough to meet her vigorous demands for conjugal love. She boasts that she wore them out, nagged them constantly, and governed them rigorously. And she tells us how she accomplished the latter feat—through means known to every smart woman, who is always more than a match for any mere man. Admit nothing (even when it is true), counter with charges (even when they are false), make claims (even when they are inordinate). Point to the fine clothes of your neighbor's wife and complain that you simply haven't a thing to wear. Accuse your husband of skirt-chasing when he makes similar charges against you. Above all, put him in the wrong first.

> ". . . O Lord, the pain I gave them and the woe,
> All guiltless, too, by God's grief exquisite!
> For like a stallion could I neigh and bite.
> I could complain, though mine was all the guilt,
> Or else, full many a time, I'd lost the tilt.
> Whoso comes first to mill first gets meal ground;
> I whimpered first and so did them confound.
> They were right glad to hasten to excuse
> Things they had never done, save in my ruse . . ." (p. 262b)

The above amounts to an advice to women—or young wives. There is also a serious defense of women against the typical male charges of frivolity, extravagance, and fickleness. The good wife asserts that women should have free access to the family money, and freedom to come and go as they please. Otherwise men incur their rightful enmity.

> " 'But tell me this, why do you hide, with sorrow,
> The keys to your strong box away from me?
> It is my gold as well as yours, pardie.
> Why would you make an idiot of your dame?
> Now by Saint James, but you shall miss your aim,
> You shall not be, although like mad you scold,
> Master of both my body and my gold;
> One you'll forgo in spite of both your eyes;
> Why need you seek me out or set on spies?
> I think you'd like to lock me in your chest!
> You should say: "Dear wife, go where you like best,
> Amuse yourself, I will believe no tales;
> You're my wife Alis true, and truth prevails."
> We love no man that guards us or gives charge
> Of where we go, for we will be at large . . .' " (p. 261c)

It is ridiculous to think that fine clothes lead to unfaithfulness or that watchmen can keep a woman faithful. The good wife is furious against the male slander of woman—why, they even take "a hateful wife" as an example of one of the three worst things in the world! (See Prov. 30:21-23.)

By sheer determination and cussedness, she got the better of her first three husbands. She taught them

> " '. . . That it is well to leave a wife in peace.
> One of us two must bow, to be at ease;
> And since a man's more reasonable, they say,
> Than woman is, you must have patience aye . . .' " (p. 263c)

Her fourth husband was more of a problem, since he had a mistress on the side and the good wife was passionately jealous. But she paid him back in kind, by assuming the appearance of unfaithfulness herself, and she hurt him in many secret ways known to man and wife alone. She gave him hell before he died—"on earth I was his purgatory."

Her fifth husband was the worst—and the best—of the lot. He beat her black and blue, and tried to tell her what to do. But he was "so fresh and gay" in bed that he could always win her love back, even after giving her a hard beating. Although in certain ways he was the worst of her husbands, she loved him the best of all. The reason lies, she thinks, in the feminine tendency to value most the love that is given most sparingly, the man who is most aloof and least importunate.

> ". . . I guess I loved him best of all, for he
> Gave of his love most sparingly to me.
> We women have, if I am not to lie,
> In this love matter, a quaint fantasy;
> Look out a thing we may not lightly have,
> And after that we'll cry all day and crave.
> Forbid a thing, and that thing covet we;
> Press hard upon us, then we turn and flee.
> Sparingly offer we our goods, when fair;
> Great crowds at market make for dearer ware,
> And what's too common brings but little price;
> All this knows every woman who is wise . . ." (p. 264b)

But, love or no love, she was not going to surrender her freedom and sovereignty. When she married him, she signed over all her wealth to him, but she soon regretted it when he tried to tell her what to do and when to go out, and to correct her faults. And, to add insult to injury, he would read selections to her from a collection of writings on wicked wives. This infamous work—written by some dried-up old cleric, she avows—starts out with Eve and goes down the list to portray the evils of womankind. She got so mad one night that she tore three pages out of the book and gave her husband a punch that sent him sprawling into the fireplace. He returned her a clout in kind that put her on the floor. This was his undoing, for it provided her with the opportunity she needed to put her house in order. As she shammed death for a few moments, her man was afraid he had killed her and he became so contrite that

> ". . . He put the bridle reins within my hand
> To have the governing of house and land;
> And of his tongue and of his hand, also;
> And made him burn his book, right then, oho!
> And when I had thus gathered unto me
> Masterfully, the entire sovereignty,
> And he had said: 'My own true wedded wife,
> Do as you please the term of all your life,
> Guard your own honour and keep fair my state'—
> After that day we never had debate . . ." (p. 269d)

Thus, in the end, her fifth and last marriage was a happy one. She and her late husband lived in amity and faithfulness until the end of his life.

But even this hearty, resourceful woman, eager for life and experience, and always on the lookout for another husband, has to acknowledge the inexorable encroachments of time. In the midst of her recollections of her married lives, she stops to cry,

> "But Lord Christ! When I do remember me
> Upon my youth and on my jollity,
> It tickles me about my heart's deep root.
> To this day does my heart sing in salute
> That I have had my world in my own time.
> But age, alas! that poisons every prime,
> Has taken away my beauty and my pith;
> Let go, farewell, the devil go therewith!
> The flour is gone, there is no more to tell,
> The bran, as best I may, must I now sell . . ."
> (pp. 263d-264a)

The wife of Bath's story illustrates one of the main points of her prologue. A knight, sentenced to death for rape, is promised his life if within a year's time he finds out what it is women most desire. His year is nearly up, when he chances upon an old hag who gives him the answer on condition that he grant whatever request she makes of him. Back at the court he gives the right answer—that women want most of all to rule over their menfolk—and he is granted his life. But the old hag demands in return that he marry her, and despite his protestations about her ugliness, age, and low station, he has to comply. On their wedding night, the old hag answers his moroseness and aloofness with an edifying discourse on the true gentility that may be found in persons of low station, and vice versa, and on the virtue of poverty and the honor of age. She then gives him the choice of having her beautiful and young but faithless, or old and ugly but faithful. He leaves the choice in her hands, acknowledging her sovereignty. Whereupon she decides to become young and beautiful (which she does through her magic powers) and good and true at the same time. And they live happily ever after, beginning with the warmth and pleasure of that night. The good wife drives home the point of her tale with the prayer that

> . . . Jesus to us send
> Meek husbands, and young ones, and fresh in bed,
> And good luck to outlive them that we wed.
> And I pray Jesus to cut short the lives
> Of those who'll not be governed by their wives;
> And old and querulous niggards with their pence,
> And send them soon a mortal pestilence! (p. 277c)

V

The clergy play an important role in the *Canterbury Tales* as storytellers and as the subjects of stories and comments. England was still staunchly Catholic in the fourteenth century, and the Church was taken for granted. With the exception of the Jews, everyone was born into it, just as he was born an Englishman. Already in Chaucer's time, however, reformers such as John Wycliffe and the Lollard evangelical movement had arisen, calling for a purification of religious life, which they announced had declined in spiritual and moral quality. The famous poem *Piers Plowman,* also written in the fourteenth century, is a serious spiritual allegory on the contemporary religious corruption and the way to purification. Let us see how Chaucer treats the Church and the clergy in the *Canterbury Tales.*

Just as the miller and the reeve antagonistically tell stories against one another's colleagues, so the friar and the summoner contend with one another in exchanging invidious tales. According to the friar, summoners are blackmailing extortionists who make money out of various charges, the most common being fornication and adultery, charges that may be true or false. In the friar's tale, a most villainous summoner meets the devil in the form of a bailiff—and the latter accompanies the summoner when he attempts to extort twelvepence from a poor old widow on a false charge of adultery. When the old lady says of the summoner, "The Devil . . . take him . . . unless he will repent," and he does not repent, the devil takes him down to Hell, where summoners have a special place. The moral, says the friar, is that summoners should repent before the devil takes them down to Hell. The infuriated summoner tells a story against friars in return. This is a tale of how an avaricious and hypocritical friar is paid back in foul fashion for his graspingness.

The pardoner himself in his prologue takes off on the ways of pardoners. This is another fine piece of character creation and revelation of contemporary English society. The pardoner pictures himself as a cunning charlatan and supersalesman. He tells how he plays on the feelings and desires of the congregations he addresses, with his phony relics and cures, and offers of absolution for sins in return for donations of money. He gains great sums by preaching against covetousness, which is the sole motivation for his preaching. He may save others from avarice, but that is not his intention.

> ". . . Think you that because I'm good at preaching
> And win me gold and silver by my teaching
> I'll live of my free will in poverty?
> No, no, that's never been my policy!

For I will preach and beg in sundry lands;
I will not work and labour with my hands,
Nor baskets weave and try to live thereby,
Because I will not beg in vain, say I.
I will none of the apostles counterfeit;
I will have money, wool, and cheese, and wheat,
Though it be given by the poorest page,
Or by the poorest widow in village,
And though her children perish of famine.
Nay! I will drink good liquor of the vine
And have a pretty wench in every town. . ."
(pp. 373d–374a)

In keeping with his talent for preaching what he does not practice, and in response to the company's request for a "moral" tale, the pardoner tells the story of three revelers who kill each other off out of avarice for a treasure they have agreed to share equally. Through covetousness they find death, whom, personified, they had sought to find and slay.

Many of the stories and side remarks are directed to the sexual activities of clergymen. In the *Shipman's Tale,* it is a sly monk who buys the lady's favor with money lent from her husband. There are many allusions throughout the work to the earthy ways of monks and friars with the ladies. The pardoner confesses his own conquests with self-satisfaction (pardoners were not always under holy vows, and summoners were usually laymen). The host, in his admiration for the strength and manliness of the monk, regrets that the vows of celibacy remove the pick of manhood from fathering children. Hence,

". . . we laymen are but shrimps!
From feeble trees there come but wretched imps.
That's why our heirs are all so very slender
And feeble that they may not well engender.
That's why our goodwives always will essay
Religious folk, for you may better pay
With Venus' payments than we others do;
God knows, in no light weight of coin pay you! . . ."
(p. 433d)

This ribald, eugenic criticism of monastic celibacy occurs in the *Monk's Prologue,* fittingly subtitled: "The Merry Words of the Host to the Monk."

Such storytellers as the pardoner represent the seamier side of fourteenth-century clerical life. However, there are other more seemly storytellers from the religious vocations. The clerk tells the famous story of the patient Griselda. Although the *Prioress's Tale* is in substance a typical medieval anti-Semitic story of ritual murder of a Christian boy by the Jews, it is a beautifully told tale and is preceded by a prologue that is a tender and deeply moving prayer. The *Monk's Tale* amounts to a series of laments on the tragic fall of famous characters, from Lucifer and Adam on down. The prologue to the *Second Nun's Tale* is impregnated with sincere religious virtues and in her story she gives us a serious prayerful interpretation of the legend of St. Cecilia.

Another profession that gets attention and ironic raillery from Chaucer is alchemy. The *Canon's Yeoman's Prologue* and *Tale*, in which alchemy is ridiculed, are among the most masterly and delightful of the pieces in this work. The *Canon's Yeoman's Tale* is generally believed to be one of the few original stories by Chaucer in the work. Possibly it is based on sad personal experience. The yeoman's master, the canon, is an experimental alchemist who has reduced himself and his yeoman to penury through his vain, expensive experiments. The yeoman tells us of what went on in those experiments, of all the apparatus and substances that were involved, and of the explosions which shake the laboratory when something goes amiss. He gives a poignant picture of the endless frustration and constant effort toward the mirage of the "philosopher's stone."

> The thing has caused us to spend all we had,
> For grief of which almost we should go mad,
> Save that good hope comes creeping in the heart,
> Supposing ever, though we sorely smart,
> The elixir will relieve us afterward;
> The tension of such hope is sharp and hard;
> I warn you well, it means go seeking ever;
> That future time has made men to dissever,
> Trusting that hope, from all that ever they had.
> Yet of that art they cannot well grow sad,
> For unto them it is a bitter-sweet;
> So it appears; for had they but a sheet

With which to wrap themselves about by night,
And a coarse cloak to walk in by daylight,
They'd sell them both and spend it on this craft;
They can withhold naught till there's nothing left
And evermore, wherever they'll be gone,
Men know them by their smell of foul brimstone;
For all the world they stink as does a goat;
Their savour is so rammish and so hot
That, though a man a mile away may be,
The odour will infect him, trust to me!
Thus by their smell and their threadbare array,
If men but wish, these folk they'll know, I say.
(p. 477c)

The *Canon's Yeoman's Tale* is of a canon-alchemist who does others, not himself, out of wealth. That this charlatan is a canon, like his master, does not mean that all canons are charlatans, the yeoman hastens to add.

But most religious canons, just and true,
Don't think I'm slandering your house, or you,
Although my tale may of a canon be.
Some rogue's in every order, pardon me,
And God forbid that for one rascal's sake
Against a group we condemnation make.
To slander you is nowise my intent,
But to correct what is amiss I'm bent.
This tale I tell here not alone for you,
But even for others, too; you know well how
Among Christ's twelve disciples there was not
One to play traitor, save Iscariot.
Then why should all the rest be put to blame
Who guiltless were? Of you I say the same.
Save only this, if you will list to me,
If any Judas in your convent be,
Remove the man betimes, I counsel you,
Lest shame or loss or trouble should ensue.
(p. 479c)

The clever mountebank in the yeoman's story sedulously cultivates the confidence of a good priest, who is quite gullible and eager to get something for nothing. The canon tricks the priest into believing that he has made silver from baser metals, and then agrees to sell his "secret" for an extravagant sum. That is the last the priest sees of the canon or of silver made out of baser metals. The moral is obvious.

Meddle no more with that base art, I mean,
For if you do, you'll lose your savings clean.
(p. 486a)

VI

The ambitious plan proposed by the host, that each pilgrim tell two stories, is not fulfilled. Only Chaucer, in his character in the story, tells two tales, and one of these he is compelled by the bored host to leave unfinished. The cook's tale is left unfinished also, just after it has begun, and not everyone gets to tell a tale. The three priests accompanying the prioress are reduced to one priest with one story, and we never hear at all from the five master craftsmen. Undoubtedly, the *Canterbury Tales* is an unfinished work, and Chaucer sketched out more to begin with than he was able to accomplish.

The tales told in the work vary greatly in kind and in source. The ribald stories come from word-of-mouth sources or Boccaccio's *Decameron.* Beautiful stories of chivalry and romantic love are told by the knight, the lawyer, the squire, and the physician—derived from Boccaccio, John Gower's *Confessio amantis* (a fourteenth-century work), the *Roman de la Rose* (a thirteenth-century French romance), and unknown sources. Chaucer's *Sir Thopas* is a burlesque of contemporary, hackneyed stories of chivalric romance.

The clerk, the nun, the pardoner, the prioress, and Chaucer himself tell edifying moral and religious tales, some of which, in the telling, are exquisite works of art. Chaucer admits getting the clerk's tale of the patient Griselda from Petrarch—who in turn got it from Boccaccio. The *Second Nun's Tale* may be a translation from one of the lives of St. Cecilia, and the *Pardoner's Tale* may be based on an Italian collection of stories. The *Prioress's Tale* is apparently based on the thirteenth-century case of Hugh of Lincoln—the alleged victim of ritual murder by the Jews—who became the subject of ballads and poems, which may have been the source for Chaucer's story. The *Monk's Tale* of the fall of men of high degree is based on various sources, and follows in form a Latin work by Boccaccio. Chaucer's *Tale of Melibeus* is a translation of a long French story on the forgiveness of enemies.

The stories include two charming retellings of ancient fables. The *Nun's Priest's Tale* is about the sly fox who devises the capture of a gullible cock, who in turn tricks the fox into letting him escape. This story, known to all children, may be based on the French story of *Reynard the Fox*. The *Manciple's Tale*, which goes as far back as Ovid, is about a snow-white crow who can sing and speak and who informs his master of the infidelity of his wife. The master kills his wife and then hates the crow so much that he pulls out his white feathers, and takes away his ability to sing and speak. Hence all crows are black now and cry a harsh caw-caw. The moral of each of these fables is obvious, but Chaucer does not neglect to point them out to us.

Chaucer frankly admits and even justifies his borrowing of stories originated by other authors. He compares his version of *Melibeus*, which differs from previous tellings of the story, with the various versions of the words and deeds of Jesus in the New Testament. (See pp. 400b-401c.) Besides, the common people love old stories best. (See p. 373d.)

Like Dante, Chaucer is by no means backward about having his characters sing his praises as a literary artist. The man of law lists some of Chaucer's works, and praises his narrative and poetic powers. (See p. 235c-d.) True, the host objects to Chaucer's verse in *Sir Thopas* as "worthless speech . . . doggerel . . . dirty rhyming . . . not worth a turd" (p. 400b). But here he is probably expressing Chaucer's own opinion of the contemporary chivalric romance which he mocks in this story. And the parson expresses scorn for the alliterative niceties of chivalric romance: "I can't romance with 'rum, ram, ruff', by letter" (p. 494b). The *Monk's Prologue*, on the other hand, includes a learned discussion on the nature of tragedy and the ideal verse form for its expression—hexameter (six-foot lines).

VII

Are Chaucer's ribald stories and expressions offensive or indecent?

Chaucer presents us with the same kind of question that we faced in regard to Aristophanes' comedies—the publication of direct, unreserved, and coarse descriptions of and allusions to sexual love and the excretory processes. One of the usual answers to this problem is to link such frank expressions to the ways of a bygone age. But this seems rather questionable, since a good many of us still know and use Chaucerian expressions or similar ones in private life, nor would it be hard to find them in twentieth-century literature, from James Joyce down to the latest novelists and poets. Moreover, the question of possible offense is raised and answered by the author himself "in the olden days." He pleads authenticity, faithfulness to actual life and speech, as his excuse.

> But first, I pray you, of your courtesy,
> You'll not ascribe it to vulgarity
> Though I speak plainly of this matter here,
> Retailing you their words and means of cheer;
> Nor though I use their very terms, nor lie.
> For this thing do you know as well as I:
> When one repeats a tale told by a man,
> He must report, as nearly as he can,
> Every least word, if he remember it,
> However rude it be, or how unfit;
> Or else he may be telling what's untrue,
> Embellishing and fictionizing too.
> He may not spare, although it were his brother;
> He must as well say one word as another.
> (pp. 171d-172a)

And Chaucer repeats this plea in the *Miller's Prologue*—to "hold not what I say/ Evilly meant," for the miller must be allowed to speak in his own fictitious person, to tell his admittedly "churlish" tale. The wife of Bath offers another excuse, that this is all in fun.

> ". . . But yet I pray of all this company
> That if I speak from my own phantasy,
> They will not take amiss the things I say;
> For my intention's only but to play . . ." (p. 259c)

Furthermore, the lawyer says in praise of Chaucer that *he* would never write wicked stories of incest and perversion.

> ". . . [He] Would never write, in one of his creations,
> Of such unnatural abominations . . ." (p. 235d)

Chaucer in person and through his characters thus pleads

authenticity, amusement, and healthy normality in favor of his ribaldries. Do you find such arguments convincing? Does an author have to reproduce the typical form and style and expressions of the actual language used in the various walks and levels of life? Can't an author suggest enough with artful allusions and metaphors, as even Chaucer does occasionally? Would such artfulness be too "suggestive" and more titillating than direct, even coarse, language? How would it sound if Chaucer used polite or clinical equivalents for his bluff English words? Think of the stories and passages that might be offensive and try substituting words like "posterior," "vagina," "copulate," "feces," and "flatulence" for Chaucer's terms. Does it decisively change the tone and meaning? For better or worse? What would this genteel renovation do to the *Wife of Bath's Prologue*?

But these are only questions of expression, of form. What of the substance of these tales? Should they be told at all in print? Even if the tales of the miller, reeve, merchant, and shipman were "cleaned up" as far as language is concerned, would that still leave their stories indecent and harmful to morals? Is the effect of these stories to induce people to act as characters in these stories act, to commit acts of adultery, for instance, or to view such acts indulgently or permissively? Do the stories arouse intense sexual images and desires? Do they make the sexual act seem ugly, degrading, or ridiculous? If the answer to these last three questions is in the affirmative, does this mean that the stories are "obscene" or "pornographic," and should, therefore, be banned from publication?

The wife of Bath raises the question of context and intent with the plea that her talk and tales are all in fun. (See p. 259a.) Does this element of "play" make any difference, decreasing offensiveness and the chance of leading to imitative action? Are Chaucer's ribaldries just a healthy, normal release, harmless to sensibilities and morals? Does the absence of pathological and perverse incidents "clear" Chaucer of any charges of offensiveness? Or should these, too, be permitted?

Is Chaucer anticlerical?

What is Chaucer's purpose in his portraits of the friar, summoner, and pardoner, and in the many references to the corruption and impure life of the clergy throughout the *Canterbury Tales*? Is he expressing his personal antagonism to the Church or the Christian religion? Or is he imbued by a reforming spirit like John Wycliffe and the Lollards? Is this a work like *Piers Plowman*, which was written in the same period and which aims at the purification of religious life? Or was Chaucer trying to portray authentically the actual conditions of life, as he claimed to do with his sexual and scatological descriptions and expressions? Does he want us to take his rascally clerics as typical or exceptional—as the canon's yeoman expressly does with his fraudulent canon-alchemist? Does he balance his worldly clerics with holy and pure ones? Or does he portray the rascals with so much more gusto that the good clerics do not stand out as well? Is he interested as much or more in the rascals because they make a good story as in their authentic reproduction of actual conditions? Is Chaucer's portrait of corrupt clergy likely to lead to religious bigotry? Would it necessarily be offensive to a devout Catholic?

How does Chaucer create living characters?

Let us assume that Chaucer's characters in the prologues and joining pieces strike you as vivid, life-sized human beings. How does Chaucer accomplish this, or what is it specifically about these people that comes home to you, that rings a bell, so that you recognize and believe in them as real persons? Does he do this by his description of their appearance—the face, the body, the gait, the voice, idiosyncrasies? Or is it by showing them in action, in the encounter with other characters, or retrospectively with regard to events in their past? Or does their conversation—the way they talk, their peculiar words and expressions—make the difference? Or is it all of these together, plus something more, that go to make up these characters in their wholeness? Did Chaucer have some idea or image of these people in his mind before he went into the details of their appearance, acts, and talk? If any of them were based on real persons, would that make his artistic accomplishment less or greater, or no different from what it would have been if they were wholly imaginary? Is there any development in the characters, or in our knowledge of the characters, as the journey proceeds, or are the essential character patterns given in the *Prologue*?

Possibly you do not find Chaucer's characters living, believable, and authentic. Or perhaps you think that his description and analysis do not go very deep. What would you criticize specifically? Do you think "realistic" portraiture is shallow and does not deal with the essence of the human person? Do you think external appearances are too easy to handle and not really revelatory? Are Chaucer's characters caricatures, "corny," conventional types? If so, which of the pilgrims do you think is merely a "made-up" job? Which do you think is the deepest portraiture?

Does Chaucer's verse form add to or detract from the story?

Would you rather have this work in prose? Is the verse form merely a conventional device of Chaucer's time, not essential to the telling of the story? Why not have a modern prose translation, as we have with the *Odyssey* and the *Divine Comedy*? Why is this one in heroic couplets? Does the verse form express anything unique in sense and tone that could not be just as adequately conveyed in prose? What, for instance—humor, deftness, sensitivity? Can the meaning of words lie in their sound as well as their sense? How, then, is translation possible? Is it merely equivalent, analogous, or proportionate to the original? Try reading aloud Chaucer's original text and the translation, pronouncing the *e*-endings in the original. Are the two texts pretty much the same, or do they differ markedly, and if so, how? Does reading aloud add anything to your appreciation of the poem? Do the beat and rhythm carry the story, or are you annoyed by the singsong quality?

Does Chaucer's use of other men's stories detract from his originality as a creative writer?

With one or two exceptions, Chaucer's stories in his *Canterbury Tales* are not really Chaucer's—as far as the original idea, characters, and events are concerned. Does this make him a mere "copycat," if not a rank plagiarist? Don't we usually expect from a contemporary author an original story instead of a reworking of some hoary and hackneyed theme? What exactly is creative originality in literature? Why should Chaucer have become so famous, while some of the sources for his tales are known only to literary scholars?

The modern emphasis on originality of plot or story was absent from writers of the past, such as the Greek dramatists, the Roman poets, and the medieval and Renaissance writers. You may remember that Euripides dealt with themes that were derived from ancient myths and had been handled by his great predecessors. Virgil openly "stole" ideas and scenes from Homer and other sources, and Dante owed a lot to Homer and Virgil. Why, then, were the Greek dramatists awarded prizes, and Virgil and Dante rated so highly? Merely for felicities of style, the beautiful sound of their poetry, some elegant rhetorical niceties? Or is there original, constructive genius in their peculiar rendering and arrangement of ancient themes? Can a story idea be merely raw material, which, along with other stuff, is worked up into artistic wholeness by the shaping power of the poet? Is "invention" distinct from "creation"? Consider this statement by Sir Henry Newbolt:

> The more a writer struggles to invent the less he is likely to create. His true way is a different one; he finds his material among the accumulated stories of the race, whether ancient or modern; he sets to work to reject all that he judges unnecessary or unfit, to add all that is lacking; and finally, without effort, almost without consciousness of his power, he endows his work with his own personal quality in the act of making it serve his own purpose. (*The Poet's Craft*, A. F. Scott, p. x)

What then becomes of the primacy of plot, announced by Aristotle? Or is the "plot" of a work something more than the story line that the poet has borrowed from others? If so, what makes a plot a new creation?

SELF-TESTING QUESTIONS

The following questions are designed to help you test the thoroughness of your reading. Each question is to be answered by giving a page or pages of the reading assignment. Answers will be found on page 232 of this Reading Plan.

1 In the *Knight's Tale,* what deities intervene against Arcita, the favorite of Mars?

2 In the *Man of Law's Tale,* why is the Sultan's mother opposed to his marriage to Constance?

3 In the *Clerk's Tale,* who is the maiden whom the marquis pretends he will take as his second wife?

4 In the *Squire's Tale,* what power does the ring give to Canace?

5 In the *Franklin's Tale,* what impossible task does Dorigen impose on Aurelius as a condition for winning her love?

6 In the *Physician's Tale,* what legal fiction provides the wicked judge with the opportunity to possess the chaste Virginia?

7 In the *Monk's Tale,* what figure from Greek mythology is an example of the fall of the mighty?

Seventh Reading

RABELAIS

Gargantua and Pantagruel

Vol. 24

The term "Rabelaisian" commonly brings to mind earthiness or obscenity in speech and writing. It usually connotes ribaldry, bawdy stories, and coarse language. But the writer from whose name the term was derived was one of the titans of European literature. François Rabelais is the one French writer who has undoubtedly achieved world stature. He ranks with Dante, Shakespeare, and Goethe among the giants of modern European literature. Coleridge, the English poet and critic, classed him "with the greatest creative minds of the world."

The reason for this universal eminence and appreciation lies in his tremendous vitality, encyclopædic scope, fantastic imagination, and incredible ability with words. He liked the sound and shape and tone and color and weight of words. He liked to throw them up and play with them and see the pattern of sense and sound that resulted. He also had an irresistible, belly-shaking sense of humor and a tremendous joy in the things of this world. Rabelais celebrated human life and the human faculties—both physical and spiritual.

A true man of the Renaissance, he was passionately interested in learning in all its forms. This work, besides being a fascinating and amusing account of the wonderful deeds of the great Gargantua and Pantagruel, contains advertisements for the new learning and plans for an ideal system of education. This combination of seemingly disparate and contradictory facets of existence gives this work its remarkable quality and flavor. Serious piety accompanies mocking irreverence, tender sentiment goes with coarse sensuality, the quest for truth is interspersed with merry and sometimes cruel pranks. And yet these various elements are welded together into a vital and harmonious whole through the literary power and personal genius of this lusty and learned monk, physician, scholar, and poet, all rolled into one.

GUIDE TO

Seventh Reading

I

Like Chaucer, Rabelais worked in the vernacular of his day, and he contributed greatly to the making of the French language. But, unlike Chaucer, he had many illustrious literary contemporaries, for he wrote in the springtime of the French Renaissance. Literary historians usually consider the seventeenth century the Golden Age of French literature, the time of the "classic" French writers, such as Racine and Molière. But this classic perfection is the culmination of the tremendous literary creativity of the preceding century, the time of Rabelais, Calvin, St. Francis de Sales, Marot, Ronsard, Du Bellay, and Montaigne, the time of great and original works in all fields of literature.

One of the great achievements of these writers was the making of a language and a style that would express fully what they had to say. They took the simple, limited language that they had inherited and worked it into the rich and supple medium that became the inspiration and the model for modern French literature. It was a wonderful time for a man of literary originality and a creative sense of language to be writing. The language was not yet fixed or formalized into rules, as it was in the seventeenth century. It was changing all the time, and constantly being enriched, in both its spoken and its written forms.

Rabelais was one of the most powerful forces in giving shape to the emerging language. His contemporary Étienne Pasquier called him "the father of our idiom." Rabelais is more than the master of a style, he is the master of many styles, from the subtle and tender to mock-heroic bombast, and is so much in control of his language that he can give all his characters the dialogue exactly suited to their personalities and traits. Our translation, by Urquhart and Motteux, captures a good deal of the verve, spirit, richness, and flexibility of Rabelais's original text. It is, in its own right, so good and original a piece of writing that it is considered a masterpiece of English prose style.

Again like Chaucer, Rabelais borrowed his original idea and many of his characters from earlier writers. In 1532 there appeared a burlesque romance about King Arthur and the Knights of the Round Table, entitled *The Great and Prodigious Tales of the Great and Enormous Giant Gargantua.* Rabelais was probably the editor of this anonymous work, which was a great popular success. He apparently wrote the first book about Pantagruel (Book II of the present work) as a continuation of the earlier story. When *Pantagruel,* published in 1533, also found popular favor, Rabelais went back and wrote his own version of the tales of Gargantua, to give his Pantagruel a worthy introduction. *Gargantua,* published in 1535, became Book I of the present work.

The publishing dates of the copies now extant are not conclusive as to the order of the books, but there is internal evidence which indicates that Book I was written after Book II. In the title to Book I, notice that Gargantua is called the "father of Pantagruel" and note the reference to the work *Pantagruel* on page 1. Also, in the original text, the first book about Pantagruel is not called "the second book," but the next book is called "the third book," and the next after that "the fourth book," indicating that Rabelais decided on the numbering only after he had written *Gargantua* and made it the first book. Also Friar John, an important character in Book I, is completely absent from Book II, but suddenly reappears in Book III, to play a role through the rest of the work, indicating the probability that Books I and III were written in succession.

The names of Gargantua and Pantagruel are apparently derived from popular medieval tales about giants. Gargantua first appears in French literature in a satire published in 1526. In the anonymous Arthurian romance of 1532 appear Gargantua, Gargamelle, Grangousier, and the great mare of the present Book I. Pantagruel's companions are drawn from a work by the sixteenth-century Italian comic poet Merlino Cocai (Teofilo Folengo). Panurge, Rabelais's finest creation, is borrowed from the buffoon of Cocai's poem. Nevertheless, the characters in the work, from whatever source Rabelais borrowed them, are his own, as re-created and used for his own literary purposes.

This veteran of two monastic orders, the secular priesthood, the medical profession, and humanistic studies not only tells us fantastic and merry tales, but communicates his typical Renaissance lust for learning and the vast knowledge he possessed. When Rabelais goes into anatomical detail on the wounding and slaughter of soldiers in battle, he speaks as a skilled medical man, not as a bombastic epic poet. He makes fun of the epic poets, including Virgil, in some of his battle scenes. He also makes fun rather vigorously of scholastic logicians and pedants, theologians, monks, judges and lawyers, militarists, picayune and fantastic literary scholarship, and a great many other things. He offers pronouncements in favor of the new learning and a program of education that he considers proper to man and more wholesome than the old learning which he attacks.

Rabelais's age was the time of the Reformation as well as of the Renaissance. John Calvin was his countryman and his contemporary. This work is filled with references to the new Protestant movement and attacks on various aspects of Catholic organization and practices, particularly against the Papacy and externality in worship. But Rabelais never renounced Catholicism and never adopted Protestantism. His writings were attacked by both Catholic and Protestant authorities. As the various books of this work appeared they were regularly condemned by the Theological Faculty of the Sorbonne (the University of Paris). Both the Catholic saint Francis de Sales and the Protestant reformer John Calvin denounced his work as evil and blasphemous. Rabelais's fortunes oscillated with the state of relations between the French court and the Papacy—going up when the king was antipapal, going down when the court and the Papacy were reconciled. If Rabelais belongs to any religious party, he belongs with the

Gallican movement which insisted on the autonomy of the French Church in ecclesiastical matters and of the French court in political matters, as against the supremacy of papal authority.

II

Rabelais opens this work with a poem and a prologue which deal with its comic aspect. He pleads for the saving powers of laughter, as the quality which "is proper to the man," and begs the reader not to take offense. The poem disclaims that this book will teach us anything of value, but the prologue invites us to seek for the serious substance underneath the comic trappings. It compares the book to a Silenus, an ancient box decorated with gay mirth-provoking figures, but containing rare substances within. Don't judge a book by its cover, pleads Rabelais. Don't be

> . . . too ready to judge that there is nothing in them but jests, mockeries, lascivious discourse, and recreative lies; because the outside (which is the title) is usually, without any farther inquiry, entertained with scoffing and derision . . . you must open the book, and seriously consider of the matter treated in it. Then shall you find that it containeth things of far higher value than the box did promise; that is to say, that the subject thereof is not so foolish, as by the title at the first sight it would appear to be. (p. 2a)

There is much in the book, he admits, that corresponds with the title if we take it "in the literal sense." But he pleads with us to interpret his "ridiculous" tale "in a sublimer sense," to go for the underlying substance with the tenaciousness of a dog sucking the marrow out of a bone.

> In imitation of this dog, it becomes you to be wise to smell, feel, and have in estimation, these fair, goodly books, stuffed with high conceptions, which though seemingly easy in the pursuit, are in the cope and encounter somewhat difficult. And then, like him, you must, by a sedulous lecture, and frequent meditation, break the bone, and suck out the marrow; that is, my allegorical sense, or the things I to myself propose to be signified by these Pythagorical symbols; with assured hope, that in so doing, you will at last attain to be both well-advised and valiant by the reading of them: for, in the perusal of this treatise, you shall

find another kind of taste, and a doctrine of a more profound and abstruse consideration, which will disclose unto you the most glorious doctrines and dreadful mysteries, as well in what concerneth our religion, as matters of the public state and life economical. (p. 2b-c)

After this extravagant claim, he plunges into the tale of the great Gargantua, the father of Pantagruel. For Gargantua's genealogy we are referred to the first chapter of the first book of *Pantagruel* (Book II), with its many "begats." Here in Book I we are given an account of the great archaeological discovery of the genealogy dug up from an ancient monument along with some drinking cups. Gargantua's father is named Grangousier literally "Big Gullet," or "Glutton." Befitting the nature of a prodigious hero, Gargantua is carried in his mother's belly for eleven months and is born out of her left ear. Her overeating of tripe has made it difficult for him to come forth in the usual manner. The moment the giant baby is born, he cries for drink. Whereupon Grangousier cries out, "*Que grand tu as . . . le gousier!*" ("What a big throat you have!"). And from these first words comes his name "Gargantua." He also gets a good stiff drink to quiet him down and this form of pacifier is often used on him in his infancy: "the sounds of pints and flagons" put him in an ecstasy, and the nursemaids cheer him up by playing a tune on the mugs and bottles,

. . . at the sound whereof he became gay, did leap for joy, would loll and rock himself in the cradle, then nod with his head, monocordising with his fingers, and barytonising with his tail. (p. 10b)

Tremendous quantities of cloth are needed to clothe Gargantua and his various members fittingly. His colors are white and blue—white for joy and blue for faith. Here Rabelais has fun with "experts" who dogmatically lay down the law on the meaning of colors, and he rails against the presumptuous arrogance that dares to prescribe "without reason, without cause, or without any appearance of truth," by mere "private authority." He ridicules the whole conventional symbolism of heraldry.

By the same reasons . . . might I cause paint a pannier, to signify that I am in pain—a mustard-pot, that my heart tarries much for it—one

> pissing upwards for a bishop—the bottom of a pair of breeches for a vessel full of farthings—a codpiece for the office of the clerks of the sentences, decrees or judgments, or rather, (as the English bears it,) for the tail of a cod-fish—and a dog's turd, for the dainty turret, wherein lies the heart of my sweetheart. (p. 12c)

Then he proceeds to expound what the colors white and blue mean by a combination of ridiculous formal logic and phony scholarship.

This preliminary portion of Book I takes up the first ten chapters. Chapters 11-24 deal with Gargantua's upbringing and education. Chapter 11 includes a wonderful piece on the natural life of the child from three to five, that is far more eloquent and graphic than Spock or Gesell. Young Gargantua invents a new type of "torchecul," or toilet paper, that signals to his father his precocious intelligence. Thereupon, Grangousier hires tutors to teach him his ABC's, Latin, and other subjects. These "sophisters" dull his mind with dreary texts of scholastic and sermonic literature. Gargantua is put to shame by a pageboy trained in the new learning, and Grangousier thereupon sends him to Paris with the pageboy's tutor, Ponocrates, to get a real education.

Gargantua rides to Paris on "the most hideous great mare that was ever seen, and of the strangest form." Among his exploits in Paris are his stealing of the great bells from the towers of Notre Dame Cathedral to use as jingle bells around his mare's neck. When a dull academic doctor, accompanied by half a dozen artless masters of the arts, arrives to argue for the recovery of the bells, Gargantua gets them drunk and the foolish doctor delivers his harangue before the town officials, invited by Gargantua to see the performance. A suit at law by the doctor to recover sausages and breeches promised to him by the University of Paris, in payment for his oratory, provides sidesplitting ridicule of contemporary litigation.

Chapters 22-24 give us a picture of the old and the new in education, and are inspired by the Renaissance ideal of the many-sided man. Ponocrates starts out by having Gargantua proceed in the way his old instructors had taught him, in order to find out how he has become such an ignorant lout.

The boy arises late in the morning, remains unkempt and unwashed, starts the day by drinking copiously, and eats tremendous meals. His religious acts are extravagant and mechanical, mere formal rote and display. His study consists of a half-hour of distracted reading in the morning and another short time in the afternoon. Most of the afternoon is spent in playing all kinds of games (hundreds of them are listed in Chapter 22). The rest of the afternoon consists of drinking and sleeping. After supper there are more gaming and supper parties. And so to bed.

Ponocrates decides to change Gargantua's "vicious manner of living," but proceeds gently and indirectly, in order not to harm him through a sudden and violent change. A drug purges his brain of its perverted habits and makes him forget all he has learned from his former teachers. Then association with learned men inspires in him the desire to imitate them through study and self-improvement. Now he is ready to submit to the new regimen that Ponocrates imposes on him.

Up at 4:00 A.M., he begins his day with Scripture reading and prayer. Every moment is filled wisely. Readings and previous lessons are expounded while he goes through his early morning excretion, washing, and dressing. Then he is lectured or read to for three hours. Following that, comes morning athletics—tennis, handball, or catch—until he has worked up a sweat and feels like quitting. Then comes a good lunch, accompanied by a pleasant story of ancient valor and a merry conversation about the nature and properties of all the foods served, with citations from various scientific works, which were often brought to the table to be consulted. He also learns mathematics from card games and geometrical drawings after the meal. Then comes singing and the playing of musical instruments. Now with the digestion of the meal well begun, he applies himself to three hours of solid study.

This long period of mental labor is followed by physical exercise, which includes horsemanship, various military arts, hunting, jumping, swimming, boating, running up and down hills, tree-climbing, rope-climbing, weight-lifting, and other activities. On the way back from the exercise field, he observes trees and plants, compares them with what various ancient authorities have said about them, and brings home specimens for further study. A hearty meal follows, accompanied by reading and conversation. Then come games, music, and juggling tricks—a merry time before going to bed. Before retiring he and Ponocrates go out to observe the heavens, recapitulate all that has been learned and observed during the day, and, finally, praying to God in gratitude and hope, they go to bed.

Even the rainy or intemperate days are filled. Instead of outdoor exercise, Gargantua works in the barn bundling hay or chopping wood. He visits the various workshops and learns how the mechanical crafts are practiced; he also observes the druggists, to learn the pharmaceutical arts. He listens to lectures, arguments, and sermons, to learn rhetoric.

It is a hard regimen, but Gargantua gets used to it and grows to enjoy it.

> Which, although at the beginning it seemed difficult, became a little after so sweet, so easy, and so delightful, that it seemed rather the recreation of a king than the study of a scholar. (p. 30b)

But Ponocrates knows that all work and no play will make Gargantua a dull boy. So once a month they take a vacation from books and go to some nearby country town to spend the day just having fun. But even then, they quote relevant lines from the ancient poets or experiment in separating the wine from the water, as taught by Cato and Pliny. Even this time of recreation is not completely unprofitable for learning and study. Such is Ponocrates' post-scholastic program of education—the wholesome "after" replacing the horrible "before."

Almost all the rest of Book I is concerned with the war between Gargantua's countrymen and the people of Lerné. Here again Rabelais ridicules stupid and vicious practices, sanctioned by custom and tradition, and points to a more rational and humane mode of behavior. The war starts over some silly dispute between the bakers of Lerné and the shepherds of Gargantua's land over the purchase of some cakes. Picrochole, the king of Lerné, in a fit of rage over the battering his bakers have taken, dispatches his forces into Grangousier's domain, where they pillage their unprepared neighbors unmercifully. Only the redoubtable Friar John of Sevillé beats them back—he kills 13,622 singlehanded (not counting the women and children).

Grangousier is distressed at this sudden and unprovoked attack, but determined not to go to war until every attempt to make peace has failed. In an expressive letter to his son Gargantua, urging him to come to the aid of his people, he states his ends and means in this conflict.

> My deliberation is not to provoke, but to appease—not to assault, but to defend—not to conquer, but to preserve my faithful subjects and hereditary dominions, into which Picrochole is entered in a hostile manner without any ground or cause. . . The exploit shall be done with as little effusion of blood as may be. And, if possible, by means far more expedient, such as military policy, devices and stratagems of war, we shall save all the souls, and send them home as merry as crickets unto their own houses. (p. 36a-c)

But Grangousier is unable to abate Picrochole's "pugnative choler" by the most courteous and generous gestures. The only way to peace now is through "sharp and fierce wars." Picrochole's advisers swell his ego with pictures of world conquest that, so they say, now lies open before him.

Meanwhile Gargantua, with his squire Gymnast, rides to the rescue. His marvelous mare drowns a corps of the enemy forces by urinating and flooding the countryside. When the enemy cannon shoots at him, the cannon balls bounce off him; he thinks they are grape seeds, and regards the bullets as annoying flies. He finally disposes of the enemy stronghold with a few swipes of a great tree which he is using as a lance. When he later combs his hair, the cannon balls fall out, and his father mistakes them for lice, picked up at a notoriously filthy college of Rabelais's time.

Gargantua, accompanied by the lusty Friar John, leads a picked force of knights and gunners against Picrochole. They score a speedy and complete victory over the vanguard of Picrochole's forces. Grangousier tells an officer prisoner his war aims and his philosophy of war and peace. Conquering a neighboring kingdom, he says, is now considered "robbing, thievery, and wickedness," not a sign of valor and strength. When neighbor takes up arms against neighbor, this is not war but sedition, as Plato pointed out in *The Republic.* There has been no real ground for war, and the trivial occasion that started the conflict can be settled by good will on both sides. Grangousier sends the officer away with many gifts to transmit this message to his king, but Picrochole remains adamant.

In the next battle, Gargantua leads his father's army to a final victory over the enemy, and addresses the vanquished in his father's spirit. Gargantua appeals to the example of his forefathers, who have preferred to build monuments in conquered men's hearts through clemency rather than erect victory memorials of stone in the conquered lands. Liberality to a man of reason, when you have him down, is remembered with gratefulness for a long time to come. Hence, he will free all the prisoners, give them three months' pay, and see that they are escorted safely out of the country. Since Picrochole has fled and his heir is only five years old, he will appoint Ponocrates as viceroy to administer the country until the child comes of age. However, the war criminals—those who started the war and egged Picrochole on—shall be held and punished.

The last chapters of Book I (Ch. 52-58) concern the utopian community of Theleme, which Gargantua builds as a reward for Friar John's services. It is to be a unique religious order—without walls, comprising both sexes, and without set hours and required duties. As against the traditional vows of chastity, poverty, and obedience, members would be allowed to marry, to have wealth, and to do as they willed. Only whole, comely, and well-dispositioned men and women were to be admitted. Beautiful and elaborate abbey buildings are built and on the gate is inscribed a long poem, forbidding entry to all vile persons and welcoming joyous, life-loving, truthful, courteous persons. The abbey contains both well-stocked libraries and facilities for all kinds of athletics and recreation. Both the men and women are richly appareled and suit their clothes to match one another.

There is only one rule at the Abbey of Theleme: DO WHAT THOU WILT.

> All their life was spent not in laws, statutes, or rules, but according to their own free will and pleasure. They rose out of their beds when they thought good: they did eat, drink, labour, sleep, when they had a mind to it, and were disposed for it. None did awake them, none did offer to constrain them to eat, drink, nor to do any other thing; for so had Gargantua established it. (p. 65c)

The reason given is that men are inclined naturally to virtue, and that freedom opens the way to virtue, while constraint arouses the perverse desire to do what is forbidden. The spur of virtue is that noble disposition, honor, not "base subjection and constraint."

III

In Book II, Pantagruel duplicates many of the educational and military experiences of his father, Gargantua. As we have pointed out, if literary scholarship is right, this book was written first, and Pantagruel is the model for Gargantua. Book II starts out with the ancient genealogy which we were promised in Book I. The origin of the race of Gargantua and Pantagruel came at a remarkable time when there was no March in Lent and the middle of August was in May. In this marvelous and portentous time the members of men's bodies grew to enormous size. From those who grew in length of body came the giants, the ancestors of Gargantua and Pantagruel. The first was Chalbroth, who, through a series of fifty-nine "begats," eventuated in Gargantua and Pantagruel.

"The Nativity of the most dread and redoubted Pantagruel" takes place when his father is 524 years old, and comes at a time of catastrophic drought. Hence the name "Pantagruel," meaning All-Thirsty, signifies both the contemporary drought and Pantagruel's future lordship over the thirsty world. Pantagruel is born as hairy as a bear, which prompts a prophecy of the wonders he will accomplish. Unfortunately, the first thing he does is to kill his mother by being born, being "so wonderfully great and lumpish" that he could not emerge "without thus suffocating his mother." There follows, in Chapter 3, a lovely, tender, humorous mixture of sorrow and joy, as Gargantua contemplates his dead wife and his newborn son.

> When Pantagruel was born, there was none more astonished and per-

plexed than was his father Gargantua; for, of the one side, seeing his wife Badebec dead, and on the other side his son Pantagruel born, so fair and so great, he knew not what to say, nor what to do. And the doubt that troubled his brain was to know whether he should cry for the death of his wife, or laugh for the joy of his son. . . Shall I weep? said he. Yes, for why? My so good wife is dead, who was the most this, the most that, that was ever in the world. Never shall I see her, never shall I recover such another, it is unto me an inestimable loss! O my good God, what had I done that thou shouldest thus punish me? Why didst thou not take me away before her? Seeing for me to live without her is but to languish. Ah Badebec, Badebec, my minion, my dear heart, my sugar, my sweeting, my honey, my little coney,—yet it had in circumference full six acres, three rods, five poles, four yards, two feet, one inch and a half of good woodland measure,—my tender peggy, my codpiece darling, my bob and hit, my slip-shoe-lovie, never shall I see thee! . . .

With these words he did cry like a cow; but on a sudden fell a laughing like a calf, when Pantagruel came into his mind. Ha, my little son, said he, my childilolly, fedlifondy, dandlichucky, my ballocky, my pretty rogue! O how jolly thou art, and how much I am bound to my gracious God, that hath been pleased to bestow on me a son, so fair, so spriteful, so lively, so smiling, so pleasant, and so gentle! Ho, ho, ho, ho, how glad I am! Let us drink, ho, and put away melancholy! . . .

As he spake this, he heard the litanies and the *mementos* of the priests that carried his wife to be buried, upon which he left the good purpose he was in, and was suddenly ravished another way, saying, Lord God, must I again contrist myself? This grieves me. I am no longer young, I grow old, the weather is dangerous; I may perhaps take an ague, then shall I be foiled, if not quite undone. By the faith of a gentleman, it were better to cry less, and drink more. My wife is dead, well, by G—, (*da jurandi*) I shall not raise her again by my crying: she is well, she is in Paradise, at least, if she be no higher: she prayeth to God for us, she is happy, she is above the sense of our miseries, nor can our calamities reach her. What though she be dead, must not we also die? The same debt which she hath paid, hangs over our heads; nature will require it of us, and we must all of us some day taste of the same sauce. Let her pass then, and the Lord preserve the survivors; for I must now cast about how to get another wife. (pp. 73b-74a)

Pantagruel's infancy is quite remarkable, far surpassing the fabled feats of Hercules. It takes 4,600 cows to supply him with milk for one meal. Giving him a cow to suck on turns out to be a bad idea. He tears the poor creature apart and eats up a good share of it before his elders rescue it. Cable ropes and iron chains cannot bind him, so great is his strength.

Pantagruel's adolescence is spent wandering through various schools and universities and having fun. Tennis courts and brothels, as well as faculties of law and medicine, are included in his itinerary. "As for breaking his head with over much study, he had an especial care not to do it . . . for fear of spoiling his eyes" (p. 77a). However, at the University of Paris he studies the seven liberal arts industriously, for he is possessed of an excellent understanding and a remarkable memory. It is here that he receives a letter from his father proclaiming the light of the new learning and the desirable educational program. (See Ch. 8.)

In this remarkable father-to-son letter, Gargantua says it is his dream to have his son become "completely well bred and accomplished, as well in virtue, honesty and valour, as in all liberal knowledge and civility," a worthy representative of his father's immortality. Pantagruel, he says, has the advantage of living in an enlightened age. Gargantua's own youth was a time that

> . . . was darksome, obscured with clouds of ignorance, and savouring a little of the infelicity and calamity of the Goths, who had, wherever they set footing, destroyed all good literature, which in my age hath by the divine goodness been restored unto its former light and dignity, and that with such amendment and increase of knowledge, that now hardly should I be admitted unto the first form of the little grammar-school boys. . .
>
> Now it is, that the minds of men are qualified with all manner of discipline and the old sciences revived, which for many ages were extinct. Now it is, that the learned languages are to their pristine purity restored, *viz.*, Greek, without which a man may be ashamed to account himself a scholar, Hebrew, Arabic, Chaldæan, and Latin. Printing likewise is now in use, so elegant and so correct, that better cannot be imagined, although it was found out but in my time by divine inspiration, as by a diabolical suggestion on the other side, was the invention of ordnance. All the world is full of knowing men, of most learned schoolmasters, and vast libraries; and it appears to me as a truth, that neither in Plato's time, nor Cicero's, nor Papinian's, there was ever such conveniency for studying, as we see at this day there is. Nor must any adventure henceforward to come in public or present himself in company, that hath not been pretty well polished in the shop of Minerva. I see robbers, hangmen, free-booters, tapsters, ostlers, and such like, of the very rubbish of the people, more learned now than the doctors and preachers were in my time. (pp. 81d-82b)

Gargantua himself is learning Greek in his old age. He advises his son to learn the ancient languages (Greek, Latin, Hebrew, Chaldean, and Arabic) perfectly, as well as history, the liberal arts of geometry, arithmetic and music, astronomy, civil law, philosophy, the natural sciences, medicine, and the Bible in its original languages. He advises Pantagruel to become a "bottomless pit of knowledge" now in his youth while he still has time to study, for he will soon have to learn the military arts and assume mature responsibilities. He cautions him to love and serve and fear God, for "knowledge without conscience is but the ruin of the soul." He must set his heart on Heaven, not on worldly things, and serve and love his neighbor, and fulfill the gifts which God bestowed on him. When he has learned all there is to learn in Paris, he is to return to his father for his blessing before he dies. The letter is datelined Utopia, the name of Gargantua's country.

Taking seriously the suggestion of his father that he test his knowledge in public debate, Pantagruel takes on and bests the foremost humanists, theologians, and legal scholars of Paris, and so acquires city-wide fame. At this time the most learned judges in the land are baffled by the abstruse questions involved in the lawsuit between Lord Kissbreech and Lord Suckfist, and they call on Pantagruel to help them out. The latter goes to the heart of the matter, brushing aside paper work and technicalities.

> But Pantagruel said unto them, Are the two lords, between whom this debate and process is, yet living? It was answered him, Yes. To what a devil, then, said he, serve so many paltry heaps, and bundles of papers and copies which you give me? Is it not better to hear their controversy from their own mouths, whilst they are face to face before us, than to read these vile fopperies, which are nothing but trumperies, deceits, diabolical cozenages of Cepola, pernicious slights and subversions of equity? For I am sure, that you, and all those through whose hands this process hath past, have by your devices added what you could to it *pro et contra* in such sort, that, although their difference perhaps was clear and easy enough to determine at first, you have obscured it, and made it more intricate, by the frivolous, sottish, unreasonable and foolish reasons and opinions of [various ignorant authorities]. . . (p. 86c-d)

He does not favor unlearned ignorance in applying the law.

On the contrary, he insists that knowledge of Greek and Latin, of moral and natural philosophy, and of antiquities and history is necessary to understand the laws. But the plaintiff and defendant involved must be heard from personally in this matter, and "these records, bills of inquests, replies, rejoinders, exceptions, depositions, and other such diableries of truth-intangling writs" only work against justice and prolong the case. Hence, burn them and bring forth the contending parties.

The Lords Kissbreech and Suckfist present their cases through two whole chapters, and, like the assembled judges and jurisconsults, the reader may say, "We have indeed heard it, but have not understood the devil so much as one circumstance of the case." But the great Pantagruel does, and he renders the judgment of a Solomon which satisfies both parties, a most wondrous conclusion which has not happened since the Flood, nor is likely to "occur in thirteen jubilees hereafter." The assembled counselors and jurisconsults are so rapt in admiration at the superhuman wisdom of Pantagruel that they have to be awakened from their trance by vinegar and rose water. When the admiring citizens offer to bestow the offices of Master of the Requests and President of the Court on Pantagruel, he graciously refuses on the ground that he might become a slave to office, incur corruption, and fail of salvation. He requests instead a few barrels of the best wine in town.

Chapters 14-22 of Book II are concerned with the amazing exploits of that remarkable, scandalous, amusing, terrible rascal Panurge, Pantagruel's crony, "whom he loved all his life-time." When Pantagruel first encounters him (in Chapter 9), he is in a bad way, looking as wounded and tattered as if he had been in a dogfight. But his face and body are so obviously noble and handsome that Pantagruel is anxious to hear from him about his misadventures. Panurge answers him in German, Italian, English, Basque, Dutch, Spanish, Danish, Hebrew, Greek, Latin, and a few nonsense languages, the import of all of which is "For God's sake, give me something to eat!" It turns out that he is a Frenchman, just back from a remarkable escape from the Turks. The narrator signals

Panurge's extraordinary "qualities and conditions" in this paragraph.

Panurge was of a middle stature, not too high nor too low, and had somewhat an aquiline nose, made like the handle of a razor. He was at that time five and thirty years old, or thereabouts, fine to gild like a leaden dagger,—for he was a notable cheater and cony-catcher,—he was a very gallant and proper man of his person, only that he was a little lecherous, and naturally subject to a kind of disease, which at that time they called lack of money,—it is an incomparable grief, yet, notwithstanding, he had threescore and three tricks to come by it at his need, of which the most honourable and most ordinary was in manner of thieving, secret purloining, and filching, for he was a wicked lewd rogue, a cozener, drinker, roysterer, rover, and a very dissolute and debauched fellow, if there were any in Paris; otherwise, and in all matters else, the best and most virtuous man in the world; and he was still contriving some plot, and devising mischief against the serjeants and the watch. (p. 97b-c)

In the twenty-six pockets of his coat he carries full equipment for his various misdeeds and practical jokes. This includes a knife to cut purses, a smarting substance to throw in people's eyes, itching powders, burning glasses, ridiculous and obscene objects to stick on people's clothes, and a picklock, a pelican, a cramp iron and other tools to break doors and coffers open. This prince of rogues makes a small fortune bestowing pennies on the pardoners who hawk their heavenly wares on the porches of the Paris churches. What he gives with one hand he filches back manyfold with the other from the pardoners' cashboxes. After all, he pleads, the pardoners say, "You will receive back a hundredfold." He claims to have made a large fortune in a papal crusade and spent it all on various pranks. "He had . . . threescore and three ways to acquire money, but he had two hundred and fourteen to spend it, besides his drinking," the author observes. When Pantagruel questions the purpose of this prodigal expenditure, Panurge replies:

My friend . . . thou hast no pastime at all in this world. I have more than the king, and if thou wilt join thyself with me, we will do the devil together. No, no, said I, by St. Adauras, that will I not, for thou wilt be hanged one time or other. And thou, said he, wilt be interred some time or other. Now, which is most honourable, the air or the earth? Ho, grosse pecore! (p. 101a)

Panurge turns out to be a redoubtable debater as well as a skilled filcher and coarse prankster. In an uproarious scene he bests a great English scholar in a debate held in sign language.

As in Book I, the latter part of Book II is taken up with a war. Gargantua has been "translated," or borne away, to Fairyland, and the neighboring Dipsodes immediately invade the land of Utopia. Pantagruel is called back to aid his country, like his father before him. He too accomplishes great exploits. Like his father's mare, Pantagruel floods the countryside by emptying his bladder. He wins the decisive victory when he beats Loupgarou (Werewolf), the leader of the three hundred enemy giants, in a man-to-man battle. Loupgarou is armed with a mace that weighs a thousand tons and is enchanted so that it will never break but will break anything it touches, and his armor is made of Cyclopean anvils. Pantagruel, armed only with the mast of a ship, sends up a sincere prayer to heaven for protection, promising purification of the Christian faith in gratitude. Whereupon a voice from heaven responds approvingly. A tremendous struggle ensues, and finally Pantagruel uses the fallen leader as a weapon against his stone-armored followers who come to his rescue. The iron-clad leader makes an excellent battering ram against the stone and slate of his followers. In the end they are all killed. Pantagruel relieves the besieged city of the Amaurots, and invades Dipsody and puts it under his rule.

Not to be outdone by the great epic poets before him, Rabelais, too, gives us a picture of the underworld and the afterlife, in Chapter 30 of Book II. In the struggle with the Dipsode giants, Pantagruel's tutor, Epistemon, is found stark dead with his head in his arms. Laments in the grand epic style resound: "Ah, cruel death! hast thou taken from me the perfectest amongst men?" Pantagruel displays "the greatest grief that ever any man did see." But the ever-resourceful Panurge patches Epistemon together again, with the aid of some dubious drugs and a fine suturing of head and neck together. Epistemon is fully resuscitated, as evidenced by various vital noises he makes, and his only reminder of the mishap is a dry cough which he has to treat with continual drinking for a few weeks.

This Lazarus returned from the dead has quite a tale to tell of the nether regions. They have a nice place down there, and the devils are fine fellows, he asserts. There is, however, a turnabout of status between this life and the next. The great ones of the earth—the monarchs, the warlords, the prelates, and the heroes—are assigned menial occupations in Hell. On the other hand, philosophers and other needy persons in this life are great lords down there. Alexander the Great ekes out a bare existence mending breeches and stockings, while Diogenes and Epictetus are wealthy, magnificently appareled, and having a wonderful time. François Villon, who was a beggar on earth, heaps indignities on Xerxes the Great, who is a mustard hawker in Hell. There are many popes down there, including Dante's enemy Boniface VIII, and they get rather hard treatment. The poet Jean Le Maire impersonates the Pope, and while the former kings and popes kiss his feet, he gives them his benediction, pardons, and a dispensation to be good for nothing. His papal "bulls" are the cracks of a bullwhip across the suppliants' backs. In a picture worthy of Dante, the usurers go around hunting old pins and nails, but ironware is of such low value that they are lucky to earn a crust of bread once in three weeks. They keep on, in hopes of gaining a "scurvy penny" by the end of the year.

IV

The main theme of Book III is Panurge's decision to get married, or rather his decision to consult other people on whether he should get married. This gives Rabelais the opportunity for all kinds of humor, both rough and gentle, at the expense of various professions, institutions, modes of thought, and human foibles. It involves a fantastic discussion of marriage and the nature of women, and an inordinate fear on Panurge's part lest in getting married he become a cuckold.

As the book opens, Dipsody has been colonized by

9,876,543,210 Utopians (not counting women and children, of course) under the leadership of the illustrious Pantagruel. The latter binds the newly conquered land to his rule through love and justice, not through tyrannical oppression. Panurge becomes Laird of Salmygondin in the new domain, with a tremendous income which he proceeds speedily to dissipate. When upbraided by Pantagruel he delivers a hilarious, ingenious defense of spendthriftry. (See Ch. 2-5.)

When he tells Pantagruel that he has decided to get married, his friend tells him to go ahead, but that is not enough for Panurge. He wants assurance from Pantagruel against the various contingencies that a man may incur in getting married—such as being cuckolded, beaten, or robbed by his wife. Dissatisfied with Pantagruel's answers, Panurge consults various authorities for the answer to his burning question. First, he tries the device of selecting passages in Virgil's works at random. This does not work out, because whatever Pantagruel interprets as being unfavorable, Panurge interprets as favorable to his proposed marital enterprise. Next, the would-be bridegroom seeks an oracle in dream interpretation, but again there is a wide discrepancy between his interpretation and Pantagruel's. For instance, horns in the forehead are for Pantagruel the obvious sign of a cuckold, but for Panurge they are the signs of plenty—a good omen. A try at the Sibyl of Panzoust, an oracular hag in the classical tradition, results in the same clash of interpretations between Pantagruel and Panurge. A very funny consultation with a deaf-mute who talks only the "natural" language of signs reveals to Pantagruel that Panurge will be married, cuckolded, beaten, and robbed, but to Panurge only that he will be married.

Panurge keeps on trying to get the right answer. He seeks advice or good omens from a poet, an astrologer, a theologian, a physician, a lawyer, and a philosopher without attaining certainty. The most frustrating discourse of all is with the philosopher, who is an Ephectic (a man who continually suspends judgment) and a Pyrrhonian (a skeptic). Try as he may, Panurge cannot get a straight answer from him. Next, Panurge seeks counsel from the wisdom of a fool, but again the fool's cryptic utterance and acts are interpreted differently by Pantagruel and Panurge. But a gesture of the fool's, handing Panurge an empty wine bottle, leads to the quest for the Oracle of the Holy Bottle, which takes up the rest of the work.

Pantagruel leads a party composed of Panurge, the tutor Epistemon, the doughty Friar John (abbot of Theleme), the explorer Xenomanes, and others of the royal house to Sammalo (St. Malo in Brittany). Here Pantagruel gathers a fleet, crews, and provisions in preparations for the voyage to the Holy Bottle. He takes along the herb Pantagruelion, which is apparently hemp, since its most celebrated application is in the hanging of criminals. The closing chapters of Book III are devoted to a recital of the herb's many marvelous and useful applications.

V

Book IV recounts the early portion of Pantagruel's voyage in search of "the oracle of Bacbuc, alias the Holy Bottle." This narrative has the interest of any tale of a voyage to far-off and fantastic places. In addition, it is a satire on various social institutions and modes of thought. For instance, in Chapter 9, Pantagruel and his party land on the island of Ennasin ("the cut-off noses"), where the inhabitants all have noses shaped like the ace of clubs. The Ennasins are all related to one another in such complicated ways that the usual terms to distinguish parents and children, brothers and sisters, and so on cannot be used. "We have here neither father nor mother," the mayor boasts. Rabelais has a lot of fun with the terms the Ennasins do use for one another, such as "hatchet," "slipper," and "currycomb." Rabelais may be spoofing Plato's ideal republic, or utopian writers in general.

Pantagruel also visits the land of Pettifogging, inhabited by pettifoggers and catchpoles (shysters and bailiffs), "rogues that will hang their father for a groat." (See Ch. 12-16.) The catchpoles earn a living by being beaten by the person they serve summons on. Both the summoners and the summoned pay them for their pains. As a commentary on the legal profession, this belongs with the portrait of Judge Bridlegoose, the judge who decides cases by rolling dice, in Chapters 39-44 of Book III. The Papacy figures as the butt of Rabelais's satire in the visit to the islands of Pope-Figland and Papimany. (See Ch. 45-54.) The Pope-figs are so named because once upon a time one of them said, "A fig for it," at the sight of the Pope's picture in a festival on Papimany. The Papimaniacs, so named because of their idolatry for the Pope, were so incensed that they attacked Pope-Figland and made it their tributary, and reduced the inhabitants to wretched slavery.

In Papimany, Pantagruel and his party are greeted immediately by the question, "Have you seen him?"—"him" being further defined as "the god on earth," that is, the Pope. When Panurge announces that he has seen the Pope, a public holiday is called, and the adoring islanders throng around the blessed persons who have seen the Pope: "O thrice and four times happy people!" Most of the chapters on Papimany are devoted to the Uranopet Decretals (heaven-sent papal decrees), which are kept in a holy of holies and revered as written by the angels and sent down from heaven. The Bishop of Papimany praises the miraculous and edifying powers of the decretals, while Panurge and his comrades ribaldly deny them, from knowledge of the decretals they have known at home. The Bishop expresses great eagerness to crush and burn the "heretical Protestants," and gratification at the worldly power and pomp that is the reward of the official interpreters of the decretals.

In addition to this invidious satire, there are many passages of pure humor and interesting narrative. Such is the story of Dingdong and Panurge, with its authentic characterization and dialogue, biting humor, and cruel denouement (Ch. 6-8); the account of the violent storm and Panurge's terror (Ch. 18-24); the island of the Macreons, where dwell the souls of heroes (Ch. 25-28); the peculiar qualities of King Shrovetide on Sneaking Island (Ch. 29-32); the discovery and hunting of the whale off Wild Island (Ch. 33-34); the encounter with the Chitterlings, including the palaver with the colonels Maul-Chitterling and Cut-Pudding (Ch. 35-42); the Island of Ruach (Wind or Breath), where wind is food (Ch. 43-44); the thawed and frozen words (Ch. 55-56); and finally Master Gaster (Stomach or

Belly), the first master of arts in the world (Ch. 57-62).

This Master Gaster is indeed an imperious master who cannot be disobeyed, the word of the belly is law to all the other members, and all human action and the origin of the arts follow from the demands of the belly. Two kinds of courtiers surround "the master of ingenuity"—the Engastrimythes (ventriloquists) and the Gastrolaters (belly-worshipers). The latter offer viands and drink to a monstrous statue, with eyes bigger than its belly and a head larger than the rest of the body, a powerful jaw and strong teeth. Their creed is summed up by a character of Euripides: "I only sacrifice to myself (not to the gods) and to this belly of mine, the greatest of the gods" (p. 301a).

In Book V, which we do not include in *Great Books of the Western World,* Pantagruel finally reaches the oracle of the Bottle, which says one word, "Trinq" (Drink). The priestess Bacbuc explains that man is a wine-drinking animal, and gains truth through wine. The book ends with a note of praise on man's quest for knowledge of what lies hidden from obvious view and requires all future time to discover.

VI

For most people, the term "Rabelaisian" does not connote the fantastic adventures, social satire, cultural interests, and reforming spirit summarized above, but, rather, a frank and coarse handling of man's excretory functions and sexual activities. This common connotation is partly correct, for this kind of thing runs through the whole book, even in some of the most "elevated" passages, and seems essential to Rabelais's literary person and character. He does not merely mention these things in passing, or deal with them in correct, painstaking, "realistic" fashion, with the idea of making an authentic description of human life. He dwells on these things at great length, devotes all his wonderful humor, gusto, verbal power, imagination, and extreme exaggeration to the affairs of the toilet and the sexual embrace. And Rabelais was never the man to call a spade a garden implement—he does not use such euphemistic terms as "toilet" and "sexual embrace."

Urquhart and Motteux, and all other honest translators, have given us the Anglo-Saxon equivalents of Rabelais's earthy French original.

Now as to the matter of offense. Undoubtedly, many of us will be shocked, offended, and repelled by some of the passages in this work. We have to go back to Aristophanes to find anything like this, and even Chaucer may seem decorous and pure in comparison. But the situation is not quite the same as it was in the era when George Saintsbury wrote of Rabelais that "The general taste having been considerably refined since [the sixteenth century], Rabelais has in part become nearly unreadable." In a time when James Joyce is required reading in college English courses, D. H. Lawrence is read by millions of paperback readers, and writers like James Jones and Norman Mailer are best sellers, we are not likely to consider Rabelais unreadable because of his coarse language and subject matter. And not only "the times" are involved, for Rabelais was charged with obscenity as well as impiety in his own time. Of course, given the general coarseness of French popular literature in the Middle Ages and early Renaissance, Rabelais's earthiness must have been more acceptable to the general public in his time than in Victorian England or even present-day America. Whether Rabelais is indecent by some absolute standard is another matter, and open for discussion. (See the Guides to Aristophanes and Chaucer above.)

Saintsbury distinguished between Rabelais's open coarseness and the "refined voluptuousness" and "sniggering indecency" of certain other writers. We should also note the joy, the humor, the superabundant vitality that is communicated in these, as in other passages of Rabelais. Many of us may be grossly offended by certain passages, but once we start to laugh, it will be hard to stop, and hard to stop reading the passage in question. (So serious a critic as John Calvin discerned the effectiveness that Rabelais commanded through his comic power. He decried writers like Rabelais as "curs who assume the attitudes of comedy in order to enjoy greater freedom to vomit their blasphemies.")

See for instance Gargantua's invention of a new kind of toilet paper (Book I, Ch. 13); the great feats of urination by Gargantua, his mare, and Pantagruel (Book I, Ch. 17, 36; Book II, Ch. 28); Panurge's wooing of the lady of Paris (Book II, Ch. 21-22); the various rhapsodies to that strange and now obsolete piece of clothing, the codpiece; Panurge's quest for an assurance of a safe and sure marriage (Book III). As in Aristophanes, the male genital organ, the universal and obvious representative of the generative act and power, is frequently alluded to, described, and glorified.

VII

How do the seriousness and the foolery fit together in this work?

The question whether Rabelais is mainly interested in buffoonery, or in serious things such as education and social reform, has bothered many generations of readers and critics. Many people think that the buffoonery and the seriousness are two separate and incompatible elements of the work. Some of them think that Rabelais was interested in getting over a serious message, and threw in all the humor and ribaldry as sugar-coating to attract readers. Do Rabelais's introductory comments support this contention? Does he say anything elsewhere to deny it? Does he or does he not want us to seek for deep meanings in his extravaganza?

Other readers and critics think that Rabelais's main interest was in giving enjoyment through fascinating and uproariously funny stories, and that he put in the serious stuff just for the sake of respectability, or because of his disorderly and undisciplined mind or the unformed taste of the time. Does this seem more likely to you than the other hypothesis? Does this explain why Rabelais throws everything but the kitchen sink—all the known arts, sciences, and literatures of his time—into a fantastic and merry fiction?

Is Rabelais's main purpose entertainment or edification? Or is it both? How can that be? Does this mean that Rabelais and his work are confused and contradictory? Or is there something about imaginative literature, and the human faculties that produce it, which permits such various things to be fused into a unified whole? Does the combination of serious and comical elements disturb you in your reading? Do you think Rabelais presented his serious views in this comic masterpiece in order to escape persecution for unorthodox views?

Is Rabelais a good storyteller?

Is *Gargantua and Pantagruel* well plotted in the conventional or classical sense? Does the plot of the work, or the plot of each of the separate books, follow a definite order through a conflict or set of conflicts to a settlement? Or is it loose and easygoing, proceeding according to Rabelais's mood and what he feels like putting in? Do you think he plotted his story in advance? Do you like the way Rabelais proceeds? Why or why not?

What about the characters? Do they stand out as distinct, identifiable individuals? Are the two leading characters clear in your mind? Very often Rabelais seems to forget that they are giants, and they act and behave like men of normal size. Does this disturb your appreciation of the story? What about their various tutors and hangers-on? Do you remember them all clearly? Are Panurge, Friar John, Epistemon, and others consistent characters throughout the work? Is consistency necessary or desirable in literary characters? Does Rabelais use dialogue successfully to distinguish the characters, or does he have them all talking the same way? Are Rabelais's characters types rather than individuals?

What are the qualities of the English prose style in this translation?

Leaving aside the dialogues, catalogues, and parodies of other styles, what would you say are the main characteristics of the English used in this translation? Are the sentences longer than those found nowadays in expository writing? Are they more complicated or simpler than contemporary sentences? Are the words and terms more abstract or more concrete than the common written style today?

Try translating some of these passages into good, standard, mid-twentieth-century English. Which style has the most tone, color, vigor, and impact? Are our sentence rhythms more even and smoother than Urquhart's? Which is closer to speech rhythms? Try reading Rabelais aloud. Does it read well? Is it a pleasure to read aloud—in mixed or unmixed company? Which of the following modern American writers are closest to this kind of writing and which are furthest away: Thomas Wolfe, Ernest Hemingway, F. Scott Fitzgerald, and Saul Bellow?

What does Rabelais have to say about human love?

There is a lot of talk about sexual activity in this book. But what about love in the sense that transcends physical pleasure? Does Panurge express *love* for the Parisian lady? Does he seek a wife for the sake of mutual love? Are there any tender feelings for women expressed in this work? Does Rabelais have a very high opinion of womankind?

What of the relation of Grangousier and Gargantua, of Gargantua and Pantagruel, of Pantagruel and Panurge? How does Rabelais portray the love of father for son, and the love between comrades? How does it differ from the relation between men and women? Is there mother love as well as father love in this book?

What are Rabelais's religious views?

Some of the most vigorous and bitter attacks in this book are directed against the religious institutions, leaders, and practices of Rabelais's time. As a result, despite the fact that he was a Catholic priest until the day he died, many readers and critics have interpreted his mockery as evidence of skepticism or even atheism. Looking at the work as a whole, do you think that Rabelais was attacking religion as such or Christianity? Do you think he was a secret Protestant? Does he display irreverence for sacred things? Are humor and joking out of place in religious matters? Was this sort of familiarity with sacred things, like the frank coarseness about sexual matters, more permissible in sixteenth-century France than nowadays?

Why, then, was his work consistently condemned by the Theological Faculty of the Sorbonne? Are the many serious passages on religion in the work to be taken seriously—as in Book I, Chapter 23, and Book II, Chapter 8? What about the identification of Pan and Christ in Book IV, Chapter 28? Is this conformable with Christian doctrine? How does the basic assumption about human nature that underlies the rules of the Abbey of Theleme compare with the Christian doctrine of human nature? Is the religious spirit irreconcilable with an ardent appreciation of sensual joy? With earthy language and ribald tales?

What is the good of Rabelais's educational program?

What does Rabelais's ideal education seek to develop in the pupil? In the case of Gargantua, does Ponocrates aim to make him a thinker or a doer, or neither or both? Is Ponocrates trying to develop Gargantua as a whole human being or preparing him for his role as a prince? Is there anything in this gigantic program of education that would apply to the education of ordinary children and youths nowadays? Do present-day programs follow the pattern of moral, physical, intellectual, and experiential development practiced by Ponocrates? What would Rabelais approve of in present-day American education? What would he oppose?

SELF-TESTING QUESTIONS

The following questions are designed to help you test the thoroughness of your reading. Each question is to be answered by giving a page or pages of the reading assignment. Answers will be found on page 232 of this Reading Plan.

1 What happened to the six pilgrims in Gargantua's salad?

2 What is the meaning of the prophetical riddle found in the ground where the Abbey of Theleme is built?

3 Who speaks to Pantagruel in this dialect: "From alme, inclyte and celebrate academy, which is vocitated Lutetia"?

4 Why is Paris a good city to live in, but not to die in?

5 What is Panurge's new way to build the walls of Paris?

6 How is the narrator able to tell what was inside Pantagruel's mouth?

7 What, according to Panurge, is the chief piece of armor amongst warriors?

8 How does the magic ring of Hans Carvel secure his wife's faithfulness?

9 What are the five means to abate carnal desire?

10 What attitudes and actions in husbands drive wives to unfaithfulness?

Eighth Reading

SHAKESPEARE

Othello, King Lear, Macbeth

Vol. 27, pp. 205–310

William Shakespeare needs no introduction. His name is known to the ends of the earth. It immediately calls to mind poetic eloquence, compelling drama, memorable characters, and an imaginary world that is Shakespeare's alone, duplicated by no other writer.

The universal, enduring appeal of this sixteenth-century Englishman who wrote for the popular theater of his time is utterly amazing. It may be, as some critics have charged, that Shakespeare in his plays populated the whole world with sixteenth-century Englishmen. Nevertheless, the peoples of the world have accepted Shakespeare's characters and have assimilated them to their own thought and speech. The Germans, moved by the magnificent translation of Tieck and Schlegel, call him "our Shakespeare." School children in non-English-speaking countries learn the key speeches of his characters by heart—often in the original English.

The reason for the universality and permanence of Shakespeare's appeal is simple. We believe in the world and the people he has created. In each of his plays there is a pervading atmosphere, tone, or light that holds everything together and makes it wholly believable. Our enjoyment and appreciation are not disturbed by the most banal and transparent devices, suited to the theater and taste of his time. Shakespeare's mastery rises above all such trivia.

In the three plays we have selected, Shakespeare tells of the fall of Othello, Lear, and Macbeth from honor and happiness to degradation and ruin. Othello falls through ill-advised suspicion and anger, Lear through blind stupidity and sudden impulse, and Macbeth through superstition and the lust for place and power. In the end they are nothing, having betrayed and lost themselves.

These tragic figures move in a rich and complex world, peopled with unique Shakespearean characters. Black villains like Iago and Edmund, endowed with self-consciousness and eloquence, tangle the plot. Sweet young ladies like Desdemona and Cordelia offer oases of virtue in a world of evil. And the not-so-sweet Lady Macbeth walks in her sleep, bearing witness to the guilt of her horrible deeds. Finally, there is Lear's fool, into whose mouth Shakespeare has put words of wisdom, couched in wildly imaginative, beautiful poetry.

GUIDE TO

Eighth Reading

I

The English drama, like the Greek, originated in religious liturgy. At first presented by the priests in Latin in the church or churchyard, religious dramas—the miracle and mystery plays—were later taken over by the trade guilds, and presented in English in the market place. Another type of drama, the morality play, arose in the fourteenth century. In these plays, the characters represented various virtues and vices, and the dramatic conflict was between Good and Evil for the soul of man. *Everyman* is the most famous and lasting of the morality plays. Bunyan's *Pilgrim's Progress* is a later prose narrative in this tradition. Tragedy and comedy of a secular nature started in the sixteenth century under the influence of classical Latin dramatists, and were usually presented in the universities.

By this time, professional companies of actors had been formed, independent of the guilds, and under the protection of a nobleman, royal person, or a high prelate. They usually put on their performances in the courtyard of an inn or other public place, setting up a stage, with the spectators grouped around it or watching from the windows and balconies of the inn. By the time Shakespeare began writing plays, regular theaters had been built in London, designed for the performance and witnessing of plays. The new playhouses, however, kept the old model of the innyard, with galleries like the balconies of the inns. The cheapest "seats" were the standing-room-only places in the yard, called the "pit," with better places in the galleries, and real seats on the stage for the rich and highborn. The famous Globe Theater, typical of such playhouses, was an open-air, fair-weather theater. Here the company of players to which Shakespeare belonged put on their plays in the summer, transferring their performances to the Blackfriars, a roofed-in theater, in the winter. Without scenery or stage "props," the audience had to use their imagination, aided by the poetic eloquence of the playwright and the costumes and gestures of the actors.

When Shakespeare appeared on the scene, he found a professional theater and actors, as well as a regular and appreciative playgoing audience. He came at the time of an extraordinary flowering of poetic drama in England. He was the contemporary of great poets and dramatists, such as Christopher Marlowe and Ben Jonson. The types of drama which he wrote, with the exception of the plays of his last years, had been originated by previous writers. The theatrical devices and wordplay that abound in his dramas were the common stock in trade of his predecessors and contemporaries. As for his plots, he took them wherever he found them, in histories, legends, and the stories of former writers.

Yet, despite all that he borrowed from his predecessors and contemporaries, he towers above them all. Using the same language, the same forms, and the same materials, working on the same stage for the same audience, he transformed the common stock of poetic drama and raised it to a new and unique level. Shakespeare's plays are unmistakably Elizabethan, and yet of undeniable universal appeal. They are good "theater," the work of a highly successful commercial playwright, director, and producer, and yet have provided sustenance to the most thoughtful and sensitive appreciators of the literary art through the centuries. His plays have not only been translated but also played to popular audiences in all the European languages, as well as Hebrew and Japanese.

Various elements that we may pick out of Shakespeare's plays indicate something of his mastery. In the first place, he was a skilled playwright, one of the best that ever lived, with a professional sense of the right way to stage the dramas he had to tell. The setting of the scene, the introductions, the various entrances, exits, and transitions, the shifts from scene to scene, the placing of encounter and dialogue between the characters, and a good deal of the dialogue itself are the work of a master craftsman in one of the great eras of the theater. But going beyond mere technical know-how and theater wiseness, he was a great dramatist with a story to tell, an action to present. Shakespeare's plays *move* unmistakably, in a definite direction, from beginning to end. In these three plays, this quality is most evident in *Macbeth,* where the action moves swiftly, in a short straight line, packing everything into a mere 2,100 lines. But it is also true of the more elaborate *Othello* and the still more complex *King Lear,* with two plots running side by side. Shakespeare found the ideas for these three plays in ancient chronicles and in the plays and stories of previous writers, and made out of the borrowed materials unified, connected, moving dramatic plots.

Shakespeare's plays are not only well made and well plotted, but are expressed in vivid, individualized, unique characters. When we think of Shakespeare we think of Shylock, Hamlet, Richard III, Falstaff, Ophelia, and a host of other persons who not only function as characters in the plays but also have come to stand for various traits or types of human character. Human life with all its passion and purpose, its grandeur and abasement, its gaiety and its seriousness is present in these figures. And things are mixed in Shakespeare's plays and characters as they are in real life; there are comic strains in his tragedies, and his serious characters may indulge in jest, as his comic characters may utter serious and wise words. His people express some rather simple and common human tendencies—grasping malevolence or lust for power, wounded pride, guilty conscience, tender devotion, the decay of virtue and honor. Somehow in Shakespeare's characters, these common human tendencies and experiences seem unique and new, as if they had never been expressed before and now are expressed once for all. He has furnished us with a permanent gallery of villains, heroes, fools, harridans, and sweet ladies.

One aspect of Shakespeare's works that everyone notices is his soaring language, his poetic eloquence, the apt linking of sound and sense. It would be hard to imagine Shakespeare without his poetry. Indeed, Bernard Shaw asserted that this was Shakespeare's main talent, or his only one, that his plays center around "purple patches" of poetic rhetoric. However, the other aspects of Shakespeare's works mentioned above seem to be as essential to his effect as his language is, and examination of the plays selected here reveals that there is a lot more to his language than "purple patches." Not only does it contain simple, direct, still idiomatic English phrases, but Shakespeare's language is, on the whole, not of a highfalutin, technically "poetic" variety; and it is usually suited to the particular character and idea being expressed. His language serves as a vehicle and usually does not get in the way of our enjoyment and understanding.

Otto Jespersen makes an interesting study of Shakespeare's language in his work, *The Growth and Structure of the English Language.* He attributes the richness of Shakespeare's vocabulary (about three times as large as Milton's or that of the King James Bible) to the wide variety of his subject matter and characters. He points to the skillful adaptation of language to suit the variety of individual characters. He finds one of the main features of Shakespeare's English to be his grammatical "boldness," his construction of sentences without regard to the rule books, his use of a conversational English, the way people actually speak and express themselves, rather than a bookish English that will pass a pedant's examination. Shakespeare's openness to the use of colloquial English in his plays accounts for the first known appearance in written English of many words and phrases that have become part of the standard written language. Shakespeare was no prissy, "literary" writer who found his verbal sources only in books or in the language of the past.

Jespersen also points out that Shakespeare's poetic diction is very close to ordinary prose. Like Chaucer, he usually employs the same grammatical forms and vocabulary in his poetry as in his prose, save when he is trying to make a point of characterization. Much of Shakespeare's language that seems "poetical" to us was part of the common speech of his time. Indeed, Jespersen points out surprisingly that Shakespeare's influence on English poetic diction is not as important as that of Edmund Spenser and other poets. Shakespeare was simply not concerned with creating a special poetic diction. He did not feel the need to get away from stale, hackneyed common prose to express what he had to say, as later poets have felt. One reason for this was probably that the language of his time was fresh and not worn out through overuse. Another reason may have been Shakespeare's special quality as a writer and a dramatist. For him "the play's the thing," and "English as she is spoke" suffices in most cases to express the highest flights of poetry and the deepest levels of human experience.

The three plays selected here were first produced in the years 1604-1606. *Othello* (1604) was based on a story by an Italian writer named Cinthio. *King Lear* (1605 or 1606) is based on materials in the histories of Geoffrey of Monmouth and Holinshed, and resembles an old play called *The True Chronicle History of King Leir.* The Lear story is also told by Spenser in *The Faerie Queene. Macbeth* (1605 or 1606) is based on materials in Holinshed's *Chronicles of England, Scotland, and Ireland,* a favorite source of Shakespeare and other Elizabethan dramatists.

II

Othello is the story of a great and noble man who destroys himself and the woman he loves. It is the tragedy of a brave soldier and an honorable gentleman who ends up as the murderer of his beloved wife. He is led to this tragic end through the machinations of Iago, perhaps the most masterful of Shakespeare's creations of human villainy. But his downfall is also caused by his own passion, impetuosity, and pride. He rushes to his own destruction and that of all he loves, incited and seduced by the diabolical and cunning Iago. How this comes about is portrayed in a play of great dramatic force, pithiness, and eloquence of language, and illuminating perception of human character and motivation.

There is something exotic and unusual about Othello from the beginning. In the cast of characters he is described as "a noble Moor in the service of the Venetian state." A romantic figure who has survived many adventures and catastrophies, he is now a trusted and valiant general of the city-state of Venice. As the play opens he has just eloped with Desdemona, the daughter of Brabantio, a senator of Venice. Iago, Othello's "ancient," or ensign, aided by Roderigo, a disappointed suitor of Desdemona's, sets up a commotion and warns Brabantio of his daughter's disappearance with the Moor. Iago, who shouts his warnings from the darkness and keeps his identity secret, combines coarse obscenity with racial feeling in his imprecations, for Othello—as is brought out again and again in the play—is a black man in a white man's world. Iago shouts such delicacies as these to the worried father:

> . . . an old black ram
> Is tupping your white ewe . . . you'll have your
> daughter covered with a Barbary horse . . .
> your daughter and the Moor are now making
> the beast with two backs. (p. 206b-d)

Roderigo talks of "the gross clasps of a lascivious Moor," whom he also calls "the thick-lips," and Brabantio refers to "the sooty bosom." Brabantio accuses Othello before the city council of having enticed his daughter through magic spells "To fall in love with what she fear'd to look on!" (p. 210a). Othello pleads that his only magic has been the tales of his trials and adventures, which drew from the young Desdemona her pity, admiration, and love, eliciting his love in response. Desdemona supports him and acknowledges him as her lord and husband, with whom she wants to live wherever he goes. The broken-hearted father disowns her (and dies, we learn later, from his grief and disappointment at his daughter's marriage).

The Duke of Venice, presiding at the council, considers Desdemona's love quite understandable, and, as for race,

> If virtue no delighted beauty lack,
> Your son-in-law is far more fair than black. (p. 212a)

Othello himself admits that he is much older than Desdemona, "the young affects in me defunct" (see Iago's remark on "his weak function," p. 220c), and at another point in the play complains, "I'm black and old," as if these were both defects.

general remark on the wanton disposition of the Venetian ladies, then he points out how Desdemona deceived her father in marrying Othello, and lastly he raises the question of what may have underlain her strange act in entering into such an "unnatural" match.

> Foh! one may smell in such a will most rank,
> Foul disproportion, thoughts unnatural. (p. 224c)

Perhaps, he suggests, she has come to repent her hasty step, now that she has had time to consult her better judgment.

These insinuations place Othello in a state of utter agony. "Why did I marry?" he asks himself.

> . . . O curse of marriage,
> That we can call these delicate creatures ours,
> And not their appetites! I had rather be a toad,
> And live upon the vapour of a dungeon,
> Than keep a corner in the thing I love
> For others' uses. (p. 225a)

Now he wishes he had been left in blissful ignorance and trust, and he is achingly aware that his life and being are so bound up with this young woman that his whole career and future hang in the balance.

> I had been happy, if the general camp,
> Pioners and all, had tasted her sweet body,
> So I had nothing known. O, now, for ever
> Farewell the tranquil mind! farewell content!
> Farewell the plumed troop, and the big wars,
> That make ambition virtue! O, farewell!
> Farewell the neighing steed, and the shrill trump,
> The spirit-stirring drum, the ear-piercing fife,
> The royal banner, and all quality,
> Pride, pomp, and circumstance of glorious war!
> And, O you mortal engines, whose rude throats
> The immortal Jove's dread clamours counterfeit,
> Farewell! Othello's occupation's gone! (pp. 225d-226a;
> see also p. 233d)

In his agony, he warns Iago that his imputations had better be proved true, or he'll kill him for sure. He demands concrete proof, "a living reason she's disloyal." Iago points out coarsely that he can hardly expect to catch her in the act, but

Still elsewhere he uses the term "begrimed and black/As mine own face" (p. 226b) as a metaphor for evil. In his address to the council, he portrays himself as a bluff soldier, experienced only in war, rude in speech, seriously devoted to the welfare of the state he serves, and unwilling to let his honeymoon interfere with his new mission to defend Cyprus against the Ottoman Turks.

To concentrate better on the expedition against the Turks, he consigns his bride to Emilia, the wife of Iago, whom he calls "honest Iago" and "a man . . . of honesty and trust" throughout the play. This is the man who, from the very beginning, reveals himself to us as inimical to Othello and concerned only with his own advancement. He hates Othello for having chosen a Florentine mathematician, Michael Cassio, as his lieutenant in preference to himself, who must be content with being "his Moorship's ancient." He scorns devoted and selfless service.

> In following him, I follow but myself;
> Heaven is my judge, not I for love and duty,
> But seeming so, for my peculiar end;
> For when my outward action doth demonstrate
> The native act and figure of my heart
> In compliment extern, 'tis not long after
> But I will wear my heart upon my sleeve
> For daws to peck at. I am not what I am. (p. 206a)

Iago is cynical about love, and ridicules Roderigo's announced intent to kill himself because Desdemona has married someone else. Iago says love "is merely a lust of the blood and a permission of the will," not worth hurting oneself about. He advises Roderigo repeatedly above all to "put money in thy purse" (in order that he may profit from it), and assures him that Iago's wits will prove more than a match for "a frail vow betwixt an erring barbarian and a supersubtle Venetian." Thus the center of the action and the principal characters are introduced in the first act, which ends with this speech by Iago, signaling the line the plot will take, and also bringing up another motivation for his enmity:

> . . . I hate the Moor;
> And it is thought abroad that 'twixt my sheets

He has done my office. I know not if't be true;
But I, for mere suspicion in that kind,
Will do as if for surety. He holds me well;
The better shall my purpose work on him.
Cassio's a proper man; let me see now;
To get his place and to plume up my will
In double knavery—How, how?—Let's see—
After some time, to abuse Othello's ear
That he is too familiar with his wife.
He hath a person and a smooth dispose
To be suspected, framed to make women false.
The Moor is of a free and open nature
That thinks men honest that but seem to be so,
And will as tenderly be led by the nose
As asses are.
I have't. It is engender'd. Hell and night
Must bring this monstrous birth to the world's light. (p. 213a-b)

Act II is set in Cyprus, the scene of the rest of the play. Iago sets to work at once to poison Othello's newlywed bliss and to put Cassio in disfavor. The simple-minded and credulous Roderigo serves as his dupe in these machinations. Iago gets him to believe that Desdemona is carrying on an affair with Cassio, and that if he gets Cassio into trouble, then Iago will be in a better position to aid Roderigo's courtship of Desdemona. Iago is cynical and coarse about the wantonness and infidelity of women (see pp. 214c-215a, 216a-b), and has got it into his head that Othello has cuckolded him and he is getting even with him; indeed he even fears Cassio may cuckold him too.

For that I do suspect the lusty Moor
Hath leap'd into my seat; the thought whereof
Doth, like a poisonous mineral, gnaw my inwards;
And nothing can or shall content my soul
Till I am even'd with him, wife for wife,
Or failing so, yet that I put the Moor
At least into a jealousy so strong
That judgement cannot cure. Which thing to do,
If this poor trash of Venice, whom I trash
For his quick hunting, stand the putting on,
I'll have our Michael Cassio on the hip,
Abuse him to the Moor in the rank garb—
For I fear Cassio with my night-cap too—

Make the Moor thank me, love me, and reward me,
For making him egregiously an ass
And practising upon his peace and quiet
Even to madness. 'Tis here, but yet confused;
Knavery's plain face is never seen till used. (p. 216c-d)

The first part of his plan works out satisfactorily. He gets Cassio drunk, Roderigo picks a fight with him, and in the disturbance Cassio is so disgraced that Othello dismisses him. Iago, who has arranged things so that he comes out in the best light, now persuades Cassio that he may get his post back by pleading with Desdemona to intercede for him. Iago, consummate in his villainy, says to himself,

When devils will the blackest sins put on,
They do suggest at first with heavenly shows,
As I do now; for whiles this honest fool
Plies Desdemona to repair his fortunes
And she for him pleads strongly to the Moor,
I'll pour this pestilence into his ear,
That she repeals him for her body's lust;
And by how much she strives to do him good,
She shall undo her credit with the Moor.
So will I turn her virtue into pitch,
And out of her own goodness make the net
That shall enmesh them all. (p. 220c)

Iago times events so that he and Othello enter just as Cassio is leaving Desdemona, and he plants the first seeds of suspicion in the unsuspecting Moor's mind. Desdemona, with whom Othello is completely enthralled by love, quickly succeeds in gaining his promise to restore Cassio to his post. However, after the victorious bride exits, Iago suggests to her doting husband, in various subtle words, intonations, looks, gestures, and silences that the lady's intercession for Cassio is prompted by much more ardent reasons than justice. After the gullible Othello, sure of Iago's great "love and honesty," has been fired with suspicion, Iago proceeds to push the point home into the open wound, never making an open and direct accusation, always stressing, in mock justice, that nothing has as yet been proved —all of which makes Othello all the more convinced that Iago knows far more than he is willing to say. First Iago drops a

promises circumstantial evidence—"imputation and strong circumstances." This solid "proof" consists of some declaration of illicit passion for Desdemona that Iago claims he heard Cassio utter in his sleep, and of a precious handkerchief that Othello gave to Desdemona and which Iago claims he has just seen Cassio use to wipe his beard. Othello is at once convinced by his fabricated circumstantial evidence.

> Now do I see 'tis true. Look here, Iago;
> All my fond love thus do I blow to heaven.
> 'Tis gone.
> Arise, black vengeance, from thy hollow cell!
> Yield up, O love, thy crown and hearted throne
> To tyrannous hate! Swell, bosom, with thy fraught,
> For 'tis of aspics' tongues! (p. 227a)

He tells Iago to kill Cassio within three days' time, and promises to dispose of Desdemona himself. He then appoints Iago his lieutenant.

Othello becomes obsessed with the handkerchief as a symbol of his wife's fidelity. Iago has arranged it so that the handkerchief turns up in Cassio's hands. When Othello finds that Cassio indeed has the handkerchief, he works himself into a murderous fury and wants to chop his "unfaithful" wife into pieces. He accepts Iago's suggestion that he stifle her in the bed she has stained—"the justice of it pleases."

Othello is a changed man. At one point, just after Iago says Cassio has admitted he has lain with Desdemona, he gives way to incoherent speech and falls into a trance. He flies into a rage when Desdemona tells Lodovico, the newly arrived envoy from Venice, of Othello's coolness toward Cassio and refers to "the love I bear to Cassio." He strikes her, and mumbles incoherently about "goats and monkeys" (referring to Iago's previous remark about lovers "as prime as goats, as hot as monkeys," p. 226c). Lodovico, shocked at such conduct, says,

> Is this the noble Moor whom our full Senate
> Call all in all sufficient? Is this the nature
> Whom passion could not shake? whose solid virtue
> The shot of accident, nor dart of chance,
> Could neither graze nor pierce?
> ....
> Are his wits safe? Is he not light of brain? (p. 232d)

Iago is quick to arouse suspicion about Othello's sanity in the emissary's mind, and invites him to observe Othello well.

In a terrible scene with Desdemona, Othello accuses her of being an "impudent strumpet," and scorns her protestations of innocence.

> I took you for that cunning whore of Venice
> That married with Othello.
> You, mistress,
> That have the office opposite to Saint Peter,
> And keep the gate of hell! (p. 234a)

Ignorant of Iago's part in this, Desdemona pleads with him to help her win back Othello's favor. When Emilia hazards the shrewd guess that some vicious and self-seeking villain has put this slander in Othello's head, Iago shamelessly says, "Fie, there is no such man; it is impossible," and advises Desdemona to be patient until Othello gets over his bad mood. Immediately afterward, he tells Roderigo to kill Cassio, on some specious pretext, and the dull dupe is wounded in an attempt on Cassio's life. Iago, lurking in the shadows ("fear nothing; I'll be at thy elbow"), wounds Cassio from behind and exits, to come back innocently later, when witnesses gather, shout mock horror at such a villainous deed, and stab Roderigo to death in a mock-just rage. Iago realizes that it is all or nothing for him tonight.

> . . . This is the night
> That either makes me or fordoes me quite. (p. 238d)

Meanwhile Othello is in Desdemona's bedchamber, preparing to end her life. Desdemona's fear and horror mount as she realizes her husband's grim intention. She pleads desperately with him,

> O, banish me, my lord, but kill me not! . . .
> Kill me to-morrow; let me live to-night! . . .
> But half an hour! . . .
> But while I say one prayer! (p. 239d)

But the relentless Moor says, "It is too late," and stifles her. When Emilia comes in and finds what Othello has done and why, she curses him, "O gull! O dolt! As ignorant as dirt!"

Here on the scene of the murder, all things are finally revealed, as Emilia confronts Iago with his lies, and tells how it was she who picked up Desdemona's handkerchief and gave it to Iago. Iago, found out, stabs Emilia to death and runs away. As the officials pursue the villain, Othello realizes that all is up with him too, that he is nothing now, that he is no longer Othello. When Lodovico asks, "Where is this rash and most unfortunate man?" Othello answers, "That's he that was Othello." The valor and the virtue are gone out of him, but still he pleads honor as his motivation, and no base passion.

> *Lod.* O thou Othello, that wert once so good,
> Fall'n in the practice of a damned slave,
> What shall be said to thee?
>
> *Oth.* Why anything;
> An honourable murderer, if you will;
> For nought I did in hate, but all in honour.
> (p. 242b-c)

He begs for a fair report on his misdeeds.

> I have done the state some service, and they know't.
> No more of that. I pray you, in your letters,
> When you shall these unlucky deeds relate,
> Speak of me as I am; nothing extenuate,
> Nor set down aught in malice. Then must you speak
> Of one that loved not wisely but too well;
> Of one not easily jealous, but being wrought
> Perplex'd in the extreme; of one whose hand,
> Like the base Indian, threw a pearl away
> Richer than all his tribe . . . (pp. 242d-243a)

And he stabs himself, kissing Desdemona a final time before he dies. Cassio, whose murder he had plotted, magnanimously bestows the epithet that "he was great of heart." Iago, whom Othello has called "that demi-devil" who "ensnared my soul and body," is to be subjected to cruel torture and execution. As the play ends, Lodovico announces that

> Myself will straight aboard; and to the state
> This heavy act with heavy heart relate. (p. 243c)

III

King Lear is the story of an old man who is brought to grief by the vicious selfishness of the ungrateful daughters to whom he has delegated his power, authority, and possessions—and by his own complacent blindness. In one sense, it is a story of the conflict between the generations, of the miseries of old age and retirement, of the tension between parents and children. But it is much more than this, not only because of its deep insights into the complexities of human character and motivations, but because this is the story of an anointed monarch, and the hostile acts against his person are blasphemous treason. There is a double offense and a double shock in what his daughters, their men, and their servants do to Lear. For Lear is not only an abused father, he is a king. This is the story of *King* Lear, who is both the ruler of Britain and the father of three daughters.

All that will appear in the play is prepared for in the first act. This initial act is unbelievably packed with the key events, characters, and motivations that trigger the action of the rest of the play. The grand old man (eighty years of age) announces to his court his decision

> To shake all cares and business from our age;
> Conferring them on younger strengths, while we
> Unburthen'd crawl toward death. (p. 244d)

The kingdom is to be divided into three parts, one for each of his daughters, but the size of each will depend on how much love each girl expresses for her father. A strange talking contest ensues in which the older daughters, Goneril and Regan, abound with flowery eloquence and exaggerated filial devotion, while the youngest and best-beloved daughter, Cordelia, is bluntly honest. She simply avers her due love, "According to my bond; nor more nor less." Lear, who has been more than generous to the two flattering daughters, is furious at what he takes to be the hardhearted attitude of this honest girl, whose love is richer than her tongue, whose heart is not worn on the sleeve. He cuts her off without a penny, and disavows her as his daughter henceforth. He summons the two foreign suitors for her hand, the King of France and the Duke of Burgundy, and announces to them that her only dowry now is his curse and hate. The Duke prudently beats a retreat, but the French king is undismayed by Cordelia's reserve and honesty and takes her for herself alone. As Cordelia takes leave of her favored sisters, she tells them, "I know you what you are," and commits her father dubiously "to your professed bosoms." Her exit lines are

> Time shall unfold what plaited cunning hides;
> Who cover faults, at last shame them derides. (p. 247c)

Lear now divides his kingdom into two parts, one half going to Regan and her husband, the Duke of Cornwall, the other half going to Goneril and her husband, the Duke of Albany. To himself he reserves only the nominal title of king, a hundred knights, and the right for him and his retinue to be supported each month in turn by his daughters. He says to his sons-in-law:

> I do invest you jointly with my power,
> Pre-eminence, and all the large effects
> That troop with majesty. Ourself, by monthly course,
> With reservation of an hundred knights,
> By you to be sustain'd, shall our abode
> Make with you by due turns. Only we still retain
> The name, and all the additions to a king;
> The sway, revenue, execution of the rest,
> Beloved sons, be yours . . . (p. 245d)

But his sudden rejection of Cordelia has not endeared him to his other daughters, and fearing his "unruly waywardness" and "unconstant starts," they scheme together to protect their own interest. The choleric monarch has also banished his loyal and honest counselor, the Earl of Kent, for opposing his treatment of his daughter. He has, in effect, cut off his own right hand in a moment of injured vanity and pique. He has banished a loyal daughter and a trusted friend and left himself almost alone, at the mercy of his two fair-speaking daughters. And they are quick to act and let him know the harsh reality he has originated by his rash act, that to them he is no more than an

> . . . Idle old man,
> That still would manage those authorities
> That he hath given away! . . . (p. 250a)

It is his own fool who first tells him that he is a fool.

> All thy other titles thou hast given away; that
> thou wast born with. (p. 251d)

The fool is unmerciful in revealing to his master how the position of father and daughters has been reversed, with the rod now in their hands, and he reduced to nothing, "an O without a figure." That the fool speaks the truth he soon sees when Goneril, the daughter whom he is staying with, criticizes the conduct of his retinue and his own attitude, and "requests" him, in no uncertain terms, to reduce his hundred knights to a smaller number,

> . . . Be then desired
> By her, that else will take the thing she begs,
> A little to disquantity your train; (p. 252d)

The outraged Lear, finding his retinue already cut in half, immediately departs with a bitter curse on this "thankless child," bound for the castle of Regan, whom he considers a really grateful and loyal daughter. But the fool, wiser than he, tells him they are identical in nature. He tells Lear bluntly,

> If thou wert my fool, nuncle, I'd have thee beaten
> for being old before thy time . . . Thou shouldst not
> have been old till thou hadst been wise. (p. 254b)

Anxiety and dread beset Lear now, as he fights against the thought that he is losing his identity, becoming nullified, a mere nothing, "Lear's shadow," and he prays,

> O, let me not be mad, not mad, sweet heaven!
> Keep me in temper. I would not be mad! (p. 254b)

These lines mark Lear's mood as the first act ends.

The above is a skeletal summary of the initial action from which all the rest of the play derives. But there is also a second theme introduced in the first act, one that runs side by side with and crisscrosses the main story throughout the play. This is the story of another rash and stupid father, who undiscerningly favors a bad son and persecutes a good son. The characters here are the Duke of Gloucester, his legitimate son Edgar, and his bastard son Edmund. The latter is one of the great Shakespearean "heavies," a villain who knows he is evil and goes self-consciously and articulately about accomplishing his villainy. Desiring to attain his brother's place as heir to the title and domains of Gloucester, he tricks his father into believing that Edgar is plotting to do away with him, and then tricks Edgar into believing his father intends to do away with him. The result is that Edgar takes to fearful flight to save his life, and his father is intent on finding him to execute him for his "treason." Says the delighted Edmund,

> A credulous father! and a brother noble,
> Whose nature is so far from doing harms
> That he suspects none; on whose foolish honesty
> My practices ride easy! I see the business.
> Let me, if not by birth, have lands by wit;
> All with me's meet that I can fashion fit. (p. 249d)

Of course, he is unconvinced by his father's ascription of the discord and division that have just occurred in the King's and his own families to eclipses of the sun and moon. He says in a soliloquy against astronomical determinism,

> . . . An admirable evasion of whoremaster man, to lay his goatish disposition to the charge of a star! My father compounded with my mother under the dragon's tail; and my nativity was under *Ursa major;* so that it follows, I am rough and lecherous. Tut, I should have been that I am, had the maidenliest star in the firmament twinkled on my bastardizing . . . (p. 249b)

One more typically Shakespearean device is introduced in the first act. The banished Kent returns in disguise, to serve and protect his master, who, of course, never sees through the disguise—like all of Shakespeare's disguises, baldly transparent to the audience, but hidden from the other characters. Lear makes Kent his messenger, with letters to Regan and the Earl of Gloucester. Regan and her husband, the Duke of Cornwall, forewarned by Goneril, avoid the old man by a sudden journey to Gloucester's palace. This becomes the scene of the main action of Act II. Kent, following Regan, gets into a scuffle with Goneril's steward, Oswald, who has been sent to get Regan to take a common stand against Lear. Regan and Cornwall, incensed at the blunt-spoken Kent, order him put in the stocks, despite his plea "I serve the King," and not to show disrespect for "the grace and person of my master." Lear, following his daughter to Gloucester's castle, finds Kent in the stocks, and in his outraged majesty and paternity summons his daughter and his son-in-law.

> The King would speak with Cornwall; the dear father
> Would with his daughter speak, commands her service.
> (p. 259c)

A most poignant scene follows as Lear pleads with Regan to take him in, and save him from her sister's abominable conduct, but she tells him he is a doddering old man and to go back to Goneril and beg her forgiveness. For what, he asks, for being old? At this point Goneril, too, arrives at Gloucester's castle, and an ugly scene ensues as the two daughters bargain with the old man for how many men he can keep with him, beating him down from a hundred to fifty to twenty-five to none. "What need one?" asks Regan. The outraged and frustrated Lear pleads with the heavens to give him patience and "noble anger," to keep him from womanish tears. He tells his daughters,

> . . . No, you unnatural hags,
> I will have such revenges on you both,
> That all the world shall—I will do such things—
> What they are, yet I know not; but they shall be
> The terrors of the earth. You think I'll weep;
> No, I'll not weep.
> I have full cause of weeping; but this heart
> Shall break into a hundred thousand flaws,
> Or ere I'll weep. O Fool, I shall go mad! (p. 261d)

And in his emotional storm, he exits into the rising storm of the elements, accompanied by the fool.

On a bare heath, under the drenching rain and the tearing winds, the old man runs the gamut from rage and grief to the verge of madness. On this heath, in Act III, occur some of the most marvelous and memorable scenes in the play. Lear welcomes the destructive elements that may wipe out this iniquitous world.

> Blow, winds, and crack your cheeks! rage! blow!
> You cataracts and hurricanes, spout
> Till you have drench'd our steeples, drown'd the cocks!
> You sulphurous and thought-executing fires,
> Vaunt-couriers to oak-cleaving thunderbolts,
> Singe my white head! And thou, all-shaking thunder,

> Smite flat the thick rotundity o' the world!
> Crack nature's moulds, all germens spill at once,
> That make ingrateful man! (pp. 262d-263a)

He pities himself as "A poor, infirm, weak, and despised old man . . . a man/More sinn'd against than sinning." Led by the solicitous Kent, he and the fool enter a hovel for shelter against the storm. Here they come upon Edgar, who has disguised himself as a madman, "Poor Tom," naked, and with amazing speeches, such as,

> Who gives anything to poor Tom? whom the foul fiend hath led through fire and through flame, through ford and whirlipool, o'er bog and quagmire; that hath laid knives under his pillow, and halters in his pew; set ratsbane by his porridge; made him proud of heart, to ride on a bay trotting-horse over four-inched bridges, to course his own shadow for a traitor. Bless thy five wits! Tom's a-cold—O, do de, do de, do de. Bless thee from whirlwinds, star-blasting and taking! Do poor Tom some charity, whom the foul fiend vexes. There could I have him now—and there—and there again, and there. (p. 264d)

Lear, fascinated by him, philosophizes, "Unaccommodated man is no more but such a poor, bare, forked animal as thou art," and tears off his own clothes. He calls the madman his "philosopher." Kent, warned by Gloucester of the daughters' plot to kill Lear, takes him away to Dover, where the French forces, led by Cordelia, are gathered to come to his rescue.

Gloucester suffers horribly for his act of mercy and respect. He is betrayed by his "loyal and natural boy," Edmund, who reveals to Cornwall and Regan his father's trafficking with the French. In punishment for this and for saving the King, Gloucester's eyes are gouged out. This is acted out before the audience in one of the most horrible scenes ever presented on the stage. Cornwall's servants are horrified too, and one of them fights with him and wounds him mortally. The eyeless Gloucester is turned out on the highway, finally understanding now which of his sons was the good one.

> I have no way, and therefore want no eyes;
> I stumbled when I saw . . . (p. 269c)

He chooses Poor Tom for his guide—"madmen lead the blind" —to take him to the cliffs of Dover, where he intends to kill himself. But the "madman" tricks him into taking his jump at a level spot, and Gloucester gives up the idea of suicide.

Meanwhile, two lines of action are going forward to bring the play to its climax and conclusion. The first concerns the deeds of the two evil sisters and the new Duke of Gloucester, Edmund. Goneril, escorted home by Edmund, develops a passion for him and a scorn for her husband, who is morally offended by what she and her sister have done. She calls him a "Milk-liver'd man" and "a moral fool," comparing him unfavorably with the dashing and unscrupulous Edmund.

> O, the difference of man and man!
> To thee [Edmund] a woman's services are due;
> My fool usurps my body. (p. 270d)

She sends him back to her sister to lead Cornwall's forces, but at the news of Cornwall's death, she realizes the new widow also may have her eye on Edmund now, and she sends him a letter in order to hold onto him. But Regan, who is sure that Edmund is "more convenient" for her hand than for her sister's, sends him a token by the same messenger, Oswald, Goneril's steward. Only it happens that Oswald is slain in a fight with Edgar, who gets and reads Goneril's letter, begging Edmund to kill her husband and release her from "the loathed warmth" of "his bed my gaol." Edgar, still disguised, brings the letter to Albany before the great battle between the English and the French, and promises to send a champion to vouch for the letter, should Albany triumph in the battle. Meanwhile the widow Regan questions Edmund quite bluntly on the intimacy of his relations with her sister, but he avers they have been of a strictly honorable nature. When he is alone he soliloquizes

> To both these sisters have I sworn my love;
> Each jealous of the other, as the stung
> Are of the adder. Which of them shall I take?
> Both? one? or neither? Neither can be enjoy'd,
> If both remain alive. To take the widow
> Exasperates, makes mad her sister Goneril;
> And hardly shall I carry out my side,
> Her husband being alive. Now then we'll use

His countenance for the battle; which being done,
Let her who would be rid of him devise
His speedy taking off. As for the mercy
Which he intends to Lear and to Cordelia,
The battle done, and they within our power,
Shall never see his pardon; for my state
Stands on me to defend, not to debate. (p. 278c-d)

The other line of action concerns the deeds of Lear, Cordelia, and Kent. Kent succeeds in bringing Lear to the French camp, and to Cordelia's loving care. But before that Lear goes through a bout of madness, in which he says many dark things and many wise things, in the wonderful language Shakespeare bestows on him. There is the extraordinary piece on womanly lust:

. . . The fitchew, nor the soiled horse, goes to't
With a more riotous appetite.
Down from the waist they are Centaurs,
Though women all above;
But to the girdle do the gods inherit,
Beneath is all the fiends'; (p. 274c-d)

As, in the hovel on the heath, he realized how ignorant he had been of how poor wretches live (see p. 264c), now he realizes he has been shielded from reality. "They told me I was every thing; 'tis a lie, I am not ague-proof" (p. 274c). He is bitter about the great discrepancy between appearance and reality in human affairs—"behold the great image of authority; a dog's obeyed in office" (p. 275a). And he ends with a cry of murderous vengeance on his sons-in-law: "Then, kill, kill, kill, kill kill, kill!" (p. 275b). Cordelia's men find him and bring him to her camp for rest and cure. When he is able to speak to her, he tells her,

I am a very foolish fond old man,
Fourscore and upward, not an hour more nor less;
And, to deal plainly,
I fear I am not in my perfect mind. (p. 277b)

He begs her to forgive and forget. Kent leaves the old man with her and goes out to fight the crucial battle.

Here occurs an unexpected turn of events for the reader. We would expect to see virtue triumphant, and the French forces under Cordelia victorious in their attempt to restore King Lear to his rightful place. But such is not the case. The British forces, under Albany and Edmund, win, and Lear and Cordelia are taken prisoner. Lear comforts his daughter thus:

> No, no, no, no! Come, let's away to prison.
> We two alone will sing like birds i' the cage;
> When thou dost ask me blessing, I'll kneel down,
> And ask of thee forgiveness; so we'll live,
> And pray, and sing, and tell old tales, and laugh
> At gilded butterflies, and hear poor rogues
> Talk of court news; and we'll talk with them too,
> Who loses and who wins; who's in, who's out;
> And take upon's the mystery of things,
> As if we were God's spies; and we'll wear out,
> In a wall'd prison, packs and sects of great ones,
> That ebb and flow by the moon. (p. 279a-b)

Edmund secretly sends one of his officers to kill them in their prison cell. A curious scene ensues as Albany questions Edmund's authority, Regan openly makes him her lord and master, and Goneril opposes her sister's enjoying the man she wants for herself. Albany thereupon declares Edmund and Goneril under arrest on grounds of high treason, and with delicious irony tells Regan she cannot have Edmund since he is already "sub-contracted" to his wife.

> . . . And I, her husband, contradict your bans.
> If you will marry, make your loves to me,
> My lady is bespoke. (p. 280a)

Edmund proclaims he will defend his name by force of arms against anyone who calls him a traitor. The trumpet sounds, and the herald reads Edmund's challenge:

> "If any man of quality or degree within the lists of the army will maintain upon Edmund, supposed Earl of Gloucester, that he is a manifold traitor, let him appear by the third sound of the trumpet. He is bold in his defence." (p. 280b)

At the third sound of the trumpet, Edgar comes forth, and without revealing his identity calls Edmund a traitor, "False to thy gods, thy brother, and thy father." In the fight he wins and wounds Edmund mortally. Edmund handsomely admits all to Albany.

> What you have charged me with, that have I done;
> And more, much more; the time will bring it out.
> 'Tis past, and so am I . . . (p. 281a)

Edgar reveals his identity to Edmund and moralizes that divine justice worked it so that their father lost his eyes for his illegitimate love. Edmund admits, "The wheel is come full circle; I am here." Edgar reveals that Gloucester just died a short while ago when he found out that his guide was his lost son. His heart "burst smilingly" between the sudden extremes of joy and grief. At this moment comes the news that Goneril has committed suicide and that Regan has been poisoned to death by her. Says Edmund, "I was contracted to them both. All three now marry in an instant." When the bodies of Goneril and Regan are brought in, Edmund says,

> Yet Edmund was beloved.
> The one the other poison'd for my sake,
> And after slew herself. (p. 282a)

The dying man tries to do some good in his last moments, "Despite of mine own nature." He tries to save Lear and Cordelia, but he is too late. Lear enters bearing the body of Cordelia, protesting her irrevocable death: "She's dead as earth."

> *Kent.* Is this the promised end?
> *Edg.* Or image of that horror?
> *Alb.* Fall, and cease! (p. 282b)

Kent says to Lear, "All's cheerless, dark, and deadly." And Lear keens over the beloved daughter he had once rejected, thus wreaking havoc and ruin.

> And my poor fool is hang'd! No, no, no life!
> Why should a dog, a horse, a rat, have life,
> And thou no breath at all? Thou'lt come no more,
> Never, never, never, never, never! . . . (p. 282d)

And the old man, broken on "the rack of this tough world," finally dies of a broken heart at this, the hardest blow of all.

Albany ends the play with this moral,

> The weight of this sad time we must obey;
> Speak what we feel, not what we ought to say.
> The oldest hath borne most; we that are young
> Shall never see so much, nor live so long. (p. 283c)

There are many famous lines in this play, which have become common speech, literary phrases, or book titles. Besides the many passages cited above, there are such lines as "defy the foul fiend," "I'll go to bed at noon," "As flies to wanton boys, are we to the gods,/They kill us for their sport," "every inch a king," "Men must endure/Their going hence, even as their coming hither;/Ripeness is all" (pp. 265b, 267c, 269d, 274c, 278d-279a).

IV

Macbeth is a much shorter and much less complicated play than *King Lear*. It has a single plot and a single theme, which it unfolds with directness and clarity, from the first to the last scene. This short and simple play recounts with intense dramatic force the story of how a man becomes possessed and destroyed by evil. It derives much of its impact from its deep insights into human character and motivations, akin to the interpretations of modern depth psychology, and also from the sense it conveys of the tremendous change that follows from the commitment of a single act, the catastrophic weight of the present moment. There is also the sense of the more than natural powers involved in human events, presented in the weird and impressive scenes with the witches. And there is, as always, Shakespeare's language, here lean and hard, with few rhetorical or fanciful flourishes, an economical fusing of sense and sound.

As the play opens, Macbeth is at his highest point as a man, a general, and a loyal servant and kinsman of his king. He has just played a foremost role in the victorious battle against rebel armies, and Duncan, the King of Scotland, has decided to transfer to him the title of one of the defeated rebel lords, the thane of Cawdor. Thus he stands at the start—"brave Macbeth," "valour's minion," "valiant cousin," "noble Macbeth." But at this moment Macbeth, returning from the battle, encounters the three witches, "the weird sisters," who call him by his new title, of which he is not yet aware, and prophesy that he will become king. He is bewildered by this "prophetic greeting," as is his companion, Banquo, also a general, whose children, the witches predict, will become kings. From this moment, Macbeth's path is downward, and "fair is foul, and foul is fair." When the King's messenger hails him as thane of Cawdor, he is convinced that the rest of the prediction will come true, but he is tempted not to leave it to chance to make him king. He is tempted, but also disturbed and terrified by the thought that crosses his mind. This man is not a cold and calculating villain. In one of those strange speeches which reveal the inner reactions of this fascinating character, he asks himself

> . . . why do I yield to that suggestion
> Whose horrid image doth unfix my hair
> And make my seated heart knock at my ribs,
> Against the use of nature? Present fears
> Are less than horrible imaginings.
> My thought, whose murder yet is but fantastical,
> Shakes so my single state of man that function
> Is smother'd in surmise, and nothing is
> But what is not. (p. 287a)

Again, he expresses this combination of willingness and repugnance toward the evil deeds that must fulfill the witches' prophecy.

> . . . Stars, hide your fires;
> Let not light see my black and deep desires;
> The eye wink at the hand; yet let that be
> Which the eye fears, when it is done, to see.
> (p. 287d)

His wife, Lady Macbeth, to whom he has made known his promised greatness, comments sadly that he

> . . . is too full o' the milk of human kindness
> To catch the nearest way. Thou wouldst be
> great;
> Art not without ambition, but without
> The illness should attend it. What thou wouldst
> highly,
> That wouldst thou holily; wouldst not play false,
> And yet wouldst wrongly win. Thou'dst have,
> great Glamis,

> That which cries "Thus thou must do, if thou
> have it;
> And that which rather thou dost fear to do
> Than wishest should be undone" . . . (p. 228a-b)

This lady calls on the spirits to "unsex" her and make her cold, hard, and merciless to accomplish the deed that will make her husband king. The opportunity occurs shortly after the battle when Duncan visits Macbeth's castle at Inverness. But it requires the woman's constant taunting, goading, and support to bring to Macbeth the will to overcome his repugnance and do the deed. He is admittedly the prey of "vaulting ambition, which o'erleaps itself," but he realizes that deeds have consequences, that murder is not just a self-contained act, from which one leaps neatly to fame and fortune.

> If it were done when 'tis done, then
> 'twere well
> It were done quickly. If the assassination
> Could trammel up the consequence, and catch
> With his surcease success; that but this blow
> Might be the be-all and the end-all here,
> But here, upon this bank and shoal of time,
> We'd jump the life to come . . . (p. 289b)

This man thinks prudently, he estimates the consequences that will ensue if this good man and king is killed. He is also compunctious about taking the life of a kinsman, ruler, and guest who has shown him so much favor. When he tells Lady Macbeth, "We will proceed no further in this business," she berates him for his cowardice, proclaims her own cruel determination, and begs him to "screw your courage to the sticking-place." Macbeth's reluctance is overcome as she sketches out the details of how to do the deed, and he contributes a few ideas of his own. He announces himself as "settled" and directing "each corporal agent to this terrible feat," but when the time comes his dread and guilt are expressed in the hallucination of a blood-stained dagger before his eyes. When he returns from the deed done, he sees the undeniable blood on his hands, "a sorry sight," and quails before the irrevocableness of his act. He sees that Macbeth "hath murder'd sleep" and shall "sleep no more." It is Lady Macbeth who has the hardness to finish the deed and plant the evidence on the King's sleeping grooms so they will be blamed for the murder. The sight of the King's corpse does not bother her. As for the blood on her hands, why, "A little water clears us of this deed."

When the murder is discovered, Macbeth kills the two grooms in a feigned fit of rage, and when the King's sons flee from Scotland in fear of what may happen to them, it is believed that they were guilty of hiring the servants to murder their father. Macbeth, as closest legitimate kin, now becomes king. Now he wears the crown, but he does so uneasily, and feels compelled to commit further evil deeds to secure the benefit of the initial deed. Banquo, his fellow in the witches' prophecy, is murdered by Macbeth's hired assassins, but his ghost appears at the banquet table to haunt the guilt-stricken murderer. Macbeth is now steeped in blood to the point of no return.

> . . . I am in blood
> Stepp'd in so far that, should I wade no more,
> Returning were as tedious as go o'er . . . (p. 299b)

Now the three witches, under the leadership of Hecate, the dark goddess of the underworld, set about leading Macbeth to his doom, through giving him a false sense of security—"mortals' chiefest enemy." In a famous scene, they brew a noisome mess in a boiling cauldron deep in a cavern, chanting,

> Double, double, toil and trouble;
> Fire burn and cauldron bubble. (p. 300c)

At Macbeth's bidding, they summon up apparitions, which warn him to beware of Macduff, the thane of Fife, but promise that no man born of woman shall harm Macbeth, and that he will not be vanquished until Birnam wood comes to Dunsinane hill. Macbeth now feels assured that he is invulnerable and indomitable. Macduff flees to England and foils the plot to assassinate him, but Macbeth has Macduff's wife and son killed in a touching and terrible scene.

Scotland is horrified at these dreadful murders. Decent men drop away from Macbeth and join the opposition, which is organized by Prince Malcolm and the grief-stricken and revengeful Macduff. Malcolm predicts that Macbeth

> . . . Is ripe for shaking, and the powers above
> Put on their instruments. Receive what cheer you
> may;
> The night is long that never finds the day. (p. 306b)

As the end approaches Macbeth is quite alone. His wife, who earlier flaunted her hardness of heart, turns out to have been shallow and blind about her own inner reactions and the personal consequences of the evil she has done. She walks and talks in her sleep and goes through compulsive acts to rid herself of her oppressive guilt. The woman who had thought water could wash away blood and the fact of murder now cries in her sleepwalking state,

> Out, damned spot! out, I say! . . .
> Here's the smell of the blood still. All
> the perfumes of Arabia will not sweeten this
> little hand . . . (p. 306c-d)

She compulsively repeats speech and gestures of the night of the King's murder, muttering, "What's done cannot be undone. To bed, to bed, to bed!" Her physician comments,

> . . . Unnatural deeds
> Do breed unnatural troubles. Infected minds
> To their deaf pillows will discharge their secrets . . . (p. 307a)

To Macbeth's plea to

> . . . minister to a mind diseased,
> Pluck from the memory a rooted sorrow,
> Raze out the written troubles of the brain,
> And with some sweet oblivious antidote
> Cleanse the stuff'd bosom of that perilous stuff
> Which weighs upon the heart? (p. 308a)

he replies, "Therein the patient/Must minister to himself."

Macbeth has changed too. This man, who has been so superstitious, full of fear, and imaginative about consequences, is now left cold by shrieks and cries and the very news of Lady Macbeth's death, apparently at her own hands. He says,

> I have almost forgot the taste of fears.
> The time has been, my senses would have cool'd

To hear a night-shriek; and my fell of hair
Would at a dismal treatise rouse and stir
As life were in't. I have supp'd full with horrors;
Direness, familiar to my slaughterous thoughts,
Cannot once start me. (p. 308d)

He has arrived at emptiness, the world and life lie hollow before him, reality is inane. "I have lived long enough; my way of life/Is fall'n into the sear, the yellow leaf" (p. 307d). This mood gives rise to his famous soliloquy:

To-morrow, and to-morrow, and to-morrow,
Creeps in this petty pace from day to day
To the last syllable of recorded time,
And all our yesterdays have lighted fools
The way to dusty death. Out, out, brief candle!
Life's but a walking shadow, a poor player
That struts and frets his hour upon the stage
And then is heard no more. It is a tale
Told by an idiot, full of sound and fury,
Signifying nothing. (pp. 308d-309a)

Now there comes home the unintended truth of his hypocritical utterance at the time the King's murder was discovered.

Had I but died an hour before this chance,
I had lived a blessed time; for, from this instant,
There's nothing serious in mortality;
All is but toys. Renown and grace is dead;
The wine of life is drawn, and the mere lees
Is left this vault to brag of. (p. 293b)

The rest follows inevitably, as the hollow man finds he has been tricked by the powers of darkness; Birnam wood does move to Dunsinane, in a metaphoric sense, and he does encounter a man who is technically not born of woman.

. . . And be these juggling fiends no more believed
That palter with us in a double sense;
That keep the word of promise to our ear,
And break it to our hope . . . (p. 310b)

But at the end his original valor and mettle appear once more when he finds he really does not "bear a charmed life," and Macduff, born through a Caesarian operation, opposes him to administer the prophesied stroke. Macbeth cries,

I will not yield

. . . .

Yet I will try the last. Before my body
I throw my warlike shield. Lay on, Macduff,
And damn'd be him that first cries, "Hold,
enough!" (p. 310b)

The play ends on a note of liberation and light, after the oppressive miasma of dark and evil deeds. Macduff enters, holding Macbeth's severed head, announcing "The time is free," and hailing Malcolm as the new king of Scotland. Malcolm starts his plans to make things grow aright and repair the damages wrought by "this dead butcher and his fiend-like queen," as the players make their final exit.

V

Are these plays "tragedies" in Aristotle's sense?

Aristotle defined tragedy as a serious action, in which a noble person comes to an unhappy end, due to some flaw in character and judgment. The effect of the tragic drama is to evoke pity and fear in the spectator. The tragedy should have a single theme, unified rather than episodic, and should proceed through complications, sudden reversals of events, and discovery or recognition of the meaning of events. The ideal tragic deed occurs within the bonds of friendship or kinship, to arouse the greatest horror and pity. (See Second Reading, Section II.)

Now obviously these plays do not fulfill Aristotle's literal requirement of unity. All of them are episodic, jump around from scene to scene, and require far more than the day's time suggested by Aristotle. *King Lear,* we remember, is particularly complicated, and even has a subtheme or side plot accompanying the main story, so that we have to shift our attention from one to the other. The question for us is whether this shifting, episodic manner adds to or detracts from the total dramatic effect. Do the various elements of these plays contribute to the total effect so as to achieve a unified dramatic whole? Does the side story of Gloucester, Edmund, and Edgar illuminate and belong to the story of Lear and his daughters, or not? Is Shakespeare's method a new way of achieving the dramatic unity called for by Aristotle?

Perhaps Othello and Lear fit easily into the requirements for the tragic hero, but what of Macbeth? Is he a good and noble man who falls because of some "tragic flaw," or a grasping villain from the start, or just an ordinary man who comes a cropper through succumbing to common temptations? Macbeth admittedly meets with an unhappy end, but does the play about Macbeth have an unhappy ending? Doesn't it end on a note of joy? "The time is free," the murderous usurper is dead, the rightful heir is on the throne, and all will be set right in the state of Scotland. Is the spectator to cheer, as in the old melodrama when the villain gets his just deserts? What is the tragedy of Macbeth?

Which of the plays produces the most fear and pity? Which of the plays has the clearest movement to a climax and conclusion? Which depends most on "recognition" scenes?

Do you think these plays fit into Aristotle's definition of tragedy? What are the main correspondences and differences? If you consider them a different kind of tragedy, how would you describe it in terms of form, plot, characters, language, and effect?

Do you find the easy success of Shakespeare's villains unbelievable?

Edmund has no trouble in manipulating his father and brother, who accept his every suggestion with simple credulity. And Iago hoodwinks Othello and Roderigo with the utmost of ease, so that they look like perfect fools. Is this probable *in real life?* Would people be such ready dupes of these "crafty" villains? Is this believable *in the plays,* or do you just accept it as a device to keep the play going? Is stage logic and probability different from that in real life? What makes Iago tick? Why this enormous resentment against Othello? What can Iago hope to gain for himself by destroying Othello? Have you ever known any Iagos in real life, or people with a large streak of Iago in them? Is Iago a perfectly believable character in the play *Othello?*

Is the blinding of Gloucester too horrible for public performance?

In ancient tragedies, the tragic deeds and mutilations always took place off stage. The horror was transmitted through the dialogue. Is Shakespeare a "barbarian" for putting such a scene on the stage? Or is something conveyed through direct representation that could not be done through commentary and dialogue? Would you be averse to witnessing such a scene?

What is the dramatic nature and purpose of Lear's madness?

On top of the other tremendous scenes in the storm and in the hovel with "mad Tom," comes this odd, short mad scene. There is reason in this madness, an illuminating recognition of things that have been hidden from the sheltered, self-complacent monarch. But why the gross sexual references? Why must the awareness of the wide gap between appearance and reality in human relations be couched in terms of sexual behavior and desire? Is Shakespeare just putting this in for the sensational effect, or does it have some special bite and logic? How does the "mad" scene connect with the rest of the play? How would you compare Lear's madness with Hamlet's?

SELF-TESTING QUESTIONS

The following questions are designed to help you test the thoroughness of your reading. Each question is to be answered by giving a page or pages of the reading assignment. Answers will be found on page 233 of this Reading Plan.

1 What does Iago claim to find in Cassio's experience and qualifications that make him unfit for the post of Othello's lieutenant?

2 What is Iago's opinion about freedom of the will?

3 Why is Desdemona's handkerchief so precious to Othello?

4 What character in *King Lear* says, "My cue is villainous melancholy, with a sigh like Tom o'Bedlam"?

5 What does Lear pray to Nature to do to Goneril?

6 Whom does Kent call "a lily-livered, action-taking knave, a whoreson, glass-gazing, superserviceable, finical rogue"?

7 What character in *King Lear* uses this dialect: "Chill not let go, zir, without vurther 'casion"?

8 Of whom is it said in *Macbeth*, "Nothing in his life/Became him like the leaving it"?

9 Why didn't Lady Macbeth kill the sleeping King as she laid out the daggers?

10 What device does Malcolm use to test Macduff's integrity?

ANSWERS

to self-testing questions

First Reading

1. 183d
2. 183b-c, 195a-196b, 204b-c
3. 201d
4. 204d
5. 218c-d
6. 230b
7. 233a-c
8. 239a-b
9. 241d, 243c-d, 250a
10. 247d

Second Reading

1. 217c-218c
2. 223b
3. 327, *Dramatis Personae*
4. 329b
5. 330c
6. 331c-d
7. 396d
8. 402c
9. 403b
10. 408c-409a

Third Reading

1. 590d-591a
2. 551a-b
3. 497d
4. 585c
5. 495b
6. 547a, see also p. 542, note 1
7. 587c, see also p. 586b
8. 497a
9. 545a
10. 550c

Fourth Reading

1. 115b-116b
2. 168a, 172a-173a
3. 195b-196a
4. 211b-212a
5. 218b
6. 224a-225a
7. 154a, 158a, 239a-b
8. 264a-266b
9. 307b
10. 295a-b

Fifth Reading

1. 1d-2a, 3b
2. 6c-d
3. 38c-39c
4. 56a-b
5. 61a-b
6. 63a
7. 72b
8. 78d
9. 81b
10. 92d

Sixth Reading

1. 200a-b, 203d-204a
2. 240a-b
3. 315c
4. 341d, 346a
5. 355d-356a
6. 369c-d
7. 436a-437c

Seventh Reading

1. 45a-46a
2. 67c-d
3. 77b
4. 78d
5. 95c-d
6. 123c-124d
7. 143a-144c
8. 185b-d
9. 188d-191c
10. 194b-195c

Eighth Reading

1. 205b-c
2. 212b-c
3. 228a-b
4. 249b
5. 253a-b
6. 256b
7. 276a
8. 287b
9. 291b
10. 303d-304d

ADDITIONAL READINGS

I. Works included in *Great Books of the Western World*

Vol. 7: PLATO, *Phaedrus; Ion; The Republic*, Books II-III, Book X

9: ARISTOTLE, *Politics*, Book VIII; *Rhetoric*, Book III; *Poetics*

18: AUGUSTINE, *On Christian Doctrine*, Books II-IV

25: MONTAIGNE, *The Essays*, I.39, "A Consideration Upon Cicero"; II.10, "Of Books"; II.17, "Of Presumption"; II.36, "Of The Most Excellent Men"

30: BACON, *Advancement of Learning*, Book II, Section IV

32: MILTON, *Samson Agonistes*, "Of that sort of Dramatic Poem which is call'd Tragedy"; *Aeropagitica*

42: KANT, *The Critique of Judgment*, Part I, "Critique of Aesthetic Judgment"

44: BOSWELL, *Life of Samuel Johnson, LL.D.*

54: FREUD, *The Interpretation of Dreams*, VI, "The Dream-Work"; *A General Introduction to Psychoanalysis*, Part II, Chapters 10-11

II. Other Works

A. Criticism and Appreciation

ABERCROMBIE, LASCELLES, *The Theory of Poetry*. New York: Harcourt, Brace and Co., Inc., 1926

ARNOLD, MATTHEW, *Essays Literary and Critical*. New York: Everyman's Library, 1907

AUERBACH, ERICH, *Mimesis: The Representation of Reality in Western Literature*. New York: Doubleday Anchor Books, 1957

BERGSON, HENRI and MEREDITH, GEORGE, *Comedy*. New York: Doubleday Anchor Books, 1956

BOWRA, CECIL MAURICE, *From Virgil to Milton.* New York: St. Martin's Press, Inc., 1946

BRADLEY, A. C., *Shakespearean Tragedy.* New York: Meridian Books, 1955

BROOKS, CLEANTH, *The Well-Wrought Urn.* New York: Harvest Books, 1956

BROOKS, CLEANTH and WARREN, ROBERT PENN, *Understanding Fiction.* New York: Appleton-Century-Crofts, Inc., 1960; *Understanding Poetry.* New York: Holt, Rinehart and Winston, Inc., 1960

BURKE, KENNETH, *Philosophy of Literary Form.* New York: Vintage Books, 1957

BUTCHER, S. H., *Aristotle's Theory of Poetry and Fine Art.* New York: Dover Publications, Inc., 1951

COLERIDGE, S. T., *Biographia Literaria.* New York: Everyman's Library, 1908

CRANE, RONALD S., ed., *Critics and Criticism: Ancient and Modern.* Chicago: University of Chicago Press, 1952

DREW, ELIZABETH, *Poetry: A Modern Guide to Its Understanding and Enjoyment.* New York: Dell Books, 1959

ELIOT, T. S., *Selected Essays,* rev. ed. New York: Harcourt, Brace and Co., Inc., 1950

EMPSON, WILLIAM, *Seven Types of Ambiguity.* New York: Meridian Books, 1955; *Some Versions of Pastoral.* New York: New Directions, 1950

FREUD, SIGMUND, *On Creativity and the Unconscious.* New York: Harper Torchbooks, 1958

GOODMAN, PAUL, *The Structure of Literature.* Chicago: University of Chicago Press, 1954

GRANVILLE-BARKER, HARLEY G. and HARRISON, G. B., *A Companion to Shakespeare Studies.* New York: Doubleday Anchor Books, 1960

HAZLITT, WILLIAM, *Lectures on the English Comic Writers.* New York: Dolphin Books, 1960; *Lectures on the English Poets.* New York: World's Classics, Oxford University Press, 1925

HOSPERS, JOHN, *Meaning and Truth in the Arts.* Chapel Hill: University of North Carolina Press, 1947

JAMES, DAVID G., *Scepticism and Poetry*. New York: Barnes & Noble, Inc., 1960

JONES, EDMUND DAVID, ed., *English Critical Essays (16th, 17th and 18th Centuries)*. New York: World's Classics, Oxford University Press, 1922; *English Critical Essays (19th Century)*. New York: World's Classics, Oxford University Press, 1916

KER, WILLIAM P., *Epic and Romance*. New York: Dover Publications, Inc., 1957

LONGINUS, *On Great Writing (On the Sublime)*. New York: Liberal Arts Press, Inc., 1957

MARITAIN, JACQUES, *Creative Intuition in Art and Poetry*. New York: Meridian Books, 1955

MURRAY, GILBERT, *The Classical Tradition in Poetry*. New York: Vintage Books, 1957

ORTEGA Y GASSET, JOSÉ, *The Dehumanization of Art and Other Writings On Art and Culture*. New York: Doubleday Anchor Books, 1956

POUND, EZRA, *ABC of Reading*. New York: New Directions Paperbooks, 1960

READ, HERBERT, *The Nature of Literature*. New York: Evergreen Books, 1958

RICHARDS, IVOR A., *Principles of Literary Criticism*. New York: Harcourt, Brace and Co., 1925

ROSSI, JOSEPH and GALPIN, ALFRED, eds., *De Sanctis on Dante*. Madison: University of Wisconsin Press, 1957

SANTAYANA, GEORGE, *Interpretations of Poetry and Religion*. New York: Harper Torchbooks, 1957; *Three Philosophical Poets*. New York: Doubleday Anchor Books, 1953

SCOTT, A. F., *Meaning and Style*. New York: St. Martin's Press, Inc., 1938

TOLSTOY, LEO, *What Is Art? and Essays on Art*, trans. by Aylmer Maude. New York: World's Classics, Oxford University Press, 1930

VAN DOREN, MARK, *Shakespeare*. New York: Doubleday Anchor Books, 1953; *The Noble Voice*. New York: Holt, 1946

WAGENKNECHT, EDWARD C., ed., *Chaucer: Modern Essays in Criticism*. New York: Galaxy Books, 1959

WHITFIELD, J. H., *Dante and Virgil.* New York: The Macmillan Company, 1949

WILLIAMS, CHARLES, *The Figure of Beatrice: A Study in Dante.* New York: Hillary House Publishers, Ltd., 1957

B. Reference Works, Literary Histories, and Special Subjects

BENÉT, WILLIAM ROSE, ed., *The Reader's Encyclopedia.* New York: Thomas Y. Crowell Co., 1955

BRERETON, GEOFFREY, *A Short History of French Literature.* Baltimore: Penguin Books Inc., 1955

BURCKHARDT, JACOB, *The Civilization of the Renaissance in Italy,* 2 vols. New York: Harper Torchbooks, 1958

COHEN, J. M., *A History of Western Literature.* Baltimore: Penguin Books Inc., 1956

DAICHES, DAVID, *A Critical History of English Literature.* New York: Ronald Press Co., 1960

EVANS, IFOR, *A Short History of English Literature.* Baltimore: Penguin Books Inc., 1940

FORD, BORIS, ed., *The Pelican Guide to English Literature.* Baltimore: Penguin Books Inc. Volume I. *The Age of Chaucer,* 1954; Volume II. *The Age of Shakespeare,* 1955

GARDINER, HAROLD C., *The Catholic Viewpoint on Censorship.* New York: Hanover House, 1958

HADAS, MOSES, *A History of Greek Literature.* New York: Columbia University Press, 1950; *A History of Latin Literature.* New York: Columbia University Press, 1952

HALE, JOHN R., *England and the Italian Renaissance.* Chester Springs, Pennsylvania: Dufour Editions, 1954

HARTNOLL, PHYLLIS, ed., *The Oxford Companion to the Theatre,* 2nd ed. New York: Oxford University Press, 1957

HARVEY, PAUL, ed., *The Oxford Companion to Classical Literature,* 2nd ed. New York: Oxford University Press, 1937; *The Oxford Companion to English Literature,* 3rd ed. New York: Oxford University Press, 1946

JESPERSEN, OTTO, *The Growth and Structure of the English Language.* New York: Doubleday Anchor Books, 1955

KALLEN, HORACE M., *Indecency and the Seven Arts.* New York: Liveright Publishing Corp., 1930

LAWRENCE, D. H., *Sex, Literature, and Censorship,* ed. by Harry T. Moore. New York: Compass Books, 1959

MURRAY, GILBERT, *The Literature of Ancient Greece.* Chicago: University of Chicago Press, 1956

NORWOOD, GILBERT, *Greek Tragedy.* New York: Dramabooks, 1960

PATER, WALTER, *The Renaissance.* New York: New American Library (A Mentor Book), 1959

READ, HERBERT, *English Prose Style.* Boston: Beacon Press, Inc., 1955

SAINTSBURY, GEORGE, *A Short History of English Literature.* New York: St. Martin's Press, Inc. 1898; *A History of English Prose Rhythm.* London: The Macmillan Company, 1922

SEYFFERT, OSKAR, *Dictionary of Classical Antiquity,* rev. and ed. by Henry Nettleship and J. E. Sandys. New York: Meridian Books, 1956

SYMONDS, JOHN A., *The Renaissance in Italy,* 2 vols. New York: Capricorn Books, 1960

WARRINGTON, JOHN, ed., *Atlas of Ancient and Classical Geography.* New York: Everyman's Library, 1952

WHITFIELD, J. H., *A Short History of Italian Literature.* Baltimore: Penguin Books Inc., 1960